Advanced Bass Fishing

A Sunrise Book E. P. DUTTON & CO., INC. · NEW YORK

JOHN WEISS

Advanced Bass Fishing

Library of Congress Cataloging in Publication Data

Weiss, John, 1944-
  Advanced bass fishing.

  Bibliography: p.
  1. Bass fishing.   I.   Title.
SH681.W4   1976   799.1'7'58   75-40142

Dutton-Sunrise, Inc., a subsidiary of E. P. Dutton & Co., Inc.

Published simultaneously in Canada by Clarke, Irwin & Company Limited,
Toronto and Vancouver
ISBN: 0-87690-204-2
Designed by The Etheredges

*To Bill, who first introduced me to bass years ago,
and to Marianne, who has tolerated my mania
for fishing in years since.*

Acknowledgments

My sincere thanks to Bill Doerflinger, my editor at E. P. Dutton & Co., for his insightful guidance in assembling this material, and to Bill Vogt for reading the manuscript and making valuable suggestions.

Contents

List of Illustrations

Preface

In view of the incredible rate at which our knowledge of black-bass behavior has increased in recent years, putting together a book on bass fishing is undoubtedly one of the most challenging assignments any writer could consider. Black bass have lived on this globe for many millennia, or perhaps even longer. (That is often a matter of heated debate, even among ichthyologists!) But it probably would not be too inaccurate to say that 95 percent of all the factual data we have on the species—their habits in various types of bodies of water, the most productive ways to enjoy catching them, and even effective management techniques—have been learned during only the last ten years.

So where does a writer begin? Is it possible for anyone to correlate the extraordinary and continually growing amount of angling know-how with what are sometimes obscure biological facts, to produce a book that is reasonably coherent and readable? That is the assignment I have undertaken, and I have done so with full awareness that no individual person has learned, or probably ever will learn, everything there is to know about bass, but that nevertheless a periodic attempt must be made to assemble masses of new information into a single work. Such efforts can substantially help anglers across the country to enlarge their perspective, sharpen their insight and skills, and improve their levels of bassing success.

Advanced Bass Fishing, then, as the title implies, is not the usual book of basics dedicated to the beginning fisherman.

Nowhere in these pages will there appear sequential photographs showing how to tie a knot, cast a lure, or hone the blade of a fillet knife. Nor, in the chapters to follow, will the reader labor through rehashed instructions on how to spool line on his fishing reel, how to clean a fish, or how to build his own homemade poppers. Elementary topics such as these and others have already been flogged unmercifully in previous bass books and this author has no intention of further beating the proverbial dead horse.

This book, rather, is for those estimated 20 million fishermen who annually devote substantial portions of their allotted piscatorial efforts to searching out the world's most popular gamefish species. They've already, many times over, paid their dues to the angling fraternity in the form of millions of hours upon America's countless lakes, reservoirs, rivers, streams and ponds. They have survived 4-A.M. wakenings and long drives through predawn darkness to favorite waters, and they've blistered their backsides from too many hours upon hard boat seats. They've weathered extreme conditions ranging from icy coldness to searing heat to drenching rain, and they've devastated their bank accounts acquiring boats and motors and experimenting with the latest angling innovations and tackle items. All of this in the fervent hope of increasing their catches, both in numbers and in size of individual fish.

Unfortunately, a goodly majority of these same anglers all too often return disappointedly to the dock at day's end with not a great deal more to show for their efforts than a medium-rare neck and an exercised casting arm. Having mastered the basics, they do all right with "keeper" fish that range in size between ten and fourteen inches, and upon rare occasion they may even slip the meshes around one slightly larger. But the real lunkers that weigh anywhere between three and ten pounds or more, and which a few select fishermen seem to bring in with exasperating regularity, are to them forever elusive. According to a recent survey, almost 80 percent of the nation's anglers who go bassing on a regular basis have never during their fishing careers caught a largemouth weighing five pounds or better or a smallmouth of three pounds or better.

The reason for these countless unsuccessful excursions each year can practically always be stated in terms of lack of fishing knowledge. And it is for these dedicated and persevering but usually unsuccessful lovers of the sport that *Advanced Bass Fishing* has been written. It is, admittedly, not the easiest book to read. You'll find little in the way of flowery prose, witticisms, or nostalgic recollections here. What you will find is a wide range of factual, little-written-about information gleaned from the country's most proficient guides, tournament professionals, tackle manufacturers, and other highly respected bass-fishing experts.

This practical yet advanced know-how is almost certain to revolutionize your approach to the fishing strategies you employ, because it takes you step by step through many of the techniques the experts use to boat large numbers of big fish consistently. It's entirely possible that several of the first bass you catch after completing this book may be real goliaths, which previously existed only in your wildest imaginations.

We must, however, be realistic in our bassing expectations. Not an angler in the world can always, on every outing, hope to crank in a record-breaker. Ten-point whitetail bucks, to frame an analogy, are not nearly as plentiful as yearling does. And ten-pound bass are not as abundant as two-pounders. But our waters are teeming with big fish in catchable numbers, and in view of the time and money and effort expended, you should be boating your fair share.

What do I mean by "catchable" numbers? An example might be found in the case of my close friend Inky Davis, who regularly fishes the famous Santee-Cooper watershed in South Carolina. Recently, Inky called me at my home with good news: he'd finally achieved a goal he'd long been striving for. That very morning he'd successfully landed a bass which weighed two ounces over five pounds.

Now a five-pound bass might not represent anything really special to any seasoned angler. But the thing which makes this particular event so noteworthy is that this special bass was the five hundredth one over five pounds that Inky had landed during his lifetime! Inky Davis is only thirty-one years old.

Tackle manufacturer and tournament pro Tom Mann and his

partner Dave Lockhart not long ago caught during a single day twenty-five bass which weighed 155 pounds from Lake Eufaula in Alabama. The heaviest ten bass on that string averaged well over nine pounds apiece and the largest tipped the scales at better than thirteen pounds!

Tackle manufacturer Dick Kotis not long ago caught five bass over ten pounds apiece during a single day, from a small Florida lake. And the tournament pro Roland Martin once took five bass over ten pounds apiece during a single day at Santee-Cooper. In the North, bass seldom grow to such large size because of the shorter growing seasons, and the five- and six-pounders which do present themselves from time to time nearly always come from farm ponds or large reservoirs. Yet from the Ohio River, where a bass over three pounds is usually considered something of a rarity among locals, my records indicate I landed twenty-four bass over four pounds apiece during a three-month period in 1974.

The list of similar, documented catches (a substantial percentage of the fish were released unharmed) could well occupy the remaining pages of this book. But the point to be made here is that while you may elect to free every bass you catch, if that is your angling philosophy, our waterways contain big fish in catchable numbers. And there is no reason for you not to be getting in on the action. Fishery biologists usually admit that most of our waters could stand an increase in their bass populations, but they also repeatedly tell us that far greater numbers of big fish die each year of old age than ever succumb to anglers' lures.

The chapters that follow, then, will be devoted to helping any angler substantially boost his bass-catch ratio. We'll do this by looking at the various bass species and how they live through the months, in various types of waters, and at the specialized techniques that various seasons or water types dictate. Much of this information has never appeared elsewhere in print.

A good deal of the instruction that follows also entails the use of a wide variety of modern tackle, and many times even the use of highly sophisticated electronic equipment. But there is yet another

During any given month of the year, Inky Davis probably releases more big bass than most anglers catch during a lifetime. This one pulled the dial down to the nine-pound mark.

Tom Mann and Dave Lockhart show a one-day catch that rates as the best in Alabama history. Ten of the bass on this string average between nine and fourteen pounds! (*Courtesy of Mann Bait Company*)

thing we should make perfectly clear at the outset. No amount of any brand-name fishing or boating equipment, by itself, will make you a successful angler, even though the manufacturers, at times, may lead one to believe otherwise. An intimate knowledge of bass behavior is the key ingredient in heavying-up any stringer. And the many varieties of tackle and bass-locating equipment any angler may use at any given time are only tools enabling him to carry out his task more efficiently and effectively.

This philosophy is the foundation upon which this book rests. The reason I consider it crucial is that too many anglers striving to better their fishing results fall into the trap of believing they can buy fishing success.

For example, I know many consistently unsuccessful anglers who in recent years have traded their small-horsepower-equipped V-bottom craft for fancy bassboats with high-performance hulls and mills that spew out "roostertails" at only half-throttle, fully convinced at the time of the transaction they'd soon need assistance in lifting their heavy stringers onto the docks. Yet they are catching no more bass today than they were in past years when working from more primitive rigs.

Thousands of other anglers each year, in search of a quick remedy for their unsuccessful fishing outings, fall for the secret-lure advertisement. It sounds fantastic, but they actually believe that once they lay their hard-earned money on the counter for some revolutionary lure design, they need only tie the contraption to their line and big bass will turn themselves inside-out trying to get at it.

Even more frequently, the winner of a national bass tournament may reveal at the weigh-in that he made his winning catch on a chartreuse whatchamacallit, whereupon the tackle company that manufactures the bait, to their sheer delight, is overnight swamped with orders. Seldom does the tournament champ have a chance to detail the rest of the story: that the chartreuse whatchamacallit was the lure he simply happened to be throwing when he finally located the fish; that the real key to his catch was not in the particular lure itself but how he evaluated the weather and water conditions, established a pattern, and eventually began making contact with bass at eighteen feet deep on windswept rocky points; and that had he been willing to switch lures during the heat of the action, with time running out, a red-and-white thingamabob, a blue bassblastit, or almost anything else retrieved at the proper depth and speed would probably have proven equally effective.

There are no revolutionary lure designs, magic lure colors, expensive marine equipment, or precision electronic gadgetry that, *in themselves,* will pay off consistently in big bass for anyone who has their cash prices. But in all fairness to the marine and tackle manufacturers, we can admit that quality gear, compared to inferior dimestore or discount stuff, is a definite aid, *provided* the hopeful angler couples the use of these tools with a thorough understanding of how bass live and move and feed.

Truthfully, bass are not very intelligent. Nor are they clever, wily, or capable of outwitting anglers, as many of my fellow writers have tended to suggest. It is true that they possess refined survival instincts. But generally they are very stupid creatures completely at the mercy of their environments. Any angler, therefore, who is knowledgeable in the ways of bass behavior can use a leaky rowboat, antiquated rods and reels, no electronic equipment, and a carrot with hooks attached for a lure, and fully expect to catch at least a few good-sized bass now and then.

We will also in coming pages make frequent mention of bass-tournament fishing. But whether or not you are in favor of bass contests for money is unimportant here. That is an area of personal philosophy in which you'll have to make your own decisions. We will be concerned primarily with one undeniable fact that tournament fishing has brought to front-stage in recent years. That truth is that bass fishing—in fact, any type of fishing—is a skill that can be learned.

Perhaps my friend Spence Petros, an expert angler and also the Managing Editor of *Fishing Facts Magazine,* said it best when he wrote: "Bass fishing is no longer considered a blind-luck proposition but the acquisition of knowledge of bass behavior and the practical application of that learning to varying situations on the water in the consistent finding and catching of large numbers of big fish."

Unlike many other things in life you do not have to be gifted with unusual talents or predisposed with certain inherited genetic structures to become a proficient bass angler. Bassing is a sport that can be learned if the fisherman is willing to approach the subject with an open mind, invest the required time and effort, and try (difficult as it may sometimes seem) to set aside many of the bad habits or incorrect information that may have dominated his angling efforts in previous years.

It's even very possible to start from scratch, with no prior angling experience, in the hope of soon becoming an expert. And no better evidence of this can be seen than in the case of Bill Dance of Memphis, Tennessee. In 1967 Dance was a furniture salesman who didn't even own a fishing rod. Yet by late 1972, through desire, eagerness, and hard work, he had captured more national bass titles on the tournament trail than any other angler in the country.

Throughout this book it will also be imperative for the student of advanced bass fishing to keep in mind that all bass have the same needs, regardless of where they may be found. This is important because off-hand mention of bassing in Indiana may prompt some reader or other to become irate and exclaim, "To hell with bass fishing in Indiana. Tell me how to catch bass in Arkansas!"

The bass you catch in Minnesota, California, or New Jersey have the same requirements as the bass I catch in Ohio, Canada, Texas, or Florida. They need food, they need cover or some form of bottom contour or structure they can relate to, they need the proper amount of dissolved oxygen in the water, and if there is to be continued propagation of their kind, they'll require suitable water temperatures and spawning habitat. Further, their day-to-day activities will be similarly influenced by a number of other variables, such as water temperature, the amount of light penetration or degree of water clarity, the age of the body of water they inhabit, balance among themselves and other fish species inhabiting the same water, existing weather conditions, and so on. Once the angler has acquired detailed knowledge of how bass react under these varied circumstances, he should be able to visit any body of water anywhere in the country and, taking existing conditions into consideration, soon be into good bass!

With only slight exceptions in habits or reactions to unique environments, bass are the same everywhere. *Their habits do not dramatically change the moment an angler ventures across some state boundary.*

Depending upon latitude and the related length of annual growing seasons, the different bass species may vary considerably in size from one region to the next. But this is seldom the sole reason behind the extensive travel many anglers engage in these days. Too many bassmen, rather, labor under the mistaken assumption that the grass is greener and the fishing easier . . .

It may indeed be an exciting challenge to fish new waters. But as in the case of purchasing expensive boats, motors, electronic gear, and new "miracle" lures, travel seems to be still another shortcut anglers take in their search for bassing success.

Before beginning the first chapter, I should here give due credit to a man who is responsible for a great deal of what we presently know about gamefish behavior. He is Buck Perry, originally from North Carolina, where he taught physics at the state university, and those who know anything about freshwater fishing consider him to be the most knowledgeable and successful angler alive. His knowledge of the earth's composition, including its many waterways, borders on the phenomenal. In verification of this it might be worth mentioning that Buck frequently serves as a consultant to many state departments of natural resources in their fish-management programs, and even to state highway departments seeking insight into variables in the stratification of terrain which they intend to gouge in the laying of new thoroughfares. Since a good many of today's best bass waters are manmade impoundments created over previously dry land, it should stand to reason that his understanding of the earth's crust has contributed immensely to his fishing insight. This knowledge is important, as we shall see later, because bass spend the majority of their time right on the bottom and in association with some type of contour, structure, or unique composition of bottom materials.

It is Buck Perry, at first criticized and ridiculed for his highly advanced thinking, research, and understanding, who is responsible for most of what we know about the deep-water lives of bass and their movements. It was he who first coined the terms "structure," "sanctuary," and "migration route," among others—terms that now, many years later, have finally been accepted by anglers and each day on the water play an important role in their varied approaches to locating and catching big bass.

One of Buck Perry's earliest and most notable discoveries—and this is in line with our previous comments about anglers traveling widely in search of bass—had to do with the almost unbelievable numbers of trophy fish which live complacent, undisturbed lives in waters right on the outskirts of large metropolitan centers. Because these waters are usually very clear, and annually come under heavy fishing pressure, many anglers believe them to be "fished out." But Buck repeatedly proves that "fished-out lakes aren't," by using knowledge and deep-water fishing strategies to consistently bring in catches—astounding catches—from countless heavily fished and supposedly barren waters that often lie within plain view of skyscrapers and superhighways.

Not long ago, for instance, as this introduction was being

Buck Perry is one of the greatest fishermen alive in the world today. We can thank him for much of what we know about structure fishing. (*Courtesy of* Fishing Facts Magazine)

written, I received a phone call from Spence Petros. He'd only recently arrived back home from a fishing trip with Buck and thought
perhaps I would be interested in the results. I was, to be sure. But
as the tale began to unravel I did not find myself at all surprised.
What happened was just another typical Buck Perry catch under
circumstances I had heard of or personally witnessed so many times
before.

It seems they launched their boat on a shallow, expansive lake
which possessed little in the way of cover or radical bottom contours. Many other fishermen had already been on the water for
hours, and checking around revealed that beyond taking a few
yearling fish no one was having much luck.

"Somehow," Spence explained, "Buck found a small square of
hard-bottom material—a shelf—in midlake with nothing anywhere
in the area even to hint of its presence. We made forty-seven consecutive trolling passes across that shelf, which was no larger than
an average kitchen floor, and took forty-seven bass as quickly as we
could haul them in. I won't tell you their sizes because you'd just
call me a liar. But I will say that we could have divided the bass up
into five equal piles and any one of those piles would have been fully
capable of easily winning any national bass tournament."

In view of all of this, my primary goal in this book will be to
impress upon the angler reader that it is not necessarily *where* you
choose to fish on this bass-rich continent that determines your measure of success. Nor is it the amount of money you may have invested
in boats and motors or assorted other fishing gear. (Buck Perry
likes the comfort of fancy bassboats but nearly always does his most
serious fishing from a rented fourteen-foot aluminum boat obtained
on location, using his own ten-horsepower outboard.) It is *how* you
fish! It is knowledge of bass behavior and how you apply that knowledge to a myriad of fishing situations you are likely to encounter
during any given day on the water. Good reading, good learning,
and good luck!

JOHN WEISS
Athens, Ohio

Advanced Bass Fishing

CHAPTER 1

The Bass Species and How They Live

As we look at the bass species and how they live, it would be incredibly easy to get hopelessly lost in a lengthy discourse having to do with the historical-biological backgrounds of the various freshwater black basses. But few, I feel, other perhaps than ichthyologists, are deeply concerned with this facet of bass learning. Most fishermen, if I may be allowed the presumption, simply want to know how to catch more bass than they have been getting, especially those elusive rascals which are half as long as a tall man's leg.

Nevertheless, we should probably take a very brief look at the various bass species this book will be concentrating upon.

Technically, there are eleven strains and/or species, but the great majority of anglers in North America pursue only four species of bass. They are all, upon occasion, known as "black bass," though this term is gradually falling out of usage and does not, by any stretch of the imagination, mean the various species are always black in color. They include the largemouth bass (*Micropterus salmoides*), the smallmouth bass (*Micropterus dolomieui*), and the spotted bass (*Micropterus punctulatus*), which is sometimes also known as the Kentucky bass. The fourth "species" diligently sought by anglers, the Florida bass (*Micropterus salmoides floridanus*), is actually a subspecies of the largemouth.

The American Fisheries Society also recognizes the redeye bass, the Suwanee bass, and the Guadalupe bass, and if you dig still deeper into the biological textbooks you will undoubtedly find even more strains. All of these latter species, however, are very limited in distribution across the continent. And you may even have to take scale-counts, refer to anatomical charts, and uncase your set of calipers if there is to be positive identification and distinction between them.

This book will be concerned only with the northern largemouth, smallmouth, spotted, and Florida basses, since any of the other species are likely to be caught only incidentally, while fishing for any of the main four.

At present, there is only one state in the Union (Alaska) that does not possess at least one strain of bass. The various bass species were not always this widely dispersed, though; their distribution beyond their native ranges has been accomplished during only the last several decades by adventuresome, experimentally minded, and often rebel biologists associated with state and federal fishery agencies or independent fishery societies.

Today, the largemouth's range is widespread, and it is the most adaptable of all the bass species. Originally restricted to the region of the Great Lakes and their drainage tributaries, the largemouth is now found from the southern portions of the eastern Canadian provinces to as far south as the arid desert lands of Mexico and the forbidden waters of Cuba. Familiar from the brackish tidal marshes of the Atlantic seaboard to the deep, manmade impoundments of the Pacific states, the largemouth is also the most prolific of all the bass species.

Primarily an inhabitant of lakes, reservoirs, sluggish rivers, tidal marshes, and ponds, the largemouth is an occasional resident of swift rivers and streams, too. But he doesn't seem to thrive upon cooler, rushing waters, and in many types of rivers and streams he seldom grows to appreciable size. Additionally, in such environments he almost exclusively restricts his home to those quiet, deep pools out of the main current or along shorelines where heavy cover or certain bank configurations retard the velocity of the current.

Providing the water is not too cold or moving too swiftly, the largemouth may elect to set up housekeeping under almost any conditions, with only two exceptions. He is not as adaptable to high levels of pollution as are many other fish species, and given the choice he will avoid bottom areas of lakes and other waters which are overly muddy or layered with silt. But in this latter regard the largemouth is also very tolerant, and if muddy water is unavoidable from time to time he will simply make do. Otherwise the water may be clear, stained, murky, warm, cool, shallow, deep, cover-free, or infested with junglelike swamp growth and chances are excellent that *Micropterus* and his progeny will get along just fine.

While in later chapters we will spend a good deal of time discussing how to sink hooks into lunker smallmouth, spotted, and Florida bass, our primary emphasis in this book will be upon the largemouth. This is because the largemouth is the basic freshwater gamefish. Understand how the largemouth lives and moves and feeds and learn how to catch him, and you can, allowing only for minor variations in habits, easily learn how to catch the other bass species. They are individuals in their own right, to be sure, but their habits differ only slightly from the ways of largemouths.

The chief distinguishing physical characteristic of the largemouth is indeed his awesome maw, which complements his habit of dining upon almost anything he can cram into it during rampant feeding spells. As we'll see later, the largemouth spends only a very small portion of each day actually feeding, but when the time does come to stock up on groceries, he spares no effort. Countless times I've boated a fine bass only to discover a smaller fish still blocking his gullet, the tail of the hapless victim yet protruding from the bass's mouth. Living as he does, however, in an environment of constantly changing water and weather conditions, the largemouth often goes through long periods of relative dormancy in which he engages in little if any feeding.

For positive identification, close the fish's mouth; the rear of the upper jaw will extend back to a point well past a vertical line drawn down from the rear edge of his eye. The forward portion of the spiny dorsal fin and the rear soft portion are very nearly separated from one another, while in the other basses the dorsal fin is either continuous or more nearly so. Coloration of the largemouth may vary from region to region. In most cases the species takes on a vibrant grass-green color along the sides, which progressively darkens in color toward the dorsal area. The underbelly is nearly always a dirty white color. Due to the chemistry of certain waters, however, the species may appear almost totally black in color, and in others they may be very pale or silvery. A dark lateral line is usually visible on smaller fish, running from the gill flaps to the tail, but in larger specimens this line may not be so pronounced. Also, there will nearly always be dark, splotchy markings along the sides of the fish.

The Florida bass, too, engages in frenzied feeding upon occasion. But since he lives in a more stable environment, he seems to be predisposed to a more regular lifestyle, at least as far as I have been able to ascertain. The Florida bass looks almost identical to the largemouth, though in many cases the subspecies seems to take on slightly darker hues. Other than the outlandish size he often attains, he differs physiologically from the largemouth only in the number of rows of scales above and below the lateral line (see below).

The smallmouth bass is much more fussy than the largemouth in his dining habits, though this is certainly not the reason for his noticeably smaller oral cavity. The relative infrequency of cannibalistic gorgings exhibited by smallmouths can probably be attributed to the rather sparse environments in which they commonly thrive. The rear of the smallmouth's upper jaw, with the mouth closed, does not extend back past a vertical line drawn down from about the middle of the eye. The forward and rear (spiny and rayed) portions of the dorsal fin are joined. As in the case of largemouths, coloration of the species may vary from one body of water to another. Generally, smallmouths take on a greenish-bronze hue on the upper two-thirds of the body, with a sort of yellowish-brown underbelly. There is no distinct, dark lateral line but there are an average of three dark stripes fanning out from the snout to the rear of the gill cover, yielding to darker, irregular splotches along the sides of the fish.

As for the spotted bass, its feeding characteristics are often a combination of those exhibited by largemouths and smallmouths. Many times they'll go on a binge; other times they seem to feed hardly at all. Proper identification of spotted bass is the most difficult of all because the species has the same general coloration as the largemouth and smallmouth, plus some markings which are unique.

To add to the confusion, the spotted bass has the dark lateral line of the largemouth, yet its mouth is like that of a smallmouth in that the rear corner of the upper jaw extends to, but not beyond, the eye. A characteristic unique to this species is several rows of dark dots between the lateral line and ventral region, extending full-length from the gill flaps to the base of the tail. There are also spots (really, splotches) of dark gray along the dorsal region. But since all bass species may vary somewhat in appearance, according to the makeup of the water they inhabit, a margin of possible error exists if one depends upon markings and color alone.

To establish positive identity in such cases, fishery biologists often count the rows of scales between the lateral line and the front of the dorsal fin. The spotted bass has nine rows of scales, while the smallmouth has eleven, the largemouth seven, and the Florida bass from seven to nine. An equally accurate method of identification, and one which is far less time-consuming, is to run your finger over the tongue of a fish you suspect to be a spotted bass. The tongues of largemouths, smallmouths, and Florida bass are smooth to the touch. On the tongue of a spotted bass, however, you'll feel a small elliptical patch of very soft teeth.

Smallmouths, spotted bass, and the Florida subspecies are more thoroughly discussed in their own chapters, respectively 11, 12, and 13.

A "lunker" largemouth caught north of the Kentucky and Tennessee region is any fish between four and eight pounds or more, though in the southland, where anglers may encounter the Florida strain of bass, you'll have to net one of better than ten pounds to raise admiring eyebrows among locals. A smallmouth of better than four or five pounds, anywhere, is an impressive trophy, and a spotted bass tipping the balance at better than three or four pounds should be more than enough to have you feeling high for a month.

In a given body of water, however, it is always the female of each bass species which attains the greater weight. Male or "buck" bass of any species only rarely grow to any size larger than three or four pounds. The affectionate labels of "sows," "hawgs," "bucketmouths," and similar colloquialisms therefore always refer to female bass.

Finally, to set the stage for coming chapters, we should mention that except in certain environmental circumstances, as in the case of very small ponds, none of the bass species live the year around in one single location in any body of water. This is not to say they are migratory like walleyes or salmon. But within their home ranges they do periodically shift from one location to another. There are seasonal movements which see the fish sometimes travel substantial distances, though less than a quarter-mile on the average. And there are temporary movements which may occur on almost a daily basis and which are predominantly of lesser distances (sometimes as little as only twenty yards).

SPRING SPAWNING BEHAVIOR

I said in the Introduction that all bass have the same needs, regardless of where they may be found, and that their habits, for the most part, are universal. Nevertheless, any discussion of the various species must always be prefaced with words such as "usually," "most often," "generally," and similar qualifications, because the species' habits are so frequently subject to local conditions that may, at times, cause the bass to vary slightly in their ways. And such is the case, especially, when the largemouth bass spawns and annually reproduces his kind. Prolonged cold-weather spells or unseasonable heat waves may delay normal spawning or trigger early egg-laying. Radical fluctuations in water levels due to rainy spells, droughts, or even the regulation of water tables in flood-control impoundments often determine when and how deep the fish will build their nests and whether the spawning attempt will be successful or disastrous.

Generally, the largemouth can be expected to commence spawning activities almost anytime after the water temperature has passed the 60-degree mark. The most active, purposeful spawning, however, occurs when the water for the first time reaches the 65-degree mark. And everything from that point on may proceed as Mother Nature has planned if radical changes in her personality do not see the influence of other factors which may postpone, slow down, or accelerate spawning activities.

I have seen bass move onto their beds in Ohio during late May when the water temperature approached 62 degrees. Then, upon experiencing a last touch of winter in which the water temperature dropped back down to 57 degrees, the fish moved off their beds and into deeper waters where they held at "waiting stations" until the water was once again suitable for spawning. Too many times these "false spawns" or delays may ruin the reproduction cycle because

Water temperature is what regulates bass spawning activities. Here I
check the temperature in an embayment of Burr Oak Lake in Ohio.

the roe-laden females will eventually refuse to move onto the beds.
After a period of time their bodies will absorb or assimilate the
eggs.

Often, fishermen may note in the waters they frequent a
marked absence of a certain age-group of bass. Fish of one, two,
five, and six pounds may be caught regularly, with few or no three-
or four-pounders ever showing up on anglers' stringers. It is likely
the majority of one or two generations of offspring never made it
into being because of the bass's habits being drastically altered during the spawning seasons of those respective years.

Under normal conditions of water and weather, latitude is the determining factor as to when, exactly, bass will commence spawning activities in any given region. In Florida and other deep South states, the spawn may be well under way during the months of February or March if weather conditions are favorable. In fact, a certain small percentage of bass may be expected to spawn every month of the year in the southern states, due to their consistently warmer temperatures and frequent heat spells. Farther north in the Kentucky region, the spawn doesn't begin until late April or May. Yet the entire reproduction process may not begin until June in the northern border states and southern Canadian provinces.

In any large body of water, the northern and northeastern coves and shoreline banks are always more susceptible to the slanting rays of the warming springtime sun. Similarly, they are also more protected from the last cold winds of winter, and therefore will usually be the first places where bass are seen to engage in homemaking activity. The smaller bucks or male bass will move into the shallows first, but "shallow" as we are using it here and will continue to use it throughout this book is only a relative term. Male largemouths may select bedding sites and begin constructing nests in water as shallow as only six inches deep. I have seen them in shallow southern bayous, bulldogging about with their dorsal fins and the humps of their backs completely out of the water as they bloodied their tails fanning away debris from a bedding site. I have also located largemouth beds as deep as eight or ten feet in certain crystal-clear northern lakes.

The *depth* at which bass choose to spawn is determined by the degree of water clarity and the amount of underwater cover. These two factors influence the amount of sunlight which is permitted to penetrate the water, and the bass seem to know instinctively that it is the warming light which is responsible for incubation of the eggs, and further, exactly how much light is required in order to accomplish the task within a specified time period. If the water is gin-clear and little cover is present, light penetration is facilitated and the beds may be constructed somewhat deeper than usual. Conversely, if the water is murky and substantial amounts of brush are in evidence, the beds will invariably be somewhat shallower. In most cases an angler can probably expect to find largemouths spawning at depths averaging between three and five feet, though as we have already noted, there may be exceptions to the rule.

The *locations* where spawning sites will be in evidence are determined by bottom composition and wind and wave action.

Ideally, the bottom should be of hard-packed sand, shell, pea-gravel, clay, or marl (loosely packed clay and limestone), with a very thin layer of mud covering the hard material. Bass are able to sweep out their nests, however, and this allows spawning to take place when marginal amounts of soft mire cover the hard bottom materials of the lake or reservoir spawning area. At the same time, the site should be as free as possible from the influence of siltation, a condition in which continually roily water permits large amounts of finely granulated sediment to sift down and layer the bottom. Minimal amounts of sediment can be kept in "suspension" by the continual fanning action of the bass's tails. But sudden or massive amounts of sediment settling upon the eggs will suffocate them.

Because of this potential siltation factor, and also because shallow-water areas warm much faster, bass-bedding locations in lakes and reservoirs will predominantly be found in coves and bays adjacent to the main body of water. But if few such shallows are in existence, the bass will spawn right along the banks of the main waterway, usually where some type of protection is afforded the beds. Small cuts in the banks, downwind sides of points jutting out from the shore, or even the presence of felled trees lying in the water are examples of locations where wind and wave action will not disturb the beds by roiling the water unduly and covering the eggs with greater amounts of debris than the parent bass are able to keep in suspension. Keep in mind, though, that you'll probably find ten beds back in the protected embayments for every one located along the banks of the main body of water.

It should also be mentioned that while bass are typically school fish for the greater part of the year, they disperse or scatter when the mating season approaches, searching out their own bedding locations away from others of the same species. They become very territorial. Nevertheless, bass-spawning beds may still appear to be rather concentrated in certain regions in any given body of water because suitable conditions and sites are always at a premium.

Generally, the largemouth's bed will take on a circular shape, measuring from twelve to twenty-five inches in diameter by about six inches deep. The contrast which spawning beds present in comparison to surrounding bottom materials makes them easy to spot from as much as a hundred yards away if the water is clear, there's no wind ruffling the surface, and the angler has donned polarizing glasses to eliminate reflective glare. Wading carefully along the shoreline (so as not to destroy beds accidentally), sculling a lightweight skiff, or quietly maneuvering under the power of an electric motor, an angler can often select which beds he wishes to cast to. The beds present a pale, saucer-shaped appearance against a rather dark background as a result of the male bass's using his tail and pectoral and anal fins to clean away the muck, leaves, decayed vegetation, and other bottom debris, leaving clean sand, gravel, or clay.

During the period in which the males are building inshore spawning nests, females heavy with eggs have begun moving from their deep-water homes to areas near the annual spawning grounds. At certain select locations they adopt "holding stations" where they wait, though not impatiently, for their suitors. In the larger and deeper lakes and reservoirs, frequent types of holding stations are the sharply sloping points which extend from shorelines and guard the entrances to bays, coves, and "backwater" ponds. If no bays or coves are nearby and the bass are to spawn along the main banks of the lake or reservoir, the holding station for the females may be a nearby drop-off or other type of bottom contour situated directly adjacent to much deeper water. In shallower lakes and reservoirs the holding stations may be along the edges of inundated stream channels or perhaps an old riverbed.

Understandably, a drop-off or winding stream channel may extend for several hundred yards, and attempting to dope out where, exactly, the holding station is situated can be a brain-racking task. Glen Lau Productions of Ocala, Florida, has shed a good deal of light on the subject in recent months. Lau Productions engages in underwater filming of gamefish behavior. And in the case of bass they discovered that the potential holding stations female bass may elect to use are usually identified by the presence of a "rubbing log." Rubbing logs may consist of stumps, standing timber, or almost any type of felled tree lying on the bottom in the types of locations listed above. It's believed that sow bass select holding stations possessing rubbing logs for the express purpose of having some type of object which they can repeatedly bump into—an instinctive attempt to loosen the eggs from their skeins, which subsequently allows the female more easily to deposit them on the spawning beds.

Though any act of reproduction certainly requires the active participation of both sexes, many believe the male largemouth bass serves the more important (or at least the more active) role in the spawning behavior of the species. We've already seen how the buck selects a suitable bedding site and then fans out the nest. Next the male searches out a nearby "ripe" female and herds her from the vicinity of the holding station to the bedding location, oftentimes nipping pestiferously at the sometimes reluctant mama-to-be. Once on the bed he may swim continual circles around her to discourage her from leaving, and he may repeatedly bump her ventral region with his nose to trigger her into dropping her eggs.

In most cases the female will drop only a portion of her eggs at any one time. Days later, with another male, she may drop more eggs on some other bed not far away. These females usually constitute the "cruisers" seen working back and forth in shallow bays and coves or along various main-lake shorelines. Likely, they have already spawned once and are biding their time, waiting to be escorted to still another bedding site. Multiple attempts at egg-laying are probably nature's insurance policy, since a certain percentage of beds or eggs each year are sure to be accidentally destroyed. This frequently happens when land-slippage occurs, when there are radical fluctuations in water levels, or when there are abrupt changes in water temperature.

The total number of eggs dropped by any female largemouth, of course, depends upon the size of the fish. A three-pound bass may intermittently drop eight thousand eggs or more during the course of her inshore reproduction efforts. Revealing studies conducted by numerous biologists, however, have shown that bass are averse to overcrowding of their species. When such conditions occur in smaller bodies of water, male bass excrete into the water a chemical substance which prevents females from dropping their eggs (they're gradually assimilated by the female's body). Conversely, where bass populations are very low, females manufacture and deposit more eggs than usual, and the males manufacture more milt to fertilize them.

While both the male and female bass may engage in normal feeding behavior during very early spring as the water begins to warm, a later preoccupation with spawning most often causes all feeding to cease. Yet when the bass are on their beds they may still be caught rather readily. It is important for the angler to know, however, that the strikes he may receive are not the result of any type of feeding behavior, per se, but are due to assorted other reasons, and he should gear his tactics accordingly.

First consider the nonfeeding striking response of the sow bass, which may take on one of two forms. Either the female is eventually angered into striking by repeated presentations of the lure (something an angler can often accomplish with largemouths

The very largest bass caught are females, and during the spring spawn is the time to take real trophies. This "hawg" of nearly fifteen pounds came from Santee-Cooper in South Carolina. (*Courtesy of Santee-Cooper Country Offices*)

and Florida bass but seldom with female smallmouths and spotted bass) or the strike is not really a strike at all but the female bass simply engaging in her continual process of "housekeeping." What happens is that the female bass sees debris such as a twig or leaf (or an angler's lure) drift into the bedding area, whereupon she inhales it, swims a short distance from the bed and then exhales or blows it out of her mouth.

The male largemouth, on the other hand, can be coaxed most easily into striking when he is on the bedding site, though again it is not a specifically predatory feeding urge which prompts him to take the angler's lure. By instinct he is very protective of the bedding site and will attack intruders which often approach the nest with the intention of dining upon the eggs or newly-hatched fry.

If the fisherman is able to spot bass spawning beds visually, or if he has found cover and bottom conditions in those types of locations discussed earlier where beds are likely to be, he is almost certain to experience several distinct types of action. The first cast or two is sure to bring a vicious strike and a rather smallish bass will be landed. This is the male, and many anglers make the mistake of then resuming the business of moving further down the shoreline. If they would continue to fish the same area, with a much slower retrieve and with long pauses between movements of the lure, succeeding casts may eventually see them hook the much larger female bass. Her strike, or "take," however, will probably be much lighter. Look for a gentle "mouthing" of the bait and be ready to set the hook immediately! If this tactic proves unsuccessful, and the angler is convinced there is a much larger bass on or near the bed, repeated casting to the area may eventually see him rewarded with an arm-jolting strike. On numerous occasions I've located a huge sow bass on a bed and had consecutive casts to her result only in massive boils of water beneath my lure. That, in itself, is enough to make the hairs on any angler's neck bristle! But then, as many as thirty casts later, she may eventually become infuriated and really knock hell out of it. My guess is that the initial boiling of water beneath the lure is an attempt to rid the nest area of the intruder, but lack of success in this regard finally prompts her as a last resort to try to kill it, and in so doing she often hooks herself.

A few additional spring spawn-fishing tips might also be in order. First, in cases of cloudy water in which bass spawning beds cannot be spotted, it's always wise to fish the sunny sides of stumps, brush piles, felled trees, or other locations which otherwise appear as suitable for spawning. We'll see in later chapters how bass are normally quite averse to bright light and will retreat for the shaded sides of cover when in the shallows for brief visits during other seasons. But the spawning weeks are an exception to the rule, as bass will usually construct their nests so they are exposed as much as possible to the warming effects of the sun.

Also, if your shallow-water spawn-fishing efforts seem to be resulting only in small bass, the season is probably still in its earliest stages and the majority of fish in the shallows are males. Shift your efforts to the steep points at the mouths of embayments, the drop-offs, the edges of stream channels, and similar holding-station locations adjacent to deep water where there is some variation of timber, and you'll probably begin picking up the larger female bass.

Another possible explanation for the continual boating of only very small male bass is that you may not be fishing suitable spawn sites diligently enough to elicit strikes from the females. Make a minimum of twenty-five casts to those areas where beds have been located, rest the area for an hour or so, and then try again. You might also want to try alternating between a wide variety of lure sizes and lure types.

Fishing for bass during the spring while they are on or near the spawning sites can produce exciting action, large fish, and quite a number of bass on the stringer during a single day on the water. This is because the bass are much easier to locate now than they will be later on when the spawn is ended and the fish have evaporated (or so it seems, to many anglers) back into the depths.

But there has long been controversy—indeed, cursing and butting of heads—as to whether catching spawning bass does harm to future bass populations. One school claims there is no way any number of anglers, using conventional fishing tackle, can severely hurt the bass population in any large lake or reservoir, any time of year. Even many prominent biologists subscribe to this philosophy, having investigated the matter on behalf of certain state and federal fishery agencies or at the request of concerned tournament officials.

But many other fish and game departments in the United States and Canada, on the other hand, believe otherwise and maintain closed seasons in their areas during those periods in which bass are expected to be spawning.

To be sure, more research is needed in this area. But one thing is certain. If you release bass taken during the spawning season, they will return to their bedding sites and very shortly resume their reproduction efforts. If you carefully release bass caught at any time of year, you will not be depleting the bass population in that particular body of water.

As a final note on the subject, many anglers release all female bass in the two-to-four-pound category but feel little remorse in keeping fish that are much larger. The theory, which has not yet been conclusively proven one way or the other by biologists, is that the younger females are more fertile and that a much larger percentage of their eggs will hatch into healthy fry than will those deposited by some monarch which may be in the last months of her life. A good philosophy for any angler to adopt is simply never to waste this continually renewable but very valuable natural resource; keep only those fish you really need and can make good use of, and turn the rest loose.

After depositing her eggs, the female largemouth plays no further role in that particular reproduction or egg- or fry-rearing process, and she gradually begins to drift away from the bedding site. The eggs may hatch anytime from two to five days after they have been fertilized by the buck. And while the male largemouth will remain near the bed to protect the young fry from predators for a short while, he eventually succumbs to his increasingly ravenous hunger and becomes a leading predator himself, gobbling up as many of the fry as possible. This response—a well-planned scheme on the part of Mother Nature—causes the offspring to scatter and for the very first time begin fending for themselves. Self-preservation is usually accomplished by remaining in or around heavy shoreline cover, hiding from those who would make a meal of them in short order.

The hatched fry, when completely free of the yolk sacs which have nourished them until this time, experience growth rates determined by many factors. Initially they feed upon plankton and other minute aquatic organisms, later switching to the smallest of crustaceans and terrestrials, including various insect forms which commonly flit about most shallow-water areas during the spring and summer. And when they are about five inches long, they may also be seen feeding heavily upon small minnow species.

Growth rates of any of the bass species, then, are in direct proportion to the fertility of the waters they inhabit, the length of the growing season each year, and the numbers of other fish competing for the food supply the body of water is capable of sustaining. If all "influences" are in balance, the young bass may rapidly begin achieving weight and length in little time.

Other times, just the reverse may occur. In many smaller lakes and reservoirs across the country, and especially in farm ponds and ranch tanks, bluegill and crappie populations also inhabiting the water are not controlled, and their numbers soar. This has a devastating effect upon the bass population in two ways. First, the swarms of small panfish invade the bass nests to dine upon the eggs and newly hatched fry, preventing the bass population from replenishing itself as it would if the massive numbers of panfish were not present. Also, the panfish devour the available food supply that the small bass also require during their early growth stages. Resultantly, the small waterway may harbor a certain number of large bass, but there are few smaller ones continually growing to take their places. When the largest bass are eventually caught or die of old age, the lake or pond is left with nothing other than panfish which continue to reproduce, outrun their available food supply, and become even more stunted. Sometimes the only solution is to drain the pond and start all over.

So there can be no doubt that the lives of young bass are laced with uncertainties, threats to their well-being, and oftentimes disastrous whims of always unpredictable Mother Nature. They are cast into a precarious environment from the minute they are dropped onto a gravel bed in an encapsulated form, through the remainder of their development and existence in the water which will forever be their home. Panfish and crayfish, among many predators, will try to make a meal of them while they are still dependent and struggling under the burden of their yolk sacs. Larger panfish and smaller gamefish will swoop down upon them in the fry stage and decimate both their numbers and available food supply. Even their own parents cannot be trusted. Mother abandons them and several days later the father will attempt to swallow them! Only from three to five percent of any bass's spawnmates will survive these initial ravages in a watery world of survival-of-the-fittest, to be made meals of by still larger predator gamefish as he nears the yearling size. For the great majority of brothers and sisters there will be no escape and no tomorrow. But if a young bass is adept at hiding and soon accepts the philosophy of "eat or be eaten," he may eventually grow to large enough size that he will need have no fear of the other fishes and creatures which inhabit the same weedbeds and rocky drop-offs.

That will not be the end of any young bass's plight, however. He must still contend with man. There will come those sporting gentlemen who will attempt to fool him into biting upon metal, plastic, and wooden imitations of his food. They will tempt him with real food in which they have concealed hooks! Or they will capitalize upon his other vulnerability—the one which states that since he is a pugnacious gamefish he can be provoked into striking, whether he is hungry or not. They will infiltrate his domain on a regular basis, trying to hook him and hoping that he will cartwheel through the air for their pleasure, using tackle ranging from the crude to the sophisticated. He may survive many of these encounters by release during his early years, and he may survive still again in later years by using brute strength to smash their gear. But the one encounter with man which he will never survive will be that in which the ruler of the earth thoughtlessly destroys his habitat by channelization* or pollution.

Despite all of these hazards, the largemouth bass, and to a lesser extent the other bass species, continue to thrive in a majority of North American waters. They grow fat, they continue to increase in numbers, and they yield the unpredictable excitement of an often spectacular battle for those who brave the elements to search them out on their home grounds. It's not at all surprising that the various bass species are the most sought-after gamefish. That they are able to buck such seemingly insurmountable odds and still survive— even flourish—is testimony enough of the tenacity of the species.

When the spawning process is completed and the young bass fry have been left to make it on their own, the parent bass (of all species) exhibit insatiable appetites. As we said before, bass do not feed continually but usually restrict their active foraging to certain indeterminate times of day. Yet with the water continuing warm, further increasing their metabolic rates, the time periods of active feeding behavior, compared to the feeding behavior they engaged in during the previous cold-water months, become appreciably lengthened. The faster their systems burn food stores to create energy, the greater the supply of food now required during each feeding session. This, coupled with the fact that the long winter months and the subsequent act of spawning have precipitated a need to replenish lost body weight, make for fast spring fishing.

* Channelization, the straightening of a winding section of waterway to facilitate the flow of water, in the process destroys bass habitat and esthetics. A common term among anglers and environmentalists.

Since bass are averse to bright sunlight, and shallow water makes them feel ill at ease, when they leave the spawning grounds they usually hide in and around some type of cover which affords shade and seclusion. Leisurely hours can be spent drifting down shorelines studded with remnants of felled trees, stumps, rocks, submerged and emergent vegetation, and other cover with the angler, if he is careful in his approach, able to expect consistent action, either by eliciting feeding responses or by forcing the fish to strike. Now is a time of year in which explosive action can be enjoyed with a variety of surface or shallow-running plugs and other lures. The flyrodder is sure to be there, too, his line uncurling like a ballerina's arm as it ever so gently and methodically lays poppers or deer-hair bugs near suspected bass lairs.

The places where bass are found now, however, are only temporary stations, as they day by day continue gradually to drift back to their year-around deep-water homes. With each passing hour of the postspawn period, any shoreline plugger's chances of coming home with a heavy stringer progressively diminish. In lakes and reservoirs the bass are beginning to congregate along the edges of the depths. In days to follow they will actually be in the depths! Left behind will be the younger bass, in various stages of growth ranging from two to twelve inches in length (many of them from previous spawning seasons), to find whatever comfort, food, and hiding the shallow shoreline cover may provide. And the young bass will remain in these places too, at least until they have grown to respectable size and likewise discover they can no longer tolerate the bright light and unsafe conditions which prevail in the shallow haunts.

Many less-accomplished anglers are probably at this time beginning to offer explanations as to why they are no longer catching bass larger than minimum "keeper" size. As products of past, erroneous conditioning, they may sincerely believe the large bass have stopped biting. "The dog days are approaching," they claim, "and the bass are becoming inactive."

The truth of the matter is that the large bass are now more active than ever! They are feeding heavily during those certain times of day when their biological clocks tell them to replenish fuel supplies, and when they are not actively foraging they can more easily be provoked into striking. Now, they can be caught in larger numbers than at any other time of year!

The problem is that most anglers are still plugging the shallow shorelines where they found the fish during the brief prespawn, spawn, and postspawn periods. But the bass have long since moved away from those places, and won't return again until the following spring.

THE SCHOOLING DISPOSITION

Secrecy has probably been an integral component of bass fishing since those halcyon times when Dr. James A. Henshall, a Cincinnati, Ohio, physician was one day seen slipping out the back door of his office carrying an umbrella and traditional black bag. That was back in 1880, a time in which house-calls were very much a responsibility of the medical profession, but on this day the visiting of patients was far from Henshall's thoughts. Concealed in the umbrella was a four-piece bamboo flyrod. And in the medical bag were hooks, rooster-hackle, and linen lines. He was off to pursue his first love in life, and his destination was a certain pool in a nearby river which contained good numbers of "specimens" that had not yet been discovered by his compatriots. Unfortuitous was this day, however, because someone had noted something suspicious about the way he left his office from the rear door, followed him to the pool, and soon the jig was up.

It was Henshall, only a year later, who undertook the responsibility for amassing in a single volume the biological nomenclature of the various bass species he had studied in the Ohio valley tributaries, along with the research findings of other scientists throughout the bass's native ranges. His detailed textbook on the subject, entitled *Book of the Black Bass*, written nearly a century ago, has long since become a cherished classic in the home libraries of esoteric anglers.

But in Henshall's case several things must be remembered. His approach to bass fishing and his "information-gathering" sessions, as much as he loved the sport, were nearly always from a biologist's rather than an angler's standpoint. And even at that, his research pertaining to the habits of bass was often cursory and not authenticated. At one time Henshall even subscribed to a theory held at the time that bass, each evening after full dark, left the water to forage on land! To be sure, Henshall was a pioneer; but during those times, few reliable methods or tools existed such as are available to modern biologists for obtaining accurate data. As a result, from Henshall's time to about the 1940s, supposition, speculation and sometimes downright misinformation were frequently passed from one generation of anglers to another as the pastime of fishing continued to grow in popularity in this country. Competition has always been ingrained in mankind's personality. And when an angler did happen to catch several nice bass, probably more by coincidence than anything else, the tactics which contributed to the catch were often guarded and hoarded from those who, it was believed, would use them to their own advantage.

Even today an aura of secrecy or mystery still prevails in bass fishing to a substantial degree. Many anglers still cling to the hope that someday they will chance upon a "magic" lure and the empty-stringer syndrome which has eternally plagued them will forever be solved. Others allow manufacturers to convince them that obtaining a high-priced electronic depth-sounder is the key. And still others, perhaps standing dockside with a few fish to show for their efforts, may be entirely close-mouthed about any fishing tactics they employed that day. They may even steer questioning bystanders in the opposite direction!

I'm sad to say that even many of my own cohorts these days—nationally known outdoor writers—are guilty of continuing to perpetuate the secrecy associated with bass-fishing success. Pluck almost any national outdoor magazine off the newsstands and you'll see countless stories in which the authors promote bizarre casting styles or describe how to jerk your lure this way or twitch it that way. Still other articles may claim fishing after dark is the way to see success, or that adding pork rind to your lures is the "secret." The glaring error most such fishing writers make is the false assumption that their angler-readers have already located the bass.

All of the above techniques, and others, to a certain extent, may have their rightful place in bass fishing. But the truth of the matter is, if the angler is fishing where the bass aren't, he will accomplish little more than tiring his arm and shoulder muscles, regardless of his expertise in implementing countless innovative variations of lure presentation and manipulation.

Exceptional is the man who through study and research has obtained accurate information and freely divulges those findings to anyone who may ask. Such is the case with Buck Perry, who has devoted most of his life to eliminating the mystery that has for too long been a byword in bassdom. It is not even uncommon for Buck to reveal the exact locations in various bodies of water where he catches his bass, simply because he enjoys seeing other anglers bring in good fish. It is proof positive to them that angling is a sport which can be learned!

Where bass are likely to be found during each of the four seasons of the year has long been a puzzle to a good majority of this country's anglers. Buck often answers this question with simple yet highly insightful phrases like, "the bass will always be in the shallows, in the depths, or somewhere in between." This may seem to some, upon first inspection, an evasive reply. But actually, Buck is laying an important foundation to which he then commences to add building blocks of further information in an attempt to help anglers understand how bass live in the depths but occasionally travel to the shallows.

In the previous section, which focused upon the brief spring spawn, we examined the time of year in which bass are in the shallows. Now it is time to launch upon the complicated subject of how bass live and move during the remaining months of the year when they are in the depths or somewhere in between. This will constitute a critical part of our learning, because after the prespawn, spawn, and postspawn periods, each of which may last only two or three weeks, the shorelines of any given body of water (which most anglers perpetually plug) serve little purpose to bass other than to hold the water in the lake or reservoir.

We should not assume, however, that simply moving away from the shoreline means we'll find bass easily, because 90 percent of any given body of water, at any given time, is as barren of good-sized fish as your living room. This is because only 10 percent of the water at any given time possesses the combination of ideal characteristics that bass will be seeking under the prevailing water and weather conditions. Consequently, the overwhelming majority of bass will be found in that 10 percent of water.

First, therefore, as Perry says, "You have to determine where the bass are likely to be." That is the goal to which we will devote many of the following sections. Only after we have determined where to look for the bass do the questions of lures and their presentation enter the picture and influence whether or not we will be successful in eliciting feeding responses or provoking strikes.

But perhaps we should first backtrack just a bit for the sake of continuity. At the conclusion of the last section we left the bass as they were finishing their spawning activities and beginning to congregate near the edges of the depths (again, we're concentrating in this chapter on lakes and reservoirs; rivers, streams, and other waters will be covered in separate chapters). The question that immediately rises is why the bass are congregating along the edges of the depths and where they plan to go next.

To find the answer to this question, the reader must understand and accept as truth a few rules of thumb concerning bass behavior. First, all bass, once they have grown beyond the yearling size, have an instinctive desire to school with like members of their species. In numbers there is a sense of safety, and bass will group together with others of their own approximate size. In one school, for example, there will be fish averaging between two and three pounds; in another, four-to-five-pounders, and so on. The larger the size of individual fish comprising the school, however, the smaller the school in numbers and the more tightly they will group together. The very largest bass in any given body of water may sometimes group together in twos and threes, but just as often they are loners. In the case of largemouths and Florida bass, we're talking here about fish over eight or nine pounds. Seldom will you find a school of largemouths or Floridas in which the individual school members weigh much over six or seven pounds. Of course, in the cases of smallmouths and spotted bass, which typically do not grow as large as largemouths and Floridas, the individual school members will average much smaller, usually between two and four pounds.

The second fact or rule of thumb is that all bass beyond the yearling size (usually from nine to thirteen inches in length and averaging a pound in weight) are basically deep-water fish and that is where, in their respective schools, they will spend most of their time. Fortunately for anglers, schools of bass (of all species) occasionally travel or *migrate* from their deep-water haunts to shallower areas, making them easier for us to catch. But the larger the individual fish comprising the schools, the less willing they are to leave the deep water, and when they do migrate they are less likely to move as far into the shallows as some other school comprised of smaller fish.

Why are bass deep-water fish? Well, for a number of reasons. The larger any bass becomes, the more shy and retiring he is in his behavior. As we have already mentioned, bass do not possess much in the way of intelligence, at least as we refer to the term; they cannot reason, nor can they weigh the consequences of their behavior. But—and this also bears repeating—their survival instincts are highly refined. Anything which even hints that their survival may be in jeopardy causes them to retreat hastily.

Picture any lake near some metropolitan area during the summer months. The shoreline is speckled with vacation cottages, docks, and swimming beaches. Here and there kids are skipping stones across the surface, less-accomplished anglers are lashing the shallows to a froth with their futile casting efforts, there is considerable motorboat and waterskier commotion, and perhaps an occasional ominous shadow looms against the skyline as some hiker plods along a shoreline trail. Now, for a moment let's look at the world from the bass's viewpoint. From the very moment they are hatched from their eggs, all bass's precautionary instincts have told them to flee from activity or risk being eaten. In the fry, fingerling, and yearling stages of growth, they have learned they can escape larger predators by vanishing into the dark recesses of shoreline weeds and rocks, and that these places are also ideal locations to wait in ambush as predators themselves. But as they grew still older and larger, with their schooling dispositions all the while approaching maturity, they soon discovered they were faced with little choice but to retreat to deeper waters. That is the only place large enough for a group to hide from disturbance.

But there is still another reason why bass do not use the very shallow shorelines after the brief spawn weeks. Sunlight easily penetrates the shallows. And bright light, in addition to promoting still more anxieties over safety and well-being, is very uncomfortable to a bass's eyes. His are fixed-pupil eyes, meaning they cannot contract or dilate to accommodate to various light intensities (he can, however, acquire types of "night vision" and "day vision" which we'll talk about later). In effect, then, his eyes are always wide open. If you were to look toward the sun for a few seconds without dark glasses, you would simulate the discomfort bass experience in clear, shallow water on a bright day. Now, turn your head toward the shade and notice the difference. If a bass is to find relief from the bright light, he must head for the depths and remain at some level where sunlight cannot penetrate; or, if there are no depths, he must retreat into the shaded comfort of "colored" water or places where there are expanses of very heavily matted weedbeds, lily pads, submerged brush, or felled trees. (The concept of light penetration, and how it affects bass, is discussed more thoroughly in Chapter 3.)

So there is no single reason why bass are basically deep-water fish, but rather a combination of reasons which include safety, adhering to an instinct to school with like members of his species, and aversion to bright light.

We've established that bass are school fish and that in most lakes and reservoirs they will spend most of their time in the depths. But how deep is "deep"? Will the depth to which bass go remain constant throughout the coming months? Are there any exceptions to the rule?

Depth is always relative. In some expansive southern impoundment, "deep water" may be where an old stream channel winding along the floor of the reservoir drops off to ten feet. Ten feet is certainly very deep water if 95 percent of the reservoir area averages only five or six feet in depth, which is a common situation throughout much of the South and especially in Florida. Since deep water is the usual home of the fish, the bass in this particular impoundment will probably be spending most of their time in the stream channel. Unless, that is, the water is extremely clear and ten feet deep is as uncomfortable to them as five feet. Then, they will probably restrict their homes to certain portions of the stream channel where there is an undercut bank, such as an "S" turn in the channel. Or, they may even leave the channel in order to seek shade under heavily matted vegetation where the light penetration is severely impeded. In a crystal-clear natural lake in some northern state, however, where there exist depths perhaps to a hundred feet or more, ten feet would probably be classified as very shallow and therefore only infrequently see bass activity. In such a body of water the fish would probably elect to spend most of their time in depths ranging from twenty-five to forty feet, and their migrations or movements would probably see them come no shallower than 10 or 12 feet (except during the spring spawn, of course). But all of this depends upon existing water and weather conditions. Reduced light penetration, such as during low-light periods of early morning or late evening or even after dark, might see them move to shallower water upon occasion. And cold-front weather conditions might see them move considerably deeper. As a general rule, bass will go as deep as need be to feel safe and avoid bright light.

There is an exception to this deep-water behavior of bass, and that has to do with many types of *newly created* manmade lakes and reservoirs. These comprise, perhaps, as little as one percent of the bass-fishing water available in this country, but for the sake of the "complete" education of the aspiring bass angler, they should be mentioned here.

The early years of any lake or reservoir's life provide very exciting fishing. For the first five to ten years or so, the floor of the impoundment is abundantly endowed with various nitrogen compounds, and these foster not only the aquatic growth but a very prolific food-chain. Hordes of baitfish and other delectables encourage the young bass to feed ravenously, and their populations rapidly increase. Because the life-sustaining nitrogen compounds and the subsequent food-chain are both widely dispersed over the reservoir area, so too are the bass, and they continue to put on weight.

It is during these youthful years of an impoundment's life that the shoreline plugger sees fast action and is able to load his stringer on almost every trip out. The bass are not yet overly large, averaging from two to three pounds with perhaps an occasional four-, five-, or six-pounder showing up, but they seem to be almost everywhere. Because such fertile waters are abundantly supplied with vegetation, flooded brush, and standing timber, a continual process of decay creates stained or at least slightly murky water, and this reduces light penetration. The bass can feel relatively safe under these conditions, and since the shallow-water covers are teeming with food, the fish seem to delay their normal movement toward the depths. They seem to prefer, for a while at least, to seek refuge in and around the existing cover where they can capitalize upon the free eats, and this makes them easy targets for anglers. Even a lure cast by unskilled hands may see a strike. Consequently, in little time, the impoundment receives the reputation of being "hot," and voluminous amounts of national publicity in the outdoor magazines prompt anglers to flock to the site in droves.

A current example of an impoundment with this spark of youth is Toledo Bend Reservoir in Texas. If you want to take a fishing vacation with Mama and the kids, with the assurance that all of you will catch plenty of bass, that is the place to go. I have seen beginning anglers, often armed with little more than dimestore gear, land as many as twenty bass in a single day at Toledo. They may have had a total of seventy strikes! A jubilant Mardi Gras flavor permeates the air at the fishing camps and resort areas. Nothing makes anglers more happy than catching bass! But you'd better hurry. Like all good things, the fun is usually short-lived.

After about ten years, but sometimes more or less, depending upon the individual body of water and its limnological characteristics, the fishing action begins to taper off slowly for the plug-pitcher. He begins to notice he is no longer king of the mountain. His tireless casting to weedbeds, stumps, and felled trees is now resulting in fewer and fewer strikes. The bass, of course, are still in the impoundment in plentiful numbers, and they are now larger than ever. The angler has simply failed to adapt his fishing style to the changing personality of the water as it progressively continues to age.

One of the many changes a lake or reservoir experiences as it grows older is the gradual depletion of the life-sustaining nitrogen. And while this may have little noticeable effect upon the aquatic growth, it severely affects the food-chain, reducing its capability to reproduce. *A major result is that the most productive fishing areas become progressively fewer in number.* With far less food present and now concentrated only in certain areas, and perhaps with the water color even beginning to clear somewhat, the habits of the bass will also be seen to change. They are no longer roamers, nor are they widely distributed over most of the impounded area. They have begun schooling or at least loosely grouping in certain areas near the depths. Soon they will be in the depths! And the once-true situation of "a bass in every bush" is rapidly becoming so much history.

As the easy catches for the unskilled masses of anglers become rare, the national publicity will slowly dwindle, and in all likelihood the angler who must have visible, shallow-water cover to cast to will give up on this impoundment. He will begin searching for a new place to fish, another impoundment only recently constructed and now having its heyday. The angler may either sincerely believe the once-hot water is now "fished out," which is absolutely never the case, or he may simply be unwilling to work at his fishing when there may be a younger lake or reservoir nearby where the pickings are easy.

Toledo Bend, it is true, is now very hot. But, alas, it will follow the same course as the many others that have gone before. Ever heard of Bull Shoals Reservoir in Arkansas? Probably not recently. But there was a time not too many years ago when the name "Big Bull" was on the lips of every bass-angler across the nation. Everybody who ventured on Bull Shoals' waters was almost guaranteed a full stringer by day's end. Of course that is no longer true, at least not for the average angler. The water is clear now, the food chain has long since settled down into daily, predictable movements, and the bass spend nearly all of their time in the depths. Fantastic strings of bass are still caught at Bull Shoals and on somewhat of a regular basis, but never by the shoreline plugger. Those catches are logged by grizzled old deep-water hounds who long ago accepted the tenets of bass behavior.

"STRUCTURE" IS THEIR HOME

We have established that bass live in schools in the depths, and that in any given lake or reservoir there are only certain locations where those schools may be found at any given time. In the further systematic elimination of barren or unproductive water, we'll now add to our growing knowledge still another fact.

Bass live on or very near the bottom. The actual depth bass will go to will vary from time to time due to weather and water conditions. But regardless of whether the bass are in twelve or twenty-five feet of water, or shallower or deeper, they will nearly always be on the bottom. There are two exceptions to this rule. One is when the water is less than about six feet deep and the other is when the bass suspend at arbitrary depths, chasing after surface-swimming schools of baitfish. Both situations are discussed later.

Schools of bass don't live, however, on just any type of bottom. They live on what is commonly referred to as *structure*. Structure is the presence of any bottom condition which presents a noticeable difference from surrounding bottom conditions. We saw in the section about spawning behavior how bass like bottom materials consisting of coarse sand, gravel, shell, rocks, clay, or marl, and how they are usually averse to heavy concentrations of mud or silt. The same is basically true during their deep-water lives throughout the remainder of the year.

There are many types of structure which bass in any given lake or reservoir may be using at any given time. It may be an underwater hump or island which juts up from the floor of the impoundment, a long underwater bar, or perhaps a point of land which juts out from the shorline and then extends underwater for some distance. Other structures might consist of the edge of a weedline where the water rapidly drops off into the depths, a series of underwater stairstep ledges or rocky outcroppings, a place where the bottom composition changes from sand to clay, or perhaps a stream channel winding along the floor of the body of water. These are all classified as "natural" structures. Not all of them are present in every body of water, but any body of water usually has some of them.

One of the best ways to grasp the idea of underwater structure is to take an occasional drive through the country in your auto. Stop now and then along the side of the road and survey the surrounding terrain, pretending that all of a sudden the entire area is flooded with water in the creation of a manmade reservoir and that you have a picture-window view of the reservoir's floor. Now, search for places around you where the terrain exhibits radical changes of one kind or another. Note the ridgelines and how they slope at different angles. These, when underwater, will usually be the points jutting out from the shorelines. Note the flat bottom-land areas and see if you can find humps. These will be the submerged islands jutting up from the floor of the reservoir. Are there any elongated mounds spanning certain sections of the flats? These will be the bars. Do you see any depressions, cuts, or slices in the terrain? These will be the "holes," which are often bass-magnets of the first order. Are there any creeks, brooks, or streams meandering through the terrain? These too will hold many bass during most months of the year. Are there any steep banks, bluffs, or cliffs? Bass will probably be along these sheer walls during the winter months. What about cover such as brushpiles, long hedgerows, small clumps of trees, rock piles, or other structural formations which seem to be situated in open pastures or fields, or on hillsides? These, too, constitute radical changes in the bottom and would probably hold bass.

Also, as you are surveying different types of terrain in the country, continually ask yourself questions. If the area really were inundated, where would the deepest water be? Where would the bottom be hard and clean, and where would it be soft and dirty? When bass move out of the deepest water during early spring, with thoughts of spawning, what areas do you see before you that they would probably move into, according to what we learned in the spawning section of this book? After you've found what would probably be the spawning grounds, can you find locations female bass would use as holding stations? Do you see any types of structure which extend from what would be the shoreline all the way into what would be the deepest water in the area? Examples might be a long sloping point (ridge), perhaps a row of stumps, a felled tree lying on a steep hillside, intermittent piles of rocks, or even a small brook trickling down from the highlands. These many configurations, and others, as we will see later, will probably be the very best bass structures in any body of water.

In addition to "natural" structures, artificial bodies of water such as reservoirs will also possess a number of various "manmade" structures. Manmade structures afford the same radical changes in the bottom, and you may see many of them in our hypothetically created lake as you drive cross-country. An old building foundation is one example, or perhaps the supporting concrete pillars of a small country bridge crossing a small river. Are there any roads, trails, or paths winding across the terrain? These will nearly always be constructed of very hard materials, and if they are surrounded by soft marshy ground they will be fish-magnets during all seasons, but especially at spawning time if they are located near the shallows. The same applies to abandoned railroad spurs you may locate. The ties and rails may have been removed, but the limestone bedding is certain to be still intact. Are there any fencerows, borrow pits (where gravel and other materials were removed for construction purposes), drainage culverts along roads, or utility poles? Junk piles of scrap building materials such as bricks and concrete slabs, along with other trash, often hold amazing numbers of bass. When impoundments are created where farms once existed, many anglers take big fish, believe it or not, from things lying on the bottom such as hot-water heaters, abandoned stoves and refrigerators, and even rusted automobile bodies! All of these, and more, which men have created and discarded, constitute manmade "structure," and bass will use them as religiously as they do the weedbeds, felled trees, bars, points, and drop-offs.

The reason for locating either natural or manmade structure—and this is very important—is that bass, during every month of the year, are highly "object-oriented." One of Buck Perry's classical observations, and this is something no angler should ever forget, is, "You may find structure which at the moment is not holding bass, but you will never find bass without structure."

The place where a school of bass rests in deep water is called the *sanctuary*. But only in rare circumstances can bass be caught when in this resting area, for a variety of reasons. First, the sanctuary is usually a very small area where the fish, when resting, are schooling very tightly. Because the sanctuary will likely be in very deep water, pinpointing its exact location can be next to impossible.

Additionally, because of the depth, precise presentation of lures is a precarious venture at best, as various "controls" which must be exercised over the lures are lost. And finally, when in the sanctuary the school of bass is in a rather inactive state and can seldom be tempted into biting or provoked into striking.

But as we noted earlier, and this is fortunate for anglers, the school of bass will occasionally *migrate* or travel from the sanctuary to some other area a short distance away, usually located in somewhat shallower water. And during the course of this migration they can be caught in a variety of ways because they are now in a highly active state and the shallower water makes precise lure presentation easier.

In discussing the migration habits of bass, it might be interesting at this time to make brief mention of a revealing study conducted only recently. This will help to tie up a few loose ends in our previous comments about how far bass are likely to move around during the course of a year, and how they are basically deep-water fish.

Two scientists associated with Southern Illinois University slowly moved along a shoreline in a boat, using electrical shocking equipment (which only temporarily stuns fish) to capture a large number of spawning bass that were in the shallows. The fish were tagged (marked for identification) and then carefully released back into the water. Subsequent shocking programs were then carried out during following months.

The study revealed that after the spawning period—and this substantiates what we said earlier about bass moving away from the shallows after the brief spawn weeks—only 1.2 percent of the originally captured bass were back on the shoreline at any given time. What this means is that after spawning has been completed, 98 percent of the fish spend the majority of their time away from the shallows and in deeper water. In addition, it was revealed that 96 percent of the bass which at some time or other left the depths and migrated toward the shallows were recaptured within three hundred feet of where they were initially tagged. This substantiates the "home range" tendency, briefly mentioned earlier, in which we distinguished bass from some other gamefish species which are classified as migratory (seen to engage in seasonal shifts of location, often covering long distances, as in the case of salmon). The term *migration,* when discussing bass, refers to short-term and short-distance movements within the home range.

When bass migrate from their sanctuaries, however, they do not simply fan out and disperse. Nor do they travel in a haphazard manner or in random directions. Rather, they travel in an orderly fashion as a group and along types of underwater "highways," or migration routes, following "signposts" or structural variations which show them the way to their destinations.

During the warm-water months of late spring, summer, and fall (during all months in the warmer southern states), these migrations or movements within the home range may take place two or three times each day. Migrations frequently take place during the early morning hours, sometime around noon, and again during the evening (but if you will carefully study Chapter 14 you will discover they can take place at almost any time and how to determine those times precisely). A migration may last as long as two hours or be as brief as only twenty minutes. During the cold-water months of late fall, winter, and very early spring, however, migrations may often take place only once per day or once every other day, usually around noon, and they are frequently of only thirty minutes' duration or less.

Additionally, and this is very important, the season of year determines the migrational characteristics. From the sanctuary area, during the cold-water months, the bass seem to migrate more on a vertical plane as they move from the depths toward the steeper shorelines. Also, the distance of the migration is usually somewhat shorter. During the warm-water months (when the water temperature is above 50 degrees Fahrenheit), the bass have a tendency to migrate more on a horizontal plane as they move from the depths toward the shallow shorelines. Chart 1 shows how season of the year usually affects migrations. In fact, you may have already experienced this phenomenon yourself, noticing that your best catches during the colder months of the year seem to come from the steep shorelines which rapidly drop off into the depths, while your best catches during the warmer months predominantly come from gradually sloping shorelines which extend far out into the lake or reservoir.

It should also be noted that bass schools do not always migrate only because they are hungry and are in search of food. This should be obvious because it is inconceivable that every bass in every school in a given body of water would be hungry at exactly the same time. Okay, then why *do* bass migrate several times a day? Well, that is something no one has positively determined. All we really

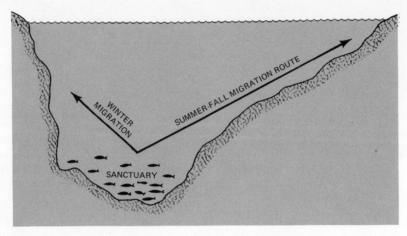

Chart 1. The shift in bass migration tendencies during various seasons

know is that bass schools do migrate at certain times and that those times are predictable. More research needs to be conducted in this area, and I have related the findings of several studies in Chapter 14. But for the purposes of this section we need only to know that when some biological clock or other mysterious force triggers an instinct to migrate, nearly all of the various schools of bass in any given lake or reservoir will simultaneously begin climbing out of their sanctuaries and traveling to their destinations. Further, that it is during these movement periods that they are most frequently caught by anglers.

This, again, is something you may have already noted during your fishing experiences. If you keep a logbook, indicating when and where you've caught your bass in the past, and if you compare that log with the catches made by your angling buddies, you'll probably discover that your peak periods of action have been quite similar. If you encountered most of your fish during, say, the hours of seven to nine o'clock in the morning on a given day, and your buddy was on the water and likewise caught fish that day, it's a good bet that most of his bass came aboard during roughly the same time period.

CHAPTER 2

More on Structure

We've outlined, very basically, a few of the behavior mannerisms of bass as they periodically migrate back and forth between their deep-water resting areas and associated shallow-water destinations. And we'll continue in this and other sections to look at bass migrations in even greater detail. But before we delve much farther into the complexities of how bass live in the depths and occasionally travel to places where they can be caught, we should spend some time acquiring map lore. The use of topographic maps and hydrologic charts is a critical ingredient in homing in upon bass in lakes and reservoirs.

MAP LORE

At first view, any type of bottom-contour map can be bewildering. But after continued use, traveling to the exact locations of specific underwater stuctures in a lake or reservoir is really not any more difficult than using a standard roadmap to travel to some neighboring town by auto.

By using contour lines and other symbols, cartographers are able to show what the bottom of any body of water looks like. The angler, in turn, after careful scrutiny and interpretation of such maps, can determine the exact locations of the deepest water in certain areas of any lake or reservoir, what structures exist and where they are located, what areas bass are likely to be using as sanctuaries, and which nearby structures they are likely to use when they migrate. He can also isolate other bottom conformations which are likely to draw and hold straggler bass (those which for some reason have become separated from their schools).

A "topographic" map shows the land contours *before* the lake or reservoir was created in the area. But the land contours are represented in different maps with varied scales. Understandably, those maps which have a scale of one inch to the mile would be almost worthless to a structure angler. It is always wise to obtain topo maps with the smallest scale or contour intervals possible. In many cases ten-foot contour intervals can be had and sometimes you'll really strike it lucky and find maps showing five-foot intervals. Regardless of what the contour interval may be, though, topographic maps are consistently more accurate than other types because they are made by professional surveyors treading across dry land.

A "hydrologic" map is a contour chart made *after* the area has been inundated, usually in the cases of natural lakes which may have existed for thousands or perhaps even millions of years. Sometimes aerial photography is used to make hydro maps, which in such cases are "generally" but not "precisely" accurate.

Whatever type of map is available for the body of water you wish to explore, also keep in mind that bottom structures that were in evidence at the time the map was made may appear slightly different now. Maps are usually made or reverified at fifteen- or twenty-year intervals. And during that time, especially in sandy regions, wind and wave action may have partially obliterated some structures and in the process created new ones. Stumps and trees on the bottom may have gradually rotted away over the years. Periodic landslides near steep shorelines, where boulders have tumbled into the water, may have created ideal structures where none previously existed.

All of this makes a good case in favor of obtaining an electronic depth sounder, turning it on when you leave the dock in the morning and not turning it off until you pull your boat out of the water in the evening. Many times you'll inadvertently discover structures not shown on the map, and these may prove to be real bass bonanzas.

Various types of contour maps for areas lying east of the Mississippi can be obtained by writing to the U.S. Geological Survey Map Distribution Center, 1200 South Eads Street, Arlington, Virginia 22202. For maps of areas west of the Mississippi, write to U.S. Geological Survey, Federal Center, Denver, Colorado 80225. Each office will send you, first, an index listing maps available for the area you request. Using this index, you can then select appropriate quadrangles of lake or reservoir areas you wish to investigate, and send in your order form. The price of each map (in all cases, less than $2.00 apiece) is listed in the map index.

Other maps of various sorts may be available through your state's department of natural resources, the District Engineers of the U.S. Army Corps of Engineers, private engineering offices, and sometimes even tackle shops and marinas near the water you intend to fish.

Whatever the source of your maps, if you receive topographic maps, which show only contour lines of an existing area before it was inundated, rather than hydrologic maps, you'll have to draw in the shorelines of the present lake or reservoir. This can be done by simply determining the maximum pool elevation of the waterway and then following that contour line on the map with a felt-tipped pen. If you don't know the maximum pool elevation, the agency that created or presently manages the waterway, or your local department of natural resources, can supply you with the information.

In certain, infrequent cases in which no maps are available, the only alternative is to explore the water with an electronic depth sounder, making your own map.

Depth sounders are probably the century's greatest boon to bass fishing, and every serious angler should own one. There are three main types, but all operate either from a pair of dry-cell batteries or the twelve-volt battery on board your craft. The first is the simple needle-gauge depth sounder. This is the least expensive, costing an average of $40, and it very simply indicates the depth of the water beneath your boat.

The most expensive type of depth sounder is the graph-recorder, which can cost many hundreds of dollars, and which actually draws a permanent picture of the lake, from the surface to the bottom, showing all depths and structural conformations.

The majority of serious bass anglers tread the middle ground, using a third type of depth sounder which costs between $75 and $200. It possesses a clocklike face which is marked in various increments indicating depths to seventy-five feet or more. Here is how it works. A probe or "transducer" mounted on the hull of the boat transmits sound waves into the water. At the same time, a high-intensity neon bulb whirls at a constant speed behind the calibrated face of the depth sounder. The sound-wave discharges are regulated to fire about twenty-four times per second at zero on the dial. This gives a constant surface reading. The bulb also fires twenty-four times per second at the point on the dial that indicates the depth, which is determined by the length of time it takes the sound waves to reach the bottom and return to the transducer. Although the bulb is rapidly firing, it appears to the human eye as an almost constant light.

Through the use of a depth sounder, an angler can determine the exact water depth beneath his boat and he can also determine the bottom composition and the location of various types of structures. For example, if the band of light indicating depth on the face of the depth sounder is very wide and bright, this means the bottom composition is hard (such as gravel or sand) and is returning a strong signal. If the band of light is thin and weak, the bottom is soft (such as mud) and is absorbing the signal. Individual spikes (thin bands of light) appearing above the bottom signal indicate that something between the bottom and the boat is interrupting the signal. These spikes may represent fish, but more often they indicate the presence of weeds, large boulders, stumps, brush, and so on. A rapid change of depth, of course, indicates a drop-off. A minor change may indicate a gradual slope or an underwater hump. Accurately reading a depth sounder takes practice but isn't all that difficult. Full instructions come with the units, which can be obtained through tackle shops, marinas and fishing-tackle mail-order houses.

BRUSH AND TREES

Brush and underwater tree signals appear similar. Underwater tree limbs at various depths return individual signals and account for the wide band of signals on the dial. Brush returns a narrower band of individual signals. Fish often gather around these submerged obstacles. To detect them, anchor bow to stern. Constant signals indicate tree limbs. Signals that come and go or shift up and down are fish.

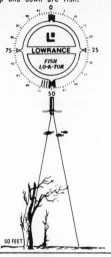

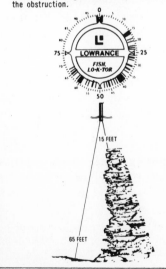

WEEDS RETURN THIN, PALE SIGNALS

Approaching an underwater weed bed creates thin, pale signals climbing up toward the zero signal — and as the boat leaves — they go back down toward the bottom signal. Weeds don't grow in water more than 12 to 15 feet due to lack of sunlight.

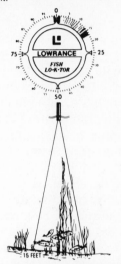

SIGNALS FROM STEEP, ROCKY LEDGES

Underwater ledges or cliffs, either vertical or inclined, will show multiple lines on the dial. Sound waves hit rough spots on the the cliff all the way down. The signals on the dial will cover an area extending from the top to the base of the obstruction.

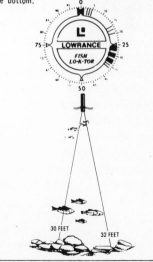

ROCKY BOTTOM SIGNALS

The dial will indicate the level of the bottom at the correct depth, but will also show clear, thin signals both above and below the wider main bottom signal. This is because the rocks near the outer edge of the cone of sound waves are farther from the transducer than those in the center, while the tops of the latter are closer than the bottom.

Interpretation of signals on depth sounder with dial face. (*Courtesy of Lowrance Electronics Corporation*)

Before we got sidetracked into a discussion of depth sounders, we were talking about bottom-contour maps.

Examining any contour map for the first time, look first at the "key" or "legend." This is a small block in one corner of the map which indicates how bottom structures are represented on that particular map. The land surrounding the water will probably be shown in either brown, yellow, or dark green. Shallow shoreline water will probably be in white, moderate depths in light green, intermediate depths in light blue, and the deepest water the lake or reservoir has to offer in dark blue. In the case of topographic maps showing areas before inundation, standing vegetation or timber is represented in dark green, while bottomlands and open fields, of either higher or lower elevation, are represented in light brown or light green.

Stream channels are usually represented as dotted lines, borrow pits or abandoned mines or quarries are usually shown by a symbol such as a crossed pick and shovel, building foundations are simple blocks, old roadbeds are dual lines, abandoned railroad spurs are single lines with perpendicular cross-marks, swampy areas are shown by symbols which look like rising suns, and standing timber or brush is represented by "puffball" marks.

Reading and interpreting the contour lines themselves is relatively easy if you go slowly and survey only small sections of the map at a time. In various places the individual lines will be broken and a number inserted. On some maps the number may be a true representation of depth. But in many cases, especially on topographic maps, only sea levels will be shown and you'll have to make mental calculations in order to determine the actual water depth. This is done by simply subtracting the sea level figure from the normal pool stage figure.* If the normal pool stage for the lake in question is 358 feet, for example, and the sea-level reading of the particular contour line you are inspecting is 338 feet, you know the water depth indicated by that contour line is 20 feet deep.

Contour lines which are spaced far apart indicate gradual underwater slopes with only modest changes in depth, while contour lines which are very close together indicate rapid changes in depth. This is one of the keys to understanding bottom contours and which

---

* The pool stage is usually clearly marked on the map in case of hydrologic charts. On topographic maps the pool stage can be determined by contacting the local agency that regulates the waterway, as described on page 35.

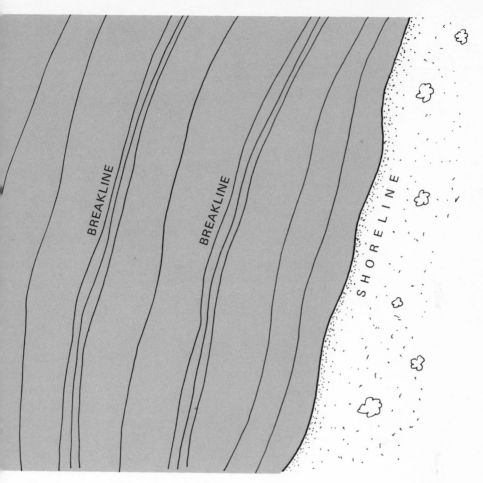

Chart 2. Breaklines off a lake shore

structures bass may or may not elect to use during the course of their migrations from the depths.

Chart 2 shows a section of shoreline as it might appear on a map, with contour lines drawn in. As you can see, several widely spaced contour lines just beyond the edge of the shoreline show how the bank begins to slope away gently underwater. Then there are several contour lines very close together, indicating a rapid change of depth. Next comes another gently sloping section of bottom and then still another drop. Nearly every body of water will have a similar shoreline configuration as the bottom slopes, either sharply in places or gradually, into the depths. The actual drops, where the

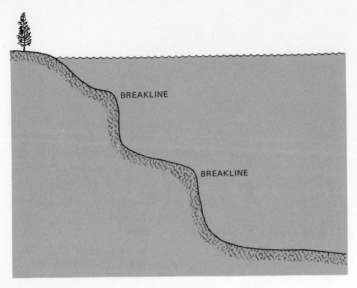

Chart 3. Configuration of a typical breakline

contour lines are close together and run for some distance, are called *breaklines*. Every body of water will have at least one break-line, usually two or three and sometimes several more. Further, these breaklines commonly extend around the entire lake, regardless of its size.

Chart 3 shows a side view of the shoreline configuration and breaklines shown in Chart 2.

Any interruption in the smooth contour of the breakline is called a *break,* and these interruptions may take on the appearance of sharp pockets or indentations or other variances in the breakline configuration, to include the presence of some structural feature (either natural or manmade) such as a stump, pile of rocks, or per-haps even a sunken boat. Examples of breaks on breaklines are shown in Chart 4.

In most cases, the largest bass in most bodies of water will be caught at breaks on breaklines.

The breaklines we have shown in Charts 2 and 4, it can readily be seen, are rather straight-line affairs and are meant only to repre-sent a single piece of shoreline. Actually, breaklines may take on many other forms, too. They will still, on contour maps, be seen as those lines which run close together for some distance and indicate rapid changes of depth. But they may meander in close to the shore-line or wander far away from the shoreline toward midlake areas,

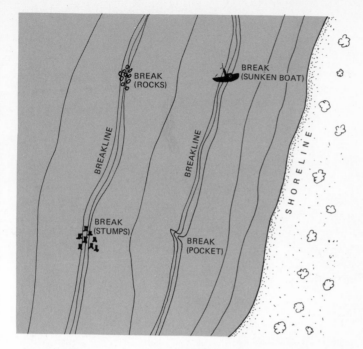

Chart 4. Typical breaks on breaklines

and in so doing they will take on the appearances of long bars, points, and other structures.

In the previous section we were talking about bass leaving their sanctuaries and migrating along underwater highways toward their destinations. Now we're going to see how they actually move.

Having departed from the resting area en masse, the first "signpost" the bass see is called the *contact point*. This is the first association they make with shallower water as they leave the depths. Usually the contact point is some type of breakline where there is a rapid change of depth, such as where the edge of a shelf drops off steeply into the sanctuary area. Bass will not rise from the depths of the sanctuary and make contact with the edge of the breakline at any arbitrary location, however. Rather, they will make contact at a specific location where there is some noticeable change in the breakline, a break!

The school will usually stop at the contact point (a break on the first breakline they encounter) for a short while before proceeding on to the next signpost. This pause takes place because they probably need to acclimate themselves to the venture into shallower

I took this photo of a lake area which was drained to perform maintenance on docks. When the water level is raised again, guess where the home of the fish will be.

waters, assuring themselves that all is safe and right with the world before proceeding onward. In fact, as we shall see later, if the school is comprised of very large fish and the water is crystal clear, they may go no farther than the contact point due to their shyness and fear of the bright shallows before them.

Let's assume, however, that the school of bass consists of twenty fish averaging four pounds apiece and they intend to "go all the way." The next signpost, or stopping place, in their migration past the contact point will probably be another breakline. And again, they will not usually contact that breakline just anywhere, but where there is a break.

The very last breakline where the bass will still be seen to be schooling is called the *scatterpoint*. From this location the school disperses, usually around cover such as an expansive weedbed, rocky shoreline, standing timber, or perhaps around the edges of submerged brush.

Bass can be caught at all of the locations described above (contact points, breaks on various breaklines, scatterpoints, and cover-formations they disperse into) either by eliciting feeding responses or by provoking strikes. As we said before, bass do not migrate because they are hungry, but nevertheless during the course of a migration they can usually be tempted into biting (though anglers usually see better success in forcing the fish to strike).

After an indeterminate amount of time, the bass will begin drifting back toward their sanctuary. Unless they are spooked (as when a careless angler bangs an oar against the side of his boat) and make mad dashes for the safety of the depths, they will usually follow the same migration route which led them toward the shallows. They can be caught during this return migration, too, but the angler has to work fast because the fish will not be pausing at the various breaks on breaklines as they did when first venturing toward the shallows.

A very common migration situation in lakes and reservoirs—and perhaps one of the easiest for anglers to find through the use of contour maps—is that of a long, sloping point jutting out from the shoreline and continuing for some distance underwater.

Chart 5 shows a contour map view of such a point. When the bass move from their sanctuary we can see the first breakline (contact point) they will associate with and the exact location where that association will occur (break). We can also see the next break on a breakline the fish will head for, and finally the last break on a

Shoreline bar exposed when a lake was partially lowered. This could be a real hot spot during certain times of year when the water level is back up.

breakline (scatterpoint) where the school disperses. Chart 6 shows a side view of the same structure, the various breaklines, and the migration route.

There are still many other types of structure bass will migrate upon, and we shall be looking at them in coming sections. But one thing we should probably emphasize about bass migrations right now is that they are not always the cut and dried, straight-line affairs we have so far indicated in several charts. The route may be very crooked, slanting off to various angles because the intermittent breaks along the way—the signposts—may not all be uniformly situated as they lead from the depths to the shallows. Upon contacting a break on a breakline, the fish may have to travel a short distance to either the right or left, following the breakline or contour change until they reach the next signpost which further directs them into the shallows. In fact, the bass may not always head for

This lake section shows still other bottom structures which might be effective when the water again covers them. The point in the foreground would probably be a good spring and winter structure, and the two bars in the background might produce during the winter.

the shallows but perhaps instead from a deep water area to an adjacent deep water area.

Chart 7 shows what a crooked migration route might look like. We can see the bass resting in their sanctuary area in about thirty-five feet of water. Adjacent to the deep water is a shelf (breakline) which extends for some distance. The first association the bass make with the shallower structure when they move from the sanctuary will be at a break (contact point) on the breakline (shelf). In this case the break or interruption in the smooth contour of the breakline is a sharp protrusion or knob. From the break there is no additional signpost immediately before them so they travel a short distance along the breakline to where there is a signpost to further direct them into the shallows. This next signpost is another break

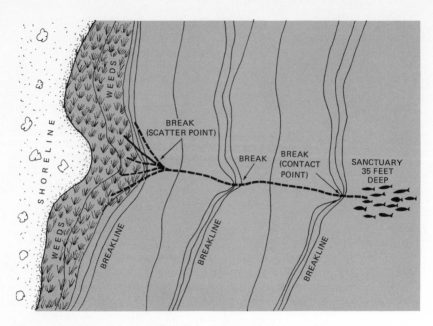

Chart 5. A common type of point continuing underwater

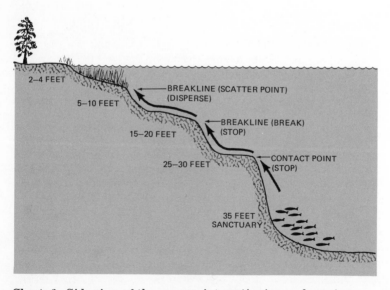

Chart 6. Side view of the same point continuing underwater

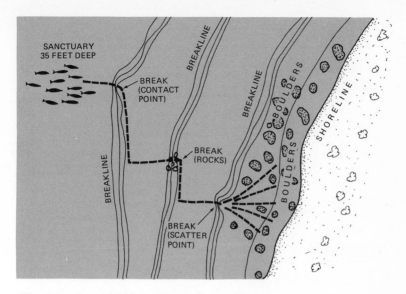

Chart 7. A crooked bass migration route

on a breakline, and in this case the interruption of the breakline is a pile of rocks. Again, there is no signpost directly before the school of bass, so they again travel a short distance to the right until they come to one—another protrusion on another breakline. Since the fish are now fully into the shallows, this final break serves as the scatterpoint and they subsequently disperse among boulders in the shallow shoreline water. All of this may be an over-simplification of bass migrations, and we'll be looking at more variations of bass movements in the future. But the point to be made here is that the fish will move in a well-disciplined manner, following "route markers," and those signposts may not always lie in a straight line as they lead from the depths to the shallows, or from the depths to adjacent deep-water areas.

We said before that bass migrations take place only during certain times of day. This means that when a good migration structure is located, such as any of those in the contour charts we have shown so far, *anglers will often have to wait for the fish to move!*

Obviously, working the contact point, the various breaks on breaklines and the vicinity around the scatterpoint can be a futile effort if the bass have only recently completed a major migration and are now resting back in their sanctuary area.

Many advanced structure anglers, being aware of the location of an ideal structure which has produced fast action in the past but seems to be void of fish at the moment, will park and wait for the next migration. This can be a worthwhile effort, especially if the angler does not know when the last migration took place (if the previous migration took place six hours ago, another one could be "scheduled" to begin in only minutes).

Other enterprising anglers, however, upon checking their favorite structures and concluding no migrations are presently taking place, use this slack time to search for additional structures which may provide even better movements when the bass begin to climb from their sanctuaries. And still others, while waiting for the fish to move, search for straggler bass. "Stragglers" are lone fish which have somehow become separated from their schools. Apparently finding themselves lost, they usually head for the nearest submerged brush pile, felled tree lying on the bottom, or other cover conformation. These fish constitute the occasional bass caught now and then by perpetual shoreline pluggers.

The straggler-angler may or may not find an occasional lone fish, and it doesn't make any difference to him one way or the other. He is simply biding his time, like the other structure anglers, waiting for the fish to move. About every half-hour, he'll take a break from his straggler fishing to check out a nearby migration route or two where he may have had success before, hoping the fish have begun to move from the depths. If they have, he'll forget entirely about stragglers and concentrate upon working the large school. And he may, if he's in the right place (which this book is all about), load the boat with whoppers in only twenty minutes' time!

In concluding this section, we should also mention that it's always wise to study a contour map thoroughly at home the evening before you plan to go fishing. In this way you can formulate a "game plan," knowing in advance about certain bottom structures you wish to locate when you slip your boat into the water in the morning. When leaving the dock I often use a compass to orient myself with my contour map and can usually motor to general locations I have in mind with no trouble.

Having arrived at the general area, an electronic depth sounder can then be used to pinpoint the precise locations of certain bottom structures you're interested in checking out. One of the best ways to determine any structure's exact conformation (remember, we said that contour maps are not always precisely accurate) is by dropping marker buoys overboard. Commercially manufactured buoys can probably be obtained through those same outlets where

Here I drop markers to outline the dimensions of a breakline. The next task will be to find breaks.

you purchase your other fishing gear. Or there are a variety of ways in which you can make the markers yourself. The ones I use are brick-size pieces of styrofoam wrapped with fifty feet of cord. A two-ounce weight tied to the end of the buoy's line will hold the marker securely in position in the face of the strongest winds. Be sure to check your state's regulations as to the use of any kind of markers. In certain areas it may be illegal to set out floating objects in navigable waters.

It's a good idea to have at least six markers on hand as you begin dropping them overboard at intervals to perfectly outline the dimensions of the structure you intend to fish. This gives you a better picture of what the structure actually looks like. On subsequent trips, however, all of the buoys do not have to be dropped. Off a long, sloping point, for example, you may need only set out one marker at its tip. On a long underwater bar two markers may suffice, one at each end. It's not a good practice to drop a marker directly on top of a breakline or a break, though. There's probably not too much chance of spooking fish which may be on the structure, but you may frequently get tangled with the buoy's line when working the bottom contour. I always place my markers a uniform distance (ten feet) to the left of the bottom configuration I'm actually working. Then, it's easy to remember with each cast or trolling pass that the true location of the structure is always ten feet to the right of the buoy.

Almost any angler who is just learning structure fishing experiences difficulty working deep contours and breaks, especially if his habits have been formed during too many years of perpetual shoreline plugging, in which there are always numerous targets such as stumps and weedbeds to cast to. Suddenly, he's in open water with no targets (none that he can see, anyway). The use of marker buoys helps to alleviate some of this initial sense of feeling lost.

LOCATING IDEAL STRUCTURE

We've seen several different kinds of structure and how bass use them. We should keep in mind, however, Buck Perry's observation that "you may find structure without bass, but you will never find bass without structure."

The various structures which exist in any body of water will far outnumber the inhabiting schools of bass. Therefore, those structures which bass elect to use will be those which possess a combination of ideal characteristics.

To qualify as ideal structure, the bottom contour in question must extend all the way to the deepest water in the area. Otherwise, when the fish leave the deep water, how would they even know the structure exists?

In Chart 8 we see two very nice points extending from the shoreline. Both have deep water nearby containing schools of bass. It's easy to see, however, that the point shown in View 1 will probably never see a bass migration. In this instance the bass would begin to climb from their sanctuary and be immediately faced with a wide flat. Remember, bass do not move in a disorderly, ran-

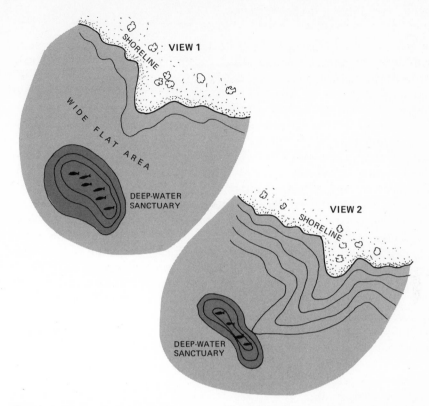

Chart 8. To be used by bass, a potential migration route must extend all the way from the shoreline to the deep water.

dom, or haphazard manner. They follow signposts along well-defined routes to their destinations. In View 1 there are no signposts for the bass to follow. In order to find the point, they would have to strike out in a wandering fashion, and this is something a school of bass simply will not do. As a result, the bass rising from the deep water in View 1 would go only to the upper edge of the hole and stop there, seeing nothing further to show them the way. This would constitute a very short migration, and if an angler were able to make contact with the fish it would probably be by bottom-bumping lures in water as deep as thirty feet or more.

Now, if there were a number of breaks or structural features interrupting the wide flat shown in View 1, the fish would proceed onward. These breaks might take the form of intermittent rock piles, stumps, felled trees, or almost anything else.

Now let's examine View 2 in Chart 8. The shoreline point in this case extends far out, all the way to the deep water. Upon rising from the sanctuary, the bass would not be faced with an open flat. There is a signpost before them, the tip of the point (breakline) and the bass would make contact wherever there was a break. As you can see, there are also the other signposts in the form of shelves (breaklines) which further show the way into the shallows.

Without intending to be redundant, we should reemphasize this very important point. For structure to be used by bass it must extend all the way to deep water and there must be intermittent signposts in the form of breaks and breaklines to show the way.

Now we'll further refine this knowledge by adding still another variable. So far, we have seen a number of breaklines in various charts, and we have said that the largest number of large bass will be caught at a break on the breakline. But that poses an interesting question. What if there are a number of breaks on the breakline?

When any given breakline possesses more than one break, the break the fish will make contact with will be the one which is the sharpest or steepest. This is important, because when bass are moving on structure, especially at the deeper levels, they will usually remain tightly grouped. And with many types of structure being so enormous in size, and subsequently possessing many breaks on breaklines, the angler may fail to make contact with the fish if he is not working the very break (of several) at which the bass are pausing. It's not at all uncommon for an angler to cast his lure toward a break and catch a good bass, cast ten feet to the right or left of the break and catch nothing, cast again to the break and boat still another bass.

Chart 9 shows a very large point extending offshore which possesses one major breakline. There are three breaks on that breakline in the form of fingers or sharp protrusions. Can you determine where the bass will be?

Finger A would probably not be a very good bet because, of the three breaks shown, it slopes away very gently into the deepest water, which in this case is twenty feet deep. Nor would Finger B be a worthwhile place to try, again, because of the way in which it very gradually descends into the depths. Finger C, however, is the sharpest and most well-defined break of the three, with radical changes as it very quickly descends into the area's deepest water. Therefore, bass migrating upon this structure from their sanctuary would contact the breakline at location C. There could be as many

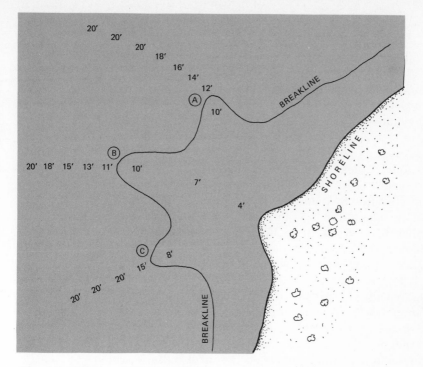

Chart 9. Where will the bass be?

as thirty large bass in the school, or more. But if the degree of
water clarity or the absence of additional signposts or other conditions prevented them from traveling any farther than location C,
an angler fishing at location A would fail to make contact with the
fish.

    Perhaps the best location on any type of structure for catching
the very largest bass in any body of water is the *contact point,* and
this can best be explained through a process of elimination.

    We've seen how it is almost impossible to catch bass in their
sanctuary. Locating bass at their shallow-water destinations is also
a precarious venture, because the bass will be dispersed at this stage
of their migration and because they will be highly spooky, since
they are in shallower water than they are accustomed to. You may
luck into a few upon occasion, but in many cases the commotion
made in landing a big fish in shallow water sends the others in the
area quickly darting for the depths.

    This leaves us with the various breaklines and associated
breaks (signposts) along the migration route from the sanctuary to
the scatterpoint as the most likely locations to catch bass in big

numbers. But we can even further eliminate most of the breaks, leaving only the contact point as the place in any body of water to catch the very largest bass. The largest bass, it was already noted, are always reluctant to leave the security of their deep-water homes (they can feed at any depth). As a result, they quite often will not travel the entire length of the migration route, even though there may well be ample signposts, unless weather and water conditions are ideal. "Ideal" might mean cloudy skies, choppy or stained water (to reduce light penetration), and water temperatures approximating those in which a bass's body metabolism is most active (remember, in cold water bass migrations of any kind will be short and of rather brief duration). Most often, however, these conditions do not exist, and the largest bass will therefore travel to the first break on a breakline (the contact point) and go no farther.

The contact point is an ideal location for big bass and bass anglers alike. The fish will actively feed when at this location, or they can be provoked into striking, and yet the depth is seldom so extreme as to prevent proper control over lures. Additionally, the contact point is a place where the largest bass still feel very safe. The amount of light penetration is still quite low, and the location affords immediate access to much deeper water in the event that something alarms them.

As a brief summary of some of the things we have learned so far, take a look at Chart 10, which is marked with various types of contour lines, structures, and depths. Before reading further, see if you can determine which structures would see the best bass migrations, and why.

Location A shows a long breakline in the form of a shelf or drop-off. This would be an ideal migration situation because there is a break on the breakline, in the form of a protrusion, where the break drops off immediately into the deepest water in the area. And upon contacting the break on the breakline, there are still additional breaks or signposts, in the form of a pile of rocks and then stumps, allowing the bass to find their way fully into the shallows.

Location B is a nice-looking point extending out from the shoreline and dropping off steeply at its tip. It does not extend all the way to the deepest water in the area, however, even though the water depth off the tip of the point is substantial. This location might see an occasional migration, but only under ideal weather and water conditions. We could therefore classify it as a "maybe" that would certainly be worth investigating when weather and water conditions

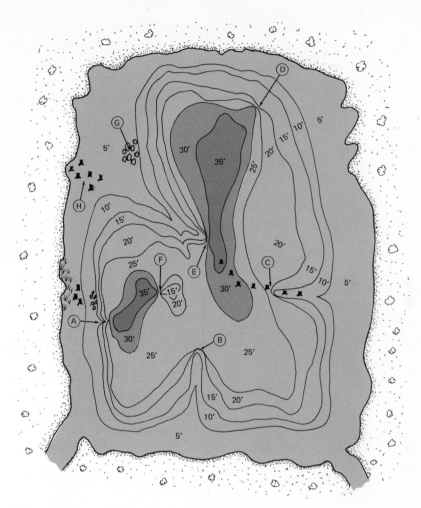

Chart 10. Some typical structures affecting migrations

are optimum. At all other times it probably wouldn't be worth the effort.

Location C is another nice point extending from the shoreline. This structure does not extend all the way to the deepest water in the area either. But in this particular case there are additional breaks or signposts in the form of a row of stumps, and they do extend all the way to the deepest water. This location would therefore be an excellent bet. But keep in mind, that after a number of years, many of the stumps will rot away. This would cause the migration route to become disconnected or separated from the depths. Bass migrating from their sanctuary would proceed along the route, following whatever signposts were still in existence. But when the stumps petered out, the bass would go no farther. They'd be faced with a barren flat and would not cross it (there would be nothing to show them the way) in order to gain access to the point.

Location D is a nice break on a breakline. And an occasional straggler fish might be adhering to this contour, so it would always be worth a cast or two if you happened to be in the immediate vicinity. But there are two things which would probably not allow a bass migration on this structure. First, while the breakline drops off sharply into deep water, there is no real connection with the deepest water in the area. Second, the inshore side of the breakline consists only of a gently sloping flat with no radical changes in the bottom contour, or any visible structure present.

Location E looks super. A point extends from the shoreline with two fingers at the end of the structure. Note that one of the fingers, however, consists only of a very gentle slope, while the other one drops sharply into the deepest water in the area. The steeper finger would be where migrating bass would make contact with the point.

Location F is another ideal structure. In midlake, a hump sticks up from the floor. The north, east, and south faces of the hump slope away very gently. But the west side is quite steep and falls directly into the deepest water the area has to offer. The west side would therefore be where bass would make contact with the hump, and they would probably travel to the hump's crest but not descend upon the north, east or south slopes, because that would be venturing out across the flats.

Location G, a pile of scattered boulders, and Location H, a number of submerged stumps, would both be good places to try to pick up straggler fish while waiting for a school of bass to move on some nearby structure. Any bass which failed to reunite with his school (which had moved up the point at Location E) during their return journey to the sanctuary would probably head for one or the other of these cover situations.

When bass migrate, we know from our previous discussions that they move on structure. But we have not spent much time talking about the types of structure they adhere to when they reach their destinations. Remember, you'll always find bass on structure, regardless of whether they are in the depths or in the shallows.

From the scatterpoint the fish may disperse into some expansive weedbed, along the perimeters of brush, or around many other types of cover. But again, this will be a well-ordered movement with the fish almost never randomly cruising about. We saw earlier that when a school of migrating bass makes contact with a breakline, they will do so at a break. A similar situation usually occurs in the shallows. When the fish disperse from the scatterpoint they do not simply seek structure but rather *substructure*. Substructure is really nothing more than a type of break or interruption in the structure, and examples are numerous. If a large weedbed along the shoreline is structure, substructure might be narrow channels or individual potholes in the weeds, or perhaps even a place along the deep-water edge of the weedline where the bottom composition changes from soft mud to coarse sand.

If structure is a small grove of flooded timber standing in the shallows, substructure might be a feeder stream channel dumping into the lake at that location and in so doing winding through the grove. If structure is a long hedgerow or brushline, substructure might be a gap or sharp indentation in the cover. If structure is a stream channel along the floor of a lake or reservoir, substructure might be a sharp "S" bend in the channel. If a submerged roadbed is structure, substructure might be a drowned bush sitting along the edge of the road or a place where the road, via a small bridge, crosses a stream.

We'll be looking at substructure again very shortly. But before we proceed any further, the angler should have some means of classifying his chosen lakes and reservoirs, because their unique physical conformations will often dictate what kinds of structure and substructure they contain.

FLATLAND AND HIGHLAND WATERS

No two bodies of water are exactly alike, and experience acquired on one is not always applicable to fishing another successfully. Each bass water has a personality all its own, and each can be considered a separate, living thing with its own individualistic water chemistry, bottom structure, plant growth, fish populations, aquatic life, and other features. As these various parts differ in design and composition, so will the required fishing techniques for successfully catching bass.

It was emphasized at the very beginning of this book that bass habits do not change dramatically with the mere crossing of state boundaries. And I don't mean to contradict that statement here. What I do mean to say is that the locations where bass may be found in one particular body of water may differ from those of another lake or reservoir. This is important because each year many anglers fish waters they are unfamiliar with, using only those few tactics that may have been successful on their home waters. The bass they are fishing for away from home are no different, but the lake or reservoir may be! At the same time, however, there are also many similarities between different bodies of water. And knowledge of these similarities may provide the enterprising angler with an occasional shortcut in making his evaluations and determining where the fish are probably located.

In this section we will classify all lakes and reservoirs as being of either the *flatland* or *highland* variety. There are always exceptions to any rule in bass fishing. And in certain rare instances some body of water may exhibit features which are characteristic of both flatland and highland waters, or perhaps even be unique in some other regard. But I am confident that any angler who thoroughly understands the nature of flatland and highland waters can venture upon any lake or reservoir in the country without experiencing too many difficulties in finding bass.

Flatland lakes and reservoirs are usually manmade impoundments, and they are commonly found in the Midwest, South, and Southwest. As the description implies, flatland bodies of water are built in rather level agricultural or grazing areas, on plains, or in swamp regions, compared to the highland type of waters, which are formed in hilly or mountainous regions.

In most cases, a flatland body of water is created by building a long dam on a major river and permitting the water to back up slowly and flood stands of southern hardwood, abandoned or government-procured farmlands, prairies, marshes, and other types of predominantly level land. The created impoundment may possess a tremendous variety of cover above or below the water's surface, or both. Stump fields, grass beds, matted expanses of weeds, standing or felled timber, brush piles, boggy islands, and other types of junglelike growth may seemingly be everywhere. Or, just the opposite may occur, with the cover being sparse and evident only in the coves and bays or dotting the edges of the shoreline.

The uniqueness of flatland bodies of water is twofold: First, the only major location of deep water is the bed of the river that

*was dammed to form the impoundment and now winds its way along
the lake or reservoir floor. Second, this inundated channel, and perhaps an occasional feeder stream which may dump into it, constitute
the major changes in bottom contour. With the exception of the old
riverbed and associated stream channels, most of the rest of the
lake or reservoir floor consists only of expansive and unbroken flats.*

The bass population in a flatland body of water will use the
main riverbed or the associated stream channels (depending upon
season of the year) as their primary sanctuary areas, and their
migrations will usually only be to adjacent or connected structures.
There may be a few exceptions to this rule, but since they occur
only in rare instances we need not mention them here.

Chart 11 shows a side view of what the bottom contour of a
typical flatland body of water might look like. The water could well
be shallower or deeper, and either more or less cover could be in
evidence. But the great majority of flatland waters across the
country will take on this appearance.

We have already discussed the general behavior of bass during
the spring spawning weeks: the males infiltrate coves and bays or
disperse along the midlake banks and begin selecting nesting sites,
while the females gather at steep points or along drop-offs where
there are rubbing logs. These mannerisms, however, are usually
characteristic of highland types of waters. In the case of flatland
waters, the bass's habits differ slightly.

As the first traces of spring make themselves known, bass in
flatland bodies of water will move out of the main riverbed that
provided their winter homes. In places where the riverbed loops in
close to the shoreline, bass may disperse along the banks (now is
the only time of year in which they will randomly cruise, their respective schools having broken up as individual fish become territorial). Even more frequently, however, the bass will leave the
main riverbed and follow the feeder tributaries. How far up the

Chart 11. Bottom contour of a typical flatland body of water

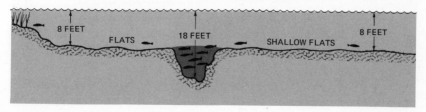

stream channels they will go is never certain, but the largest bass will seldom move as far inshore or as far back into bays, coves, and backwater ponds as the smaller fish. Those stream channels coursing along the reservoir floor that are bordered on both sides by brush-filled flats seem to provide the most-favored spawn sites. And look for a greater number of beds to line the edge of the submerged channel than to be situated far inshore against the bank.

There are two other types of spawn locations I nearly always find productive in flatland waters, and most other anglers overlook them. One is an old roadbed, which is most often comprised of hard-packed sand, clay, or gravel (there may even be concrete or asphalt roads with a light covering of sand that has settled from the water). And the other is an abandoned railroad spur left intact when the reservoir was flooded. Both structures are quite common in southern impoundments and are usually clearly marked on topographic maps. If not, the shoreline may reveal where they enter the water, and you can trace their routes with a depth sounder. Those roadbeds and railroad spurs which run near the main channel are the best bets of all, since the bass do not have to travel far to find suitable spawn sites, and if spooked they have ready access to their deep-water retreats.

Wherever the spawning grounds, the females will still select holding stations near some form of timber (rubbing logs) situated adjacent to the deep water of a stream channel or riverbed. Then, the actual spawning activity commences as we described earlier.

In flatland waters, spawn-spent bass may immediately drop off into a stream channel if it is nearby and hold there for several weeks until increased light penetration forces them deeper. Or, in their movements away from the spawning grounds to deeper waters, they may stop to hug the bases of trees or brush cover where the water is shaded. These stopovers are only for brief periods, however, as the bass continue toward the depths where they will begin schooling activity. Now is a time when successful anglers first begin experiencing very light stringers. Rather than follow the fish to their various summer, fall, and winter homes, they continue to plug the standing timber in the shallow swamp areas, the weedbeds, brushpiles, and other visible cover. They should be working cover leading away from the spawn sites to the stream channels, the stream channels themselves, or structures associated with the main riverbed.

So if you take a spring fishing vacation and arrive at some

camp on a reservoir that can be classified as "flatland," you should find out what spawning stage the bass are in. If the word you receive is, "They are not spawning yet," work those shallow, cover-filled areas immediately adjacent to the deep-water routes. If you're told, "They are on the beds," work those shallow areas where the proper bottom conditions exist, such as roadbeds, railroad spurs, or the brush-filled flats adjacent to the stream channels or main river-bed. And if the reply is, "They are about done spawning," expend no efforts at all in the shallows but instead work the cover leading away from the shallows to the edges of the depths.

Of course, if your fishing vacation comes during the summer, fall, or winter, you should forget entirely about the shallows and concentrate on the feeder stream channels and the main riverbed. There is an irony here, and that is that the main riverbeds on most of the larger flatland reservoirs are clearly marked with various types of channel buoys, usually by departments of natural resources or sometimes inland Coast Guard detachments. This is done so anglers and other boaters will know the safest routes to follow in their high-speed travel from one portion of the reservoir to another without the potential hazard of plowing into hidden stumps or sub-surface trees scattered about the adjacent flats. Anglers buzz right along the main river channel in their bassboats, seldom fishing it, and yet this is what the greatest numbers of large bass call home for most of the year.

The first contact the schools of bass have with shallower water when they migrate from the depths of the riverbed or stream channel (they'll be in the riverbed during the summer and winter, and in the stream channel in the spring and fall, in most cases) will be the edge of the channel itself. This location serves as the contact point and also the first (and sometimes only) breakline. Since the breakline may be extremely long and uniform, we know the bass will make contact with the edge of the channel at some location where there is a break. This may consist of several stumps situated on the edge of the channel, a felled tree, a pile of rocks, or some other type of substructure. If, beyond this break, there exists nothing but expansive, unbroken flats, the fish will probably go no farther. You'll either catch them at the break along the edge of the channel or not at all. But if signposts such as a row of stumps, a hedgerow, or a tree-line lead from the channel to perhaps a nearby weedbed, we could probably expect a longer migration route.

Another type of place where bass might be caught is where there is a sharp S-bend in a stream channel (a bend in the riverbed could be as much as a mile long). Due to the washing effect of the current, the bass may rest in the outside, undercut portion of the bend and migrate up the inside bend where a shoal is created by fine sand settling out. Again, the fish may go no farther than the edge of the channel, or they may follow signposts to some nearby area. Still another type of structure might be where the channel, twisting and turning on itself, loops in close to the shoreline. If any type of point extends out from the shoreline all the way to the channel and drops off steeply at its tip, we have again a classic migration situation.

Those are the natural features to look for in flatland lakes and reservoirs. They are the most prominent. But on occasion you may find still others. Where there is a substantial depth of water covering the flats, a hump sticking up from the bottom may be a real hot spot. The hump attracts straggler bass one by one, and soon there is a small school. There may also in certain locations be borrow pits or deep holes where construction crews have removed quantities of sand or gravel. The depths of the pit will serve as the sanctuary, with the bass occasionally migrating to the upper edge or breakline and then on still further if there are signposts. These latter situations, however, are exceptions to the rule. Most of the floor of a flatland reservoir, while it may be covered with trees and other cover, is basically flat and unbroken. The bass are not in the trees and other cover, however, and this is something which must be remembered. They are in deep water.

Flatland bodies of water are also abundant with manmade structures such as old building foundations, bridges, trash piles, old automobile bodies, and roadbeds. Straggler bass may be caught around these structures almost any time of year, but don't expect to find schools of larger fish unless there is deep water such as the main channel or a tributary nearby.

Two other manmade structures are also worth mentioning. One is the riprap lining both sides of a causeway where a highway may cross the impoundment. Because the slope of the riprap is usually steep, an angler can often take a certain number of straggler bass at this location any time of year. The same applies to the area of the lake where the dam is situated. There will usually be an apron made of concrete, riprap, or other hard materials which extends out into the lake and drops off in stair-step fashion. These drops constitute breaklines, and if you can find breaks you may find schools of bass moving up them from time to time.

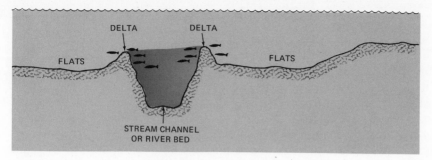

Chart 12. Side view of a common delta situation

One type of "hot spot" which Buck Perry has discovered to exist in flatland bodies of water are *deltas*. Deltas consist of ridge or lip formations, most often elongated in shape, and they are especially common in places where the land was formerly farmed on the flats, leading right up to the edges of the channels. Deltas provide ideal migration situations for bass summering in the main riverbed.

When present, deltas are marked on maps, but the angler must be able to recognize the change in contour lines signaling their locations. Chart 12 shows a side view of what a delta looks like, and Chart 13 shows the elongated shapes of close contour lines indicating the presence of deltas. A delta configuration may be covered

Chart 13. Deltas as shown by contour lines

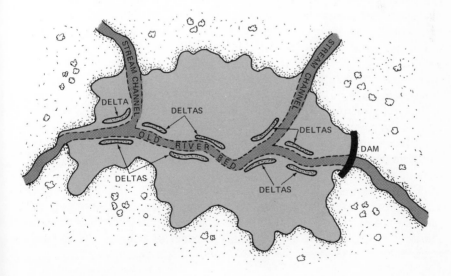

with stumps, brush, or trees and when this is the case the fish seem to remain on them a little longer, compared to migrations which may take place upon "clean" deltas. One of the hottest of hot spots in flatland bodies of water is a delta in the shape of a "saddle" or ridge separating two stream channels meandering side by side. Saddles or ridges may also be present at those locations where stream channels join each other or the main riverbed.

Throughout the summer and early fall, the greatest numbers of big bass in a flatland reservoir will be in the main riverbed. And they will also be there during the winter. But in late fall they may often be briefly on the move again. During this period, which may last up to six weeks, depending upon local weather and water conditions, I have found bass adhering to *false-spawn* tendencies, to use a term I coined several years ago. This means they will temporarily leave the main riverbed and head once again in the direction of the feeder-stream channels or other tributaries winding along the floor of the reservoir. And for a while they may be found in the same locations where they were *at the end of the spring spawn.* They will have temporarily abandoned their schooling disposition, but they won't usually be loners as they are during the spring. Look for them to appear in loose groups of from three to six fish.

Now let's look at highland bodies of water. Highland waters may be either natural or manmade, and while they may be located almost anywhere, they are most commonly found in the Northeast, Midwest, and Northwest. In comparison to the flatland bodies of water which exist over plains-type areas, old farmlands, swamps, and other level-ground terrain, highland bodies of water are characteristic of the hilly and mountainous regions. Those which are manmade are usually constructed by building a dam between rather steep mountain ridges, permitting the water to back up and flood a series of associated gorges and valleys. Highland waters of natural origin are usually nestled in a rocky chasm or basin. And while they are often supplied by a number of feeder streams which drain the high country, they are primarily fed by underground springs and seepages.

Upon immediate inspection, even the untrained eye will note a number of radical differences between a highland and a flatland body of water. The highland lake or reservoir, be it natural or manmade, will not usually possess a great deal of cover. Certain bays and coves may have lily pads and other vegetative cover. And in places along the shoreline, there may be felled or standing trees. Exceptions to this rule occur, but most highland waterways are basically cover-free. And the bottom or floor is primarily clean and appears to be sandy, gravel-strewn, and with frequent evidence of rocks and boulders. There will be mud, silt, and other debris, too, but seldom in such quantities as are present in flatland waters. The water and bottom composition in the highland lake or reservoir is rarely as rich or fertile in nitrogen compounds as the flatland water. As a result, look for it most often to be very clear, and because it is deep, much colder.

During the early years of a manmade highland reservoir or lake, the food chain and growing bass behave in much the same manner as they do in the young flatland waters. The fish are pretty well scattered and in most cases will be found abundantly in the shallows near whatever cover may be present. Of course, in the case of natural lakes which may have been formed by glaciers and other phenomena eons ago, anglers are seldom able to experience the "hot" fishing which newly created lakes and reservoirs usually provide. The only exceptions are lakes where departments of natural resources have launched massive fish-stocking programs and wilderness or private lakes which have gone for years with no anglers dimpling their waters with assorted offerings.

While the most obvious deep water in a manmade lake or reservoir in the flatlands is the old riverbed and associated feeder streams, these locations will not always be the home of the bass in the case of highland waters. Indeed, as we have already noted, those highland waters of natural origin probably don't even have such structures meandering along their floors. And in highland waters created by man, the old riverbed or feeder-stream channels may well provide the deepest water in the lake or reservoir, but it may be so deep that no bass can live there! A quick check of a contour map will either confirm or refute this possibility. If the inundated creek or riverbed lies deeper than seventy-five feet, discount it as a probable sanctuary for bass. This is often the case in the vicinity of the lake or reservoir's tailwaters (near the dam), but sometimes not true in the headwaters region, where at least a portion of the riverbed may be used as a sanctuary because of the only moderate depths there.

Likely deep-water homes for bass schools in the highland lakes and reservoirs will be the gullies, holes, bases of drop-offs, cuts, depressions, slots, and similar places. Except during the spawning weeks, these locations will be the home of the fish throughout the year (though the depth they will go to will be dictated by the season and existing weather conditions).

It is in highland bodies of water that classic fish migrations (along numerous breaks and breaklines) take place, and since most of these migration habits exhibited by schools of bass were discussed in earlier sections of this chapter, we need only briefly look at how these migrations differ through the seasons.

As bass enter their sanctuary areas for the first time after the spawning weeks, their depth will usually be determined by the amount of light penetration. Toward the beginning of the year, and then again during the winter months, the sun's rays strike the water at a sharp angle and therefore do not penetrate as deeply as they do during the late spring, summer, and early fall, when the sun is directly overhead.

What this means in the case of highland waters is that the schools of bass, when migrating from their sanctuaries during the earliest and latest months of the year, will be prone to use *on-structures*. On-structures and *off-structures* are terms I coined several years ago to describe the migrational tendencies of bass at different times of year. On-structures are in some way connected or attached to the shoreline, allowing the fish during the course of any migration to come much shallower because of reduced light penetration. Examples of on-structures are points which jut out from the shoreline, shelves, stair-step ledges, and underwater rocky outcroppings.

Off-structures are not in any way attached or associated with the shoreline, and bass will usually migrate upon these bottom configurations during the summer and early fall months when light penetration is greatest and the fish are staying much deeper. Examples of off-structures are the deeper midlake bars, reefs, shoals, humps, or islands which stick up from the bottom, or structures associated with stream channels such as deltas, saddles, substructure along the edge of the channel, or bends in the channel.

This is not to say, however, that bass will exclusively use either on- or off-structures at the various times of year just described. You'll have to ascertain the personality of each body of water you fish in order to determine which types of structures the fish predominantly use at various times of years. In some cases, for example, bass may be migrating upon the very steepest points during midsummer rather than using some nearby off-structure such as a bar.

CONSIDER WATER COLOR

The color of the water in any given lake or reservoir will have an important influence upon the success of a bass-angler. Various degrees of water clarity will determine how deep the fish will be and how easily they will be able to see the angler's offering.

Water color is generally of two basic types. There are the stable water colors which pretty much exist on a year-around basis, meaning that the angler can count upon their being in evidence before he ever climbs out of the rack in the morning. Stable water colors are direct results of the chemistry of the water and the physical composition of the bottom materials. In the rock-bound, infertile lakes of the far North, the water is often quite clear. Southern waterways, which are nearly always highly fertile, may see a variety of water colors ranging from cloudy green, a result of algae bloom, to brown/black or stained, which is a result of tannin being released into the water by decomposing brush, felled trees, and standing timber. The presence of certain types of clay or iron-ore deposits may leave the water with a red or rust color. Very shallow waters with soft bottoms may take on a muddy-brown color throughout the year.

Very clear waters are usually more in evidence during the earliest and latest months of any given year. The water is still probably very cold during these months and consequently the growth of aquatic vegetation is at a low ebb.

Unstable color conditions in water are short-term affairs which may catch the angler entirely off guard. These are caused by high winds, heavy rains, water run-off from higher ground, or increased current velocities which may roil the bottom sediment. Unstable water colors are nearly always a muddy-brown or cloudy.

There are some types of water coloration which do not make for ideal fishing, but there are no types of water coloration which should prompt an anxious angler to cancel a fishing trip. He may, however, in the case of unstable water coloration, have to use other angling strategies than he had planned upon. I have taken big bass

from water of all colors—from those which were so clear I could see
the lake floor at twenty-five feet deep to those which were so muddy
they looked like a chocolate milkshake.

It is lucky that the avid bass angler today is living during a
time in which some of the best bass fishing to be found is in the
larger lakes and reservoirs across the country. Such waterways are
often so enormous that there is rarely a time when he cannot find
water of the exact color he wishes to fish in.

Perhaps the most ideal colors of water are those which are at
neither end of the clear/muddy spectrum but somewhere in between. *Slightly murky, milky, or stained waters are probably the
very best.* Under these conditions the fish are not overly spooky, the
angler can use heavy tackle if existing cover conditions require it,
and he can expect the schools to migrate much shallower.

The most difficult of all water conditions to fish is sparkling
clear water with a preponderance of heavy cover. The fish will stay
very deep, their migrations will be over lesser distances and of only
brief duration, they will be very restless, and contact with them can
usually be made only through the use of cobweb lines and very
small lures. Yet with such tackle, it will often be impossible to
wrestle a thrashing hawg out of the tangled limbs and brush.

As a general rule, then, in clear water the bass occupy a deep
sanctuary and do not migrate far into the shallows. The more highly
colored the water is, the shallower they will sanctuary and the
shallower they will migrate. Chart 14 shows the views of three
different possible migration routes, approximate sanctuary depths,
and how shallow the fish might be expected to migrate under varying water-color conditions.

Because of the importance of water-color conditions, an angler
should eliminate from consideration those locations in any body of
water which do not provide for ideal movements of the fish. And he
should do this before he ever slips his boat into the water and begins
searching for good-looking structure.

Upon arriving at the lake or reservoir you plan to fish, it's wise
to spend a brief amount of time simply driving around the impoundment to determine what water colorations are available. If this is
not practical (some bodies of water may be more than a hundred
miles long), you can inquire at marinas and fishing camps. The op-
erators of these facilities and their guide staffs continuously keep
tabs on water conditions. This initial investigation on your part may
later save countless hours of exploring and searching for good water

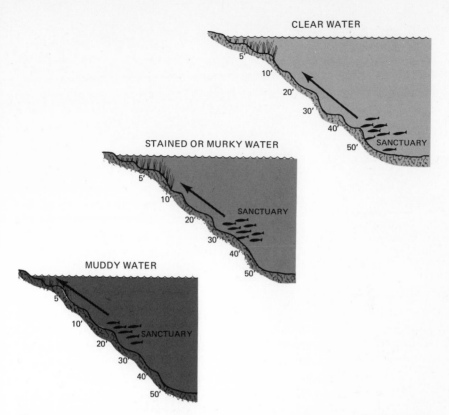

Chart 14. Bass will sanctuary shallower and migrate shallower during colored water conditions.

coloration by boat. On the smaller bodies of water, however, you may be able quickly to motor around the lake or reservoir, and in less than an hour, know exactly what conditions exist and where. Keep in mind, also, that while water color conditions are usually stable for several days or perhaps even weeks at a time, they can change overnight.

When winds lash your favorite waters and heavy rains fall, the shallower headwater areas will be the first to show a muddy appearance. Better-colored water can usually be found if you move further down lake toward the tailwaters. The deeper waters near the dam are seldom affected by brief changes in the weather.

CHAPTER 3

Light Penetration Is the Key

We stated in Chapter 1 that bass will go as deep as need be in order to feel safe. And in waters with extreme depths, that level may often be considerable, though rarely more than seventy-five feet.

Light penetration into the depth of any lake or reservoir determines not only how deep bass will seek sanctuary, however, but also how far inshore they will move during the course of any given migration on structure. The penetration of sunlight is influenced by various factors such as the color or clarity of the water, existing weather conditions, and even the season of the year.

I was not the first to offer explanations on the subject of light penetration and its effect upon bass and other fish species. Anglers, scientists, and fishery biologists down through the years have made occasional discoveries and remarks concerning the phenomenon.

Buck Perry was one of the early pioneers in this field. Another was Roland Martin, the bass tournament champ. But I do believe I was the first to combine all the available knowledge on the subject, add my own research findings, and present a single comprehensive package that anglers could use in seeking out and catching bass and other freshwater gamefish. That report was run as a special feature in *Sports Afield* magazine in early 1973.

We mentioned earlier that bass have fixed-pupil eyes and that to avoid bright light they have only two alternatives—find shaded seclusion in heavy cover or retreat to the depths. Since shallow-water, heavy-cover bassing is a specialized undertaking discussed in another section, this chapter will focus upon lakes and reservoirs with at least moderately deep water. And in these types of waters, studies have shown that an aversion to bright light takes on greater importance to bass than almost any other desire, including the survival instinct!

One such confirming study took place on Lake Mead in Nevada under the supervision of fishery biologists many years ago. It was designed to demonstrate just how deep bass would go in order to avoid bright light.

For those who are unfamiliar with Lake Mead, it is of the classical highland variety, meaning it is very deep, relatively cover-free, and possesses gin-clear water. During the course of their experimentation, biologists donned scuba gear and took floodlights underwater in search of bass. They found one school in a sanctuary area about forty-five feet deep, just off the edge of a drop-off which plummeted still further into the depths.

Previous underwater encounters with bass—and other fish, by the way—have shown that for some unknown reason, fish seldom fear skindivers. Divers can often closely approach large fish underwater and sometimes even touch them without the fish registering alarm. They seem to just slowly mosey along, continuing about their normal activity. Poke a finger at them and they may dart a few feet away, only to swing about—out of curiosity toward the webbed-footed intruders, I suppose—and return to the immediate vicinity.

When the bright floodlights were switched on in the Lake Mead study, however, the bass quickly dived for the darkness of the depths. The divers pursued them at a leisurely pace, and eventually the bass went so deep that they willingly entered the oxygen-void lower layer of water, known as the *hypolimnion*, where they suffocated. Any deal was a bargain, even death, just as long as they got away from that damned bright light!

Subsequent to this research, Buck Perry involved himself in similar studies in the Southeastern states, lowering lights underwater and observing bass reactions. His conclusions were very much the same.

During these early years, however, the only type of instrument available for actually measuring amounts of underwater light intensity was designed for photographic use and required the user to go underwater to take readings.

Fishermen who had accepted the idea of light penetration being a prime determinant of the depths at which bass would most frequently be caught therefore began resorting to many crude attempts at evaluating underwater light. One such effort was simply to tie a white china cup (a variation of the limnologist's Secchi disc) to a line and lower it over the side of the boat into the depths. When the white cup disappeared from sight, the angler measured the amount of line which had been let out, doubled that figure, and then fished no shallower than that depth (the reason for doubling the figure is because light not only has to penetrate through the water down to the cup but reflect off its shiny surface and bounce back an equal distance).

Enter Roland Martin, who for years was one of the most sought-after bass guides on the Santee-Cooper lakes in South Carolina. Martin had likewise adopted a light-penetration philosophy, but had grown frustrated with the haphazard attempts at measuring underwater light intensities. So he set to the task of building the very first underwater light meter for use in bass fishing (it was never commercially manufactured).

The meter, which he was nearly always seen carrying around in a padded suitcase, was capable of measuring the exact water clarity between a six-volt bulb and a cds light lamp cell. The bulb and the cds cell were placed at opposite ends of a plastic tube which was shaded against extraneous light. The cds cell was then connected to a millimeter which measured the exact amount of light from the bulb reaching the cds cell through the water.

With this homemade invention, Martin then proceeded to conduct tests on twenty different lakes across the country, comparing light-penetration readings with the depths at which bass were found. The results were startling: they showed that if, for example, the various percentages of light penetration into the depths on any given day were the same at Table Rock Lake in Missouri and Sam Rayburn Reservoir in Texas, the bass in both lakes would sanctuary at almost exactly the same depths. Further, the shallow-water levels they would move to during the course of a migration would also be the same. These findings, of course, depended upon all other things being equal, such as water coloration, weather, and so on.

Having long since accepted the basic facts of light penetration and their effect upon bass, I was meanwhile poring over biology books and research studies, attempting to learn as much as possible about how bass perceive colors ("color" is really only a combination of various wave-lengths of light). But again, without some form of reliable instrument (commercially available) which could be used for precisely measuring light, I was, as they say, at the end of my rope.

Fortunately, I was soon able to get further involved with the business of studying bass and their reaction to light as a result of a contact with an independent testing company in Tulsa, Oklahoma. It was Fishmaster Products, Inc., who informed me during the summer of 1972 that they were developing a light meter for fishermen called the Depth-o-Lite. I immediately launched upon a full-scale investigation of the product in cooperation with the people who had pioneered the study of this aspect of bass behavior, conducted numerous experiments myself, talked with still others involved in studies of light penetration, and eventually published my findings in *Sports Afield,* as mentioned earlier.

The small, battery-operated, hand-held Depth-o-Lite offered fantastic amounts of data previously unknown or even unsuspected by the majority of this country's bass anglers. The unit looks much like a common water-temperature gauge. Basically, you unwind a wire from the frame of the unit, lowering a sensor or probe to various depths which are indicated by a color-coding system marked on the line.

When the sensor is at each depth, you push a button and the percentage of light penetrating to the probe registers on a meter or scale. At a depth of one foot below the surface, for example, light penetration on a relatively bright day would be approximately 100 percent. As the depth increases, light penetration gradually diminishes until eventually there is total darkness. Chart 15 gives a visual representation of light penetration into the depths of a typical lake.

That level or depth where light almost ceases to exist and

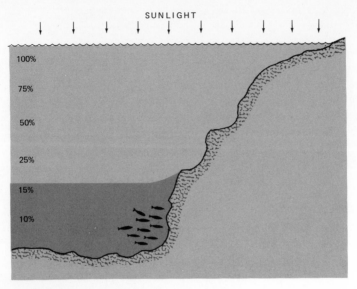

Chart 15. Light penetration forces bass into depths or shaded, heavy-cover areas

nearly total darkness begins, between 5 and 10 percent of light penetration, is usually the shallowest that bass will sanctuary, if the body of water goes that deep.

How far the fish will move inshore during a migration, as we already noted, is also dependent upon the existing amount of light penetration. But I am not yet ready to commit myself by saying that the fish will always move inshore until they reach a certain level of light penetration, whereupon they will go no farther; though it seems, from the research I've conducted, that that may very well be the case with lake and reservoir bass weighing three pounds or more. I will say that the largest bass I have caught (from a school during the course of their migration on structure) have predominantly come from depths *where light penetration was less than 25 percent.*

One of the first studies I undertook was on Dale Hollow Lake in Tennessee, where the water averages quite deep and is very clear. It was nothing more than sheer luck that I almost immediately found a school of smallmouths on a long sloping shale slide which jutted far out from the shoreline, extending all the way to deep water and then dropping off sharply at its tip end. The time was "shooting light" (the very crack of dawn), and in rapid succession I boated four bass which averaged 2½ pounds apiece. I took a break in order to measure the amount of light penetration and discovered that at fourteen feet deep—the level at which the fish had been caught—the light penetration was about 20 percent. Thorough probing of the shallows revealed that none of the fish in the school had come into water less than fourteen feet deep.

What I discovered next occurred mainly as a result of what I first thought to be misfortune. The wind had moved me just a tad too close to the shale slide, and when I attempted to back away the electric motor went on the blink. The boat I was fishing from had been borrowed from a friend and I wasn't certain what the exact nature of the problem was, so I began fiddling with wires. One of them had broken. So I dropped anchor to prevent my drifting over the shale slide and spooking the fish and launched upon the task of making a temporary repair. The splicing job took about half an hour (that is why I make my living as a fishing writer and not an electrician).

Anyway, by the time I was able to resume fishing I quickly noticed that the action had ceased. Where I had previously boated four good fish in almost as many casts, two dozen presentations now resulted in only one stray crappie coming aboard.

Curious, I took another light-penetration reading. During the course of about forty-five minutes, the light penetration at fourteen feet deep had risen from 20 to almost 50 percent!

Using the meter, I began slowly working my way farther offshore, following the same shale slide to deeper water until light penetration once again was reduced to about 20 percent. At twenty-five feet deep I started catching bass again! Three fish came aboard: two more smallmouths of about 2½ pounds and one of almost four pounds. But soon that action ceased, too.

Recounting the morning's events, the reasoning for what had happened became obvious. During the low-light period of dawn, the fish had migrated upon the shale slide. But as the morning wore on, the sun grew higher in the sky, causing light penetration to be greater; this forced the fish deeper. Naturally, they followed the same route toward deeper waters which they had used during their inshore movement. Finally, the migration completed, they dropped off the tip of the shale slide into the depths of their sanctuary. I knew I could not expect another major migration on that particular slide, or probably anywhere else for that matter, for perhaps six hours or more.

The depth to which light will penetrate, it was mentioned

earlier, is dependent upon existing water color and weather conditions. On any given day when a high overhead sun is pounding the water, the rays will more easily penetrate clear water than that which is muddy, stained, or cloudy. Fine particles suspended in the water not only block the further penetration of the rays but bounce the light back toward the surface (at various angles). A chop on the water because of wind ruffling the surface will refract the rays too, heavy cloud cover will screen out much of the light, and even conditions of rain, fog, smog, haze, and other variations of air clarity will prevent sunlight from striking the water to various degrees.

What is important to keep in mind is that varying amounts of light penetration into the water, resulting from various combinations of all of the above conditions, will see the fish sanctuary at certain levels and travel to certain other levels when they migrate.

Most anglers are very guilty of the mistaken assumption that nice days are great for fishing. Calm waters, a high overhead sun, no threatening cloud-cover, and picnic-type air temperatures prompt anglers to flock to their favorite lakes and reservoirs in droves. The day is grand for fishing, or rather for the fishermen. But it is horrid for the fish! They will live and move at much greater depths, often making themselves inaccessible for the majority of anglers.

On the other hand, the most unpleasant days for fishermen are usually the best days for bass and bass fishing. A dark, overcast sky with wind ruffling the surface and perhaps a light rain falling will all greatly reduce light penetration. This causes bass to sanctuary somewhat shallower, and when they move they will often do so upon very shallow structures (or when moving on deeper structures they will often come far into the shallows).

It is very understandable why fishing logs and record books consistently show that the very largest bass and the best catches of the season are usually brought aboard when the weather conditions keep less adventuresome anglers at home.

Then, the following day, out comes the bright sun again. There is not a single cloud in the sky to filter or diffuse the strong rays, and there is no chop on the water to refract the light further. As a result, the light penetrates to sometimes astounding depths (depending upon the degree of water clarity), forcing the fish to maintain deep sanctuaries and preventing them from moving into shallow water during their migrations.

Let's further refine some of this understanding. During the

course of any given day the sun will strike the water at varying angles. Therefore percentage of light penetration is less (during morning or evening) and bass will migrate shallower on the side of the lake or reservoir which is closest to the sun and affords less light penetration and more shade.

Since bass can be located and caught much easier when they have migrated to the shallowest level they intend to travel to, it therefore makes great sense to fish likely structures on the far east side of your favorite lake in the morning and the structures on the far west side during the late afternoon. Should you accidentally reverse this fishing strategy, during both morning and late afternoon fishing, the bass would be on very deep structures when they migrated, and your chances of bringing in a good string would probably be neatly clipped in half. Chart 16 will better enable you to visualize this concept. We've shown a side view of an old riverbed lying on the floor of a flatland reservoir. We know that during all seasons of the year (except for the brief spawn weeks, and again for a brief period during the "false-spawn" in the fall), the riverbed will be the home of the fish because that is where the deep water is. Chart 16 shows how the fish will shift locations as the sun rises in the morning, crosses the sky at noon, and then drops toward the western horizon.

I'm usually against commercial "hawkery" of fishing tackle and related gear, as the reader already well knows. But one gadget that I can highly recommend is the Depth-o-Lite.

But if you should choose not to purchase a Depth-o-Lite, that is all right, too. Just keep several things in mind. First, fish as much as possible under those conditions of low-light or reduced-light penetration; this means early and late in the year, early and late during any given day, and when weather conditions are such that you're tempted to stay home and watch television. Second, fish water of the most suitable coloration, as we discussed in the last chapter. Third, when you find yourself on the water during midsummer, during midafternoon, when weather conditions are bright, or when water conditions are predominantly clear, concentrate the bulk of your efforts upon much deeper structures than you customarily find bass upon.

Many types of lakes and reservoirs, however, simply do not possess suitable depths to which bass can retreat in search of darkness. Fortunately, in such cases, we can usually expect Mother Nature to intervene with her own set of checks and balances. Those

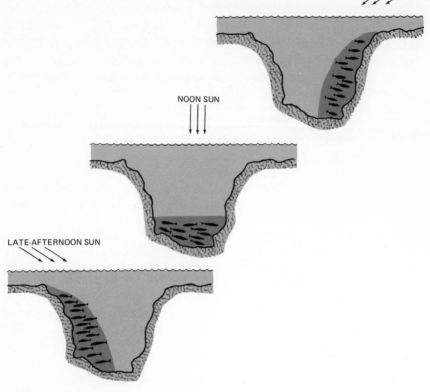

Chart 16. How bass shift locations with the sun

waters which do not possess depths nearly always possess extensive amounts of vegetation or other cover. Or there may be steep banks along the shoreline which cast shade upon the water. In rivers, turbulent waters refract the sun's rays and make conditions tolerable, if not favorable.

All of these exceptions, and more, enable bass to seek out areas of reduced light penetration where there is no deep water. How to fish for bass under these conditions is discussed in Chapter 7.

WEATHER

Weather conditions, per se, do not affect bass. It is the changing degree of light intensity associated with various weather conditions that influences their behavior.

If it were possible (sometimes it is) to select a perfect day for bass fishing, this is what it would look like: first, there would be overcast conditions: preferably a solid gray ceiling to substantially block out the sunlight, perhaps even with dark thunderheads hanging low in the sky. There would be a light breeze blowing but not enough to hamper precise boat control or presentation of lures; just enough to put a mild chop on the water to refract existing sunlight still further and prevent its penetrating the depths. The water temperature would be somewhere between 65 and 75 degrees because that is the range in which bass have very active body metabolisms. The air would be humid and hot, somewhere around 85 degrees, and the temperature would be stable and have remained that way for at least the past three or four days. The water would be slightly milky in color.

Under these conditions, regardless of when they might occur during the year, an angler could expect regular fish migrations to shallow-water structures and probably a very heavy stringer by day's end.

Now let's look at the opposite extreme. If it were possible to anticipate the worst fishing conditions (sometimes it is), here is what they would look like. First, the sky would be a pale blue, not a cloud would be in sight, and the sun would be pounding the water from directly overhead. Not a hint of even the faintest breeze would be in the air, and the surface of the water would look like a sheet of glass. The water temperature would be less than 60 degrees and the air temperature would be colder still, having dropped below the water temperature during the previous night. The barometer would be either very low or falling rapidly.

Under these conditions—a classic cold front—the fish will descend far into the depths, maybe to seventy-five feet or more if such depths are available. They will not feed, and they will not migrate.

A cold front, by definition, is a line on a weather map in which a leading edge of a mass of cooler air is advancing into an area presently containing a mass of warmer air. The difference between the temperatures of the two air masses can be great, as in the examples given above, but many other times they are barely discernible. Masses of air of varying temperatures, while there are occasional exceptions, generally move across our continent from the west to the east.

The leading edge of a cold front, however, just before it moves into any given area, can often provide fantastic fishing. The reason is that this leading edge is often associated with stormy weather or conditions which indicate that a storm will soon descend upon the region (as in the example given at the very beginning of this section).

The thing which is unique about cold fronts is that while the leading edge can provide ideal fishing conditions, once the mass of cooler air enters the area, and for several days thereafter, you may not be able to buy a strike, at any price! Even expert anglers, faced with these conditions, often give it up and go home. But it is not the cold air which has affected the fish. Rather, here is what usually happens. With the sky slightly gray and clouds beginning to form (several days before the arrival of a front) the fish begin moving somewhat shallower during their migrations. The next day there are even more clouds and the sky becomes still darker. The fish move still shallower. The next day dark thunderheads move in and the sky looks almost black. Everybody is catching bass— mainly because the fish are now quite accessible when they migrate, having moved progressively shallower each succeeding day. Suddenly, the front passes through and the next day dawns exceedingly bright and clear, causing the fish to dive for the depths.

There are numerous ways in which anglers can use weather conditions to their advantage. Let's say it's predicted that a major cold front will enter your area in four days. You have two days available for fishing. To see your best action, you would probably be wise to wait for two days and then fish on the two days just prior to the arrival of the front.

Let's say, on the other hand, that you plan to go fishing the next morning. You'd like to fish a certain lake about twenty miles to the west of your home. Before retiring that evening, however, you tune in a weather forecast and learn that a mass of cooler air is rapidly entering your area. The meteorologist says the front should arrive within ten hours. Your best bet in this case would be to eliminate from consideration your previously decided-upon lake. You'd get there just after the front had passed through that region. It would be better to select some alternate lake or reservoir located to the east of your home! I know anglers who often drive as much as a hundred miles during the night, with some destination in mind, in order to get ahead of the leading edge of a front, rather than staying at home to fish postfrontal conditions.

Sometimes, however, anglers have no choice in the matter and must fish under cold-front conditions. This is frequently the case when you're on vacation away from home at some fishing camp and a major front moves into the area the day after your arrival. Here is how to fish under such conditions—after, of course, you've uttered a few well-chosen words.

First, understand that when a cold front moves into an area full force and then passes through, leaving clear skies and bright light and causing the bass to scatter in a disorderly fashion as they beat a hasty retreat for the depths, individual fish frequently become separated from their respective schools. And once separated they exhibit characteristics of being disoriented. The usual behavior they will display under these circumstances is to seek heavy cover where they can hide. Felled trees, logs, and stumps in the shallows offer this very type of seclusion. If I am on a fishing vacation somewhere and a cold front descends upon the area, I immediately abandon all efforts to locate a migrating school of bass on structure. I head straight for those shorelines saturated with stumps, felled trees, and logs and cast my lures into the darkest, most secluded places possible, putting in my hours in the hope of picking up a lone fish here, another there, and so on. If such cover is not available, my next choice is to fish potholes and channels in the heaviest weedbeds I can find. Or I fish shorelines where some degree of shade is afforded by high rock cliffs or the branches of overhanging shoreline trees.

Sometime or other you'll probably even experience a situation in which two or three cold fronts pass through, one after the other, every three days or so. Such are the times that try fishermen's souls.

CHAPTER 4

You Need to Monitor Water Oxygen

Bass fishing's latest wrinkle is testing the oxygen content of various sections of the body of water you intend to fish, and plying your skills only in those locations found to have optimum oxygen-saturation levels.

Learning how to determine oxygen levels in any lake or reservoir is amazingly easy. And I am confident the many types of oxygen-evaluation equipment now on the market will exert the same revolutionary effect upon the sport of bassing as have electronic depth sounders for locating good structure, and light-penetration equipment for determining how deep the fish will be.

It all began when a suave, handsome young man from Austin, Texas, invented the first small-scale oxygen monitor for fishermen. His name was Dr. Martin Venneman, and his brainstorm, released in 1973, was dubbed the Sentry Oxygen Monitor.

I was the first fishing writer/scientist to test the equipment thoroughly and introduce it to anglers nationwide through a special feature article which appeared in an early 1974 issue of *Sports Afield* magazine. I found the Sentry advanced in concept and spectacular in its accuracy, and I was convinced its use would quickly spread to all corners of bassdom. Apparently I was not alone in my observations. Within a few months after my report was published, three respected manufacturers of fishing tackle had pulled out all stops, engaged in research and testing, and were preparing to introduce their own variations of oxygen-evaluation equipment. By the time you read this many more will likely have joined the parade. The monitors are even standard equipment, now, in national bass-tournament boats.

Dr. Venneman's inventiveness was spurred as a result of extensive testing of large waterways with much more sophisticated, oversize equipment. He discovered, and stated publicly, that "at any given time from 50 to 80 percent of the water in any lake does not contain enough oxygen to support fish life!" Shortly thereafter, he began work on a scaled-down version of the larger oxygen equipment he'd been using in order that anglers could take advantage of his findings.

If the bass-angler considers an oxygen monitor to be a valuable tool and uses it in conjunction with his knowledge of bass behavior, and only in this manner, he may almost immediately see a sharp increase in his level of fishing success.

In detailing how oxygen monitors work and why knowledge of oxygen-structure fishing is important to anglers, I would like to reprint, verbatim, two sentences which originally appeared in my *Sports Afield* article. They should always be kept in mind as the advanced angler commences his search for bass.

"Oxygen monitoring equipment does not guarantee you will consistently be able to find or catch fish. It does guarantee you will not waste one minute of time fishing where no fish can possibly survive."

Oxygen evaluation will take the seasoned bass angler still another step further in his scientific and systematic elimination of barren or unproductive water. All efforts may then be concentrated only in those areas most likely to contain bass.

It should also be mentioned that bass found in rivers and

Oxygen-monitoring equipment can save anglers time because it prevents you from fishing where no fish can live!

streams are not as likely to be influenced by changing oxygen levels. The waters there most often have some variation of moving current. And any depletion or reaching of saturation levels which may indeed occur are usually so short-lived as to have no effect upon the bass and so will not force them to alter their habits radically or move to other locations.

The greatest applications of oxygen evaluation are on the larger lakes and reservoirs where miles of shoreline twist and turn on themselves to form numerous channels, bays, coves, and other such areas which may be subject to wide variations in water temperature, exposure to weather, and so on. Our concern in this chapter, then, will be with bass fishing in these more expansive waterways.

All of the bass species (indeed, every species of gamefish) must have enough dissolved oxygen in the water around them in order to live. In many other respects, bass may be seen to be very tolerant (within limits) and very adaptable to varied conditions. Weather may change, light intensities will certainly vary from time to time, water temperatures may fluctuate, and water levels may rise or fall. But in the matter of minimum oxygen requirements there can be no compromise, no tolerance, and no adaptation. Bass absolutely must have certain levels of oxygen or they will be faced with an immediate alternative. Either move out of the area altogether or perish!

For the bass species, optimum oxygen levels are found in the range of 5 to 13 parts per million (PPM) though they highly prefer and will seek out the 9 to 12 PPM level. Of the four bass species covered in this book, smallmouths, according to Dr. Venneman, are an exception to the rule in that their preference is for waters somewhat less saturated with oxygen and frequently ranging from 3 to 8 PPM.

Remaining in a lake area where the oxygen level is below 3 PPM will cause bass of any species to die of asphyxiation. And if they remain in areas with more than 13 PPM they will experience symptoms of oxygen poisoning.

You may have already witnessed numerous instances of this oxygen dependency but never been aware of exactly what was happening. This may have occurred when baitfish in your minnow bucket, after several hours, began coming to the surface to gulp air. The same can occur with bass you are trying to keep alive in a closed live-well onboard. The fish have simply depleted the oxygen supply in the water, and adding fresh water or turning on an aerator usually solves the problem.

Another, more serious example frequently occurs on many northern ice-bound lakes and reservoirs during the winter months. In what is known as a "freeze-out" or "winterkill," all fish in the lake may perish. Here is what happens. During their photosynthesis (or food-making process), aquatic plants take in large quantities of carbon dioxide and in exchange release oxygen molecules into the water. The sun plays an important role in this phenomenon as it allows the plant life to remain in an "active" state. The sun's rays are easily able to penetrate clear ice, but when a heavy blanket of snow blots out the rays for prolonged periods, the plants fall into a dormant state, discontinue giving off oxgyen, and soon the fish are incapable of surviving.

Oxygen levels may also become depleted in large sections of lakes and reservoirs during the summer and fall months. In these cases, however, the cause is abrupt changes in barometric pressures, underwater "density" currents, wind direction and velocity, and other acts of Mother Nature. These forces are strong enough to deplete the oxygen even in vegetation-filled areas! The effects of oxygen depletion or over-saturation may last for only a day or two, or they may last for several weeks. This is why anglers should frequently take oxygen readings in those lake sections they fish most regularly, especially if they are experiencing difficulty finding fish.

Most oxygen meters (four or five are presently commercially available) look like a small box. Others, however, are roundish, clocklike affairs with oxygen-evaluation, light-penetration, and water-temperature gauges sometimes incorporated all in the same unit. Whatever the brand name, oxygen monitors are all battery-operated, fully portable, and about half as expensive as a quality depth sounder. Every oxygen monitor I have tested has had a probe attached to a line which is lowered over the side of the boat to various depths. A small dial is synchronized with a needle-type gauge, and then a button is pushed. The needle tells the angler the parts per million of oxygen saturation at the level to which he has lowered the probe. It is all that simple.

At the very beginning of the first day on the water, before fishing, the angler devotes a small amount of time to "research" to avoid wasting many hours fishing blindly. Motoring back and forth, he surveys sections of the lake, taking oxygen readings here and there and jotting down his findings in a notebook or on his contour map. *Now is also an ideal time to note the presence of various types of water coloration,* as was discussed in Chapter 2.

The remainder of the day's fishing then sees the angler searching for good structure, but only in those areas found to have oxygen levels most ideally compatible with the lives of the bass species. He completely eliminates from any consideration those areas he has found to be incapable of supporting fish life, regardless of how much "bassy looking" structure they may possess. On subsequent days on the water, he need only reconfirm the oxygen saturation levels upon arrival at his chosen fishing locations. It takes only a few minutes.

What a time-saving boon for anglers! No longer will the fisherman locate good structure, wait for a migration of fish, fill his stringer, return the following day, and perhaps sit there for hours without a strike and be puzzled as to why. He will be able quickly to test the water, and if something has happened to radically change the oxygen-saturation levels, he will be absolutely certain the bass have left the area.

Surveying a body of water in search of optimum oxygen levels and schools of bass should not be carried out at the expense of disregarding depths where light penetration is minimal or locations where suitable structure is present that will draw and hold bass. The point to be made here is that while both of these latter considerations, and perhaps still others as well, may seem to indicate ideal conditions for bass, if oxygen levels are not suitable, the area will be as barren of fish as the rafters in your garage.

Chart 17 shows a rather small highland-type lake we will suppose you have just completed surveying with an oxygen monitor. It's the morning of the first day of a five-day fishing trip. In which general areas should you now begin your search for suitable structure which may be holding bass? Of course, it will be in those areas where oxygen saturations are highest but not exceeding 13 PPM.

During the summer months most of the deepest lakes and reservoirs become separated into three distinct layers of water. These, which are discussed in detail in the next chapter, are commonly referred to as the *epilimnion* (upper layer), *metalimnion* or *thermocline* (middle layer) and *hypolimnion* (bottom layer).

The hypolimnion, the layer of water just above the lake floor in the very deepest sections, is generally (there are exceptions, discussed in the next chapter) completely void of oxygen, while the upper two layers are most often oxygen-saturated. Temperature

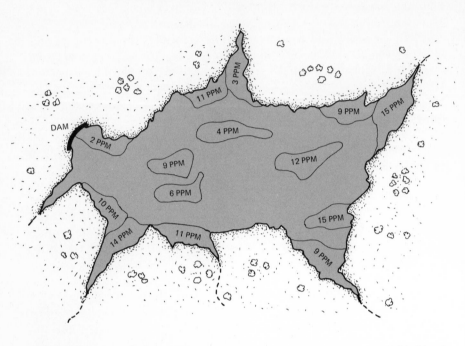

Chart 17. How oxygen levels commonly vary in a typical small highland lake

variations and other factors determine the limits or depths at which these various layers may form. And for the sake of simplicity in this chapter we may simply, therefore, combine the upper two, oxygen-rich layers of water and call them the *oxycline.*

The advanced angler will use his oxygen monitor in conjunction with his water temperature gauge to determine the exact depth of the oxycline, for he knows that if he fishes below this level he will be in the hypolimnion, where no fish can survive. To make this perfectly clear, let's look at a hypothetical example.

Let's say the angler is fishing a highland-type lake and there is an "off" structure in the form of a midlake bar. It's a very long bar that runs from relatively shallow water to very deep water—a perfect migration structure. This bar is the midsummer home of a school of largemouths. They sanctuary just off the end of the bar where the water is deepest (let's say fifty feet) and several times a day they migrate up the structure toward the shallower end of the bar, where the water is twelve feet deep. The bar possesses a number of rock piles at scattered intervals; these serve as the "breaks" or signposts which the fish follow when they migrate. The angler lucks out (actually, in modern bassing, there is little real "luck") and takes several nice bass at twelve feet deep during one of the school's migrations. This is understandable, because before fishing the area he took an oxygen reading and discovered the shallow end of the bar to possess 11 PPM of dissolved oxygen. That night, at home, he listens to the wind howling outside, and the following morning he unsuccessfully fishes the twelve-foot level of the bar for three hours without a strike. He should have taken an oxygen reading first! The wind may have pushed the oxygen-rich water further offshore or rearranged it in some other manner. Perhaps the twelve-foot level now possesses only 4 PPM of oxygen. Since the bar is quite long, the fish may still be using it. But now, when they migrate, they may be coming only to the twenty-foot level!

One particular oxygen condition all anglers should be on the lookout for is called an *oxygen inversion*. An oxygen inversion is the brief formation of a third layer of water *below* the oxygen-void hypolimnion. An oxygen inversion is usually high in oxygen content (8 to 13 PPM) and is most often found near a sharp drop-off or in association with underground springs. When wind direction, barometric changes, and types of underwater currents form an inversion pocket, the bass are trapped, usually in a fairly confined area. Until wind and wave action cause the inversion to dissipate, the bass can go absolutely nowhere, because venturing out of the pocket would mean entering the oxygen-void hypolimnion and perishing. That is something they will not do under normal circumstances (though we saw how they did indeed do this very thing when scuba divers contrived artificial conditions with floodlights).

Although only a limited number of inversions occur at any one time in a body of water, and their existence is usually only brief, the angler who stumbles onto such a situation may experience the fastest fishing of his life. You may literally catch a fish on every cast until your arm turns to rubber or until you spook the school. Even if the fish do become spooked, however, it's impossible for them to leave the area! Rest them for a short while and you can usually return to where you left off and start catching them again.

Chart 18 shows a side view of a section of highland reservoir and the general appearance of an oxygen inversion pocket.

On Lewis-Smith Reservoir in Alabama my frequent fishing

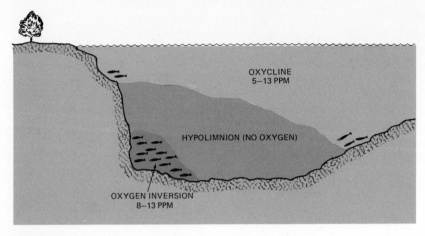

Chart 18. Oxygen inversion pocket in a highland reservoir

companion, Dave Moore, and I were one day taking oxygen readings before commencing our angling efforts. Purely by accident we found an inversion pocket at the base of a sheer underwater rock cliff. The fish were spotted bass and the action they provided is something neither of us is likely to soon forget.

I made eleven consecutive casts into the pocket and brought eleven fish to the boat. Dave made eight casts and hooked eight fish but landed only six of them. Then the action started to taper off. But before the bass school was completely spooked, we had successfully boated twenty-seven bass during a time-span of only thirty-five minutes!

We continued to work down the same shoreline but found no other inversion pockets and later returned to the first location and took still an additional twenty-one bass! A cast to either side of the inversion pocket (into the oxygen-void hypolimnion) brought no strikes. But back into the inversion and BAM!

Those fish weren't very large, averaging perhaps only 2½ pounds, but numerically they constituted the largest catch in the shortest time period that I have ever participated in. Of the forty-eight bass boated, we kept ten (six of which had been seriously injured during the course of fighting them) for a fish-fry we had planned with two other anglers. The rest of the fish were carefully slipped back into the water immediately after being unhooked. That evening a thunderstorm moved into the area and caused the inversion pocket to break up. For the next two days we could not catch a single bass from the area which had previously been so hot. Now, there was only oxygen-void hypolimnion water there.

There may be one exception in which the angler does not have to put into daily use a knowledge of oxygen levels and that is during the spring when numerous feeder creeks and tributaries continually pour in large quantities of fresh run-off water. Perhaps this is one of Mother Nature's safeguards so the bass will not be prompted periodically to abandon their nests. But about the time the spawn is ended and the body of water is beginning to settle down (or complete its "turnover," which will be discussed shortly), the angler should check the batteries in his oxygen-monitoring equipment. From this time of year through the remaining seasons, monitoring water oxygen will play an important role in his level of bassing success.

CHAPTER 5

Facts about Water Temperature

Another aspect of "water structure" to be discussed, before we get into the business of actually catching bass, is water temperature. In view of what we've already learned, it is easy to see why one area of any lake or reservoir may be teeming with fish while other areas only a short distance away may be completely barren of almost any aquatic life whatever. Understanding water temperature will help us to refine even further our knowledge as to where bass will be at certain times of year, and why they will be in those particular locations.

In this chapter we'll be disproving three bass-fishing tenets that a majority of anglers have accepted as gospel for decades. The first has to do with the hypolimnion being void of oxygen. This may be true at certain times of year, but as we mentioned in the previous chapter, there are other times when the hypolimnion may actually have more oxygen than the other water layers! The second has to do with the notion of bass seeking out certain water temperatures where they can feel most comfortable. This is pure bunk. And the third has to do with water temperature determining how deep bass will go. This, too, is entirely untrue! All of these fallacies, I'm sorry to say, have been and still are given big play in the outdoor magazines by writers and fishing editors. Perhaps they should spend a little more time actually experimenting and testing on the water than sitting behind their typewriters parroting what others have said before.

Let's begin this discussion by looking at the water-temperature changes any given lake or reservoir experiences during the seasons. You should have an electronic water-temperature gauge. These are small, hand-held, battery-operated instruments. Very simply, you unwind a wire from the instrument and lower a probe to various depths. Then you push a button and the water temperature at the depth of the probe registers on a meter on the face of the instrument. A high-quality gauge should cost about $40, and given reasonable care it will last a lifetime. Check with your local tackle dealer.

Depending upon latitude, the fall season usually arrives sometime around September in the far northern states and perhaps as late as November in the southernmost states. Usually after the first hard frost, the water begins to cool. Of course, the first water to be affected by the gradually cooling air is the upper layer, and especially that water found in shallow coves and bays.

Since this cooler surface water is molecularly quite dense, it is therefore heavier than the warmer water which lies directly below. As a result, the cooler water starts to sink, pushing the warmer water to the top, where, in turn, it is cooled and likewise starts to sink. This physical process creates density currents, commonly referred to as the "fall turnover." The turnover, along with decreasing of light penetration because of the late-season position of the sun in the sky, means the fish will begin using predominantly shallower structures.

As the cool, sinking water reaches a temperature of about 39 degrees Fahrenheit, it becomes heavier than all other water layers and therefore sinks right to the very bottom, destroying whatever thermal stratification may have been in evidence. This process continues until, eventually, in the northern states, the water is a uniform 39 degrees from top to bottom, except for the very surface, which reaches 32 degrees and freezes.

When the spring comes, another "turnover" occurs, but contrary to circulated opinion it occurs in a much different manner. The sun's rays melt the ice and warm the surface water. Since this warm surface water is lighter in molecular density than the much colder water directly beneath, *it does not sink*. The only way the lower depths warm up is by "conduction" or the downward transfer of heat from one molecule of water to the next. As we all know, heat would much rather rise than sink, and this is the reason why the water takes much longer to warm in the spring than it takes to cool during the fall. So the spring turnover is really a misnomer, because the water doesn't really turn over.

Naturally, the water closest to the shoreline and in shallow coves and bays warms more quickly, because the sunlight penetrates all the way to the bottom, where it is absorbed and then transmitted back to the water. This doesn't happen, of course, in deep water, since there the sunlight cannot penetrate all the way to the bottom, so there is no "bounce-back" effect.

The warming water of spring, we know, triggers the spawning instincts of bass and other gamefish and panfish. And the water will continue to warm through the summer months to the point where surface temperatures may often approximate air temperatures, soaring as high as perhaps 80 or even 90 degrees in certain areas of the country!

As the top layer of water warms much faster than the deeper, colder water, it eventually reaches a point in which it ceases to mix or transfer heat downward from one molecule to the next. The reason why all of this takes place is complex and we need not go into it here. But we need to know that the effect brings about the formation of the three layers of water already mentioned: the *hypolimnion* at the very bottom, the *thermocline* in the middle and the *epilimnion* on top. Sometimes these layers are well defined, but usually they appear only as fluctuating zones.

Water stratification and the formation of a thermocline do not take place in every lake or reservoir. They are usually deep, clear-water phenomena that take place in lakes and reservoirs at least thirty or forty feet deep. This means that summer stratification is usually more characteristic of highland than flatland waters.

In shallower lakes and reservoirs with an average depth of perhaps no more than fifteen feet, no thermocline will form. Mother

Nature's check, in these cases, is usually the presence of heavy cover to screen out some of the sun's penetrating rays so the shallows do not "burn themselves out" by allowing water temperatures to become exceedingly high.

In waters in which stratification takes place, a thermocline, then, defined in its most simple terms, is that middle layer of water which separates the warm water from the very cold. Within this layer or zone the temperature changes rapidly, perhaps as much as one-half a degree Fahrenheit or more with each foot of depth. Skindivers are sometimes able to hover at a certain depth and poke a toe only inches deeper and feel the sharp, biting cold of the thermocline.

A typical thermocline might appear as follows if an angler charted temperatures and depths in a notebook:

DEPTH		WATER TEMPERATURE
Surface		78 degrees
5 feet		78 degrees
10 feet		76 degrees
15 feet		75 degrees
20 feet		73 degrees
25 feet	THERMOCLINE	66 degrees
30 feet		60 degrees
35 feet		59 degrees
40 feet		58 degrees
45 feet		56 degrees
50 feet		54 degrees

Chart 19 shows another example of water stratification in which a thermocline has formed. Using a suitable water-temperature gauge, you can ascertain the thermocline's upper and lower limits in the lakes and reservoirs you frequent. Later, we'll see how you can use that information to your fishing advantage.

It should be repeated, however, that the upper and lower limits of a thermocline are not often well-defined but rather constitute zones which may vacillate upward or downward from day to day during the summer, and even from hour to hour.

Chart 20 gives a visual representation of how a thermocline, in conjunction with the other water layers, may take on varying forms.

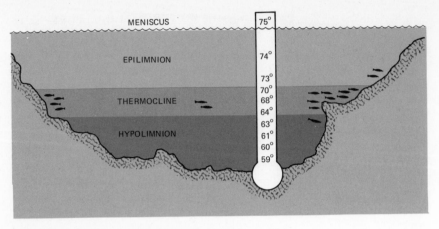

Chart 19. Water stratification with a thermocline

Most thermoclines average between seven to ten feet thick, are usually found between depths of twenty to thirty-five feet, and encompass temperature ranges of between 55 to 70 degrees. However, this is only the norm. At Lewis-Smith Reservoir in Alabama, where the depth may drop from five feet to three hundred feet just a few yards away from the shoreline, I once found a thermocline that had a lower limit of seventy feet!

In all of this, the important thing for bass-anglers is that when stratification is in evidence, the fish will be found in greater

Chart 20. A concentration of bass in a thermocline

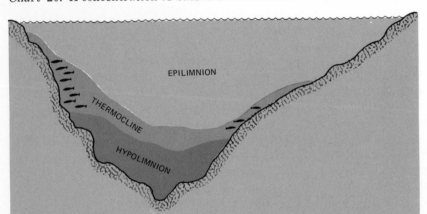

abundance within the thermocline. There are two reasons for this. First, the upper layer or epilimnion usually has too much light penetration to be comfortable for the bass. Second, the hypolimnion is usually void of oxygen. That leaves the thermocline, where there is a combination of minimal light penetration and ample oxygen.

While the thermocline is generally the best depth for the bulk of your fishing efforts, there are always exceptions to the rule. The most common exception is when you locate a long structure leading all the way to deep water which looks as though it might have good migration possibilities. A thermocline, we'll say, exists from twenty to thirty feet deep and so you decide to begin fishing at that depth. But no strikes come. You move deeper and begin catching good fish at the forty-five-foot level!

This very situation occurred two years ago when Bill Dance was competing in a Bass Angler Sportsman Society tournament. On one day of the contest, using plastic worms and 3/4-ounce slip-sinkers, Bill caught the majority of his bass from fifty feet deep! His partner, Charlie Searcy, could hardly believe it, even though he observed it firsthand.

"How can fish exist below the thermocline, where there is no oxygen?" is a common question that befuddles even the most experienced anglers.

For years fishing experts and even a few biologists stalwartly proclaimed that the hypolimnion was completely void of oxygen. Placing fish in this layer of water, it was believed, would be like throwing them on a hot sidewalk; their resultant life expectancy could be measured in minutes. And indeed, for the period in which summer stratification is in evidence, this may be true (we saw how bass entered the hypolimnion in the light-penetration study and suffocated).

But biologists have recently begun to admit that at certain times during the year, the hypolimnion may possess much more dissolved oxygen than the thermocline itself! And further, this seldom-fished layer of water may be chock-full of bass!

The reason for this phenomenon takes a bit of explaining but is not overly difficult to understand. When a lake stratifies, we know there is little or no mixing of the various layers, and therefore there is no way for the lower layer to receive oxygen from the upper layer via rain, wind, and wave action or as the byproduct of photosynthesis. This is how the upper two layers receive practically all of their oxygen. But while the hypolimnion receives no oxygen at all from these sources, this does not mean the lower layer is dead, at least, not all of the time.

You must remember that when ice-out first occurs during late winter, there is no stratification to separate one layer of water from another. As a result, the *entire* body of water will temporarily undergo an oxygenation process when strong winds lash the surface, feeder streams gush forth with spring rains, and a profusion of plant growth gets underway.

Under normal conditions, therefore, the deeper portions of any body of water are fairly well saturated with their share of oxygen at the time of stratification. And since the lower layer of water is much colder than the surface (averaging between 15 to 25 degrees cooler) the deepest portions can quite easily retain the oxygen molecules initially sent their way during the prestratification mixing process (cold water will retain more oxygen than warm water).

As the season wears on, until stratification has been evident for some time, the hypolimnion will gradually begin to lose its oxygen. But at the very outset many fish will be down in the hypolimnion and be perfectly contented, thank you.

Chart 21 gives a visual representation of this situation.

The gradual loss of oxygen in the hypolimnion, while the thermocline and epilimnion continually replenish their supplies, is

Chart 21. A lake's deeper portions sometimes hold ample oxygen

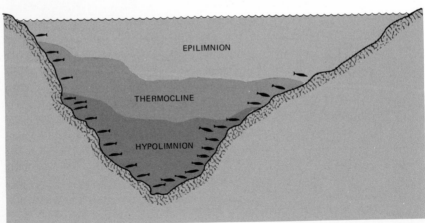

due to several factors. For one, there is almost no plant life at great depths, since beyond thirty feet at the most, even in very clear water, there is too little sunlight to support it. Moreover, the fish which were present in the hypolimnion have of course consumed part of the oxygen. And the rest is gobbled up in time by the oxygen-consuming process of decaying organic matter (dead plants and fish which sink to the bottom and slowly decompose).

It's worth noting that infertile lakes of the north country often experience stratification situations in which the bass are able to live in the hypolimnion for most of the summer. There is simply not enough decaying organic matter to consume the large quantities of oxygen present at the time of stratification. However, just the opposite becomes true as you move farther south, particularly in the Gulf States region. Here, the oxygen in the hypolimnion is rapidly consumed because of the high fertility levels of many of the waters and the vast subsequent quantities of decaying organic matter.

With this knowledge we can deduce several strategies which will help in locating bass. First, it's wise to determine whether those lakes or reservoirs you plan to fish during the late spring, summer, or fall months experience stratification. Those waters which do not stratify, of course, can be fished using the tactics we have discussed in previous chapters. Those which do stratify—and this is something which can be determined in five minutes' time with your water-temperature gauge—should be fished according to the existing upper and lower limits of the thermocline. The largest bass will usually hug the lower limit of the thermocline, simply because this is where the light penetration is lowest and because they can go no deeper without entering the hypolimnion. The two exceptions to this rule, again, are during the late spring months in clear, fertile bodies of water when the hypolimnion may contain plenty of oxygen, and during all months of stratification in the infertile northern lakes where conditions protect against the gradual depletion of oxygen in the hypolimnion.

One of the greatest handicaps from which bass fishing has suffered in this country has been the perpetuation of the myth about bass "preferring" certain water temperatures, that during the summer months they will seek out cool water where they can be comfortable and that during the winter months they will seek out warm water. Nothing could be farther from the truth! Sure, bass do indeed move into the depths during the summer and they gravitate back toward the shallows at certain other times during the fall, but water temperature has nothing to do with it.

Even tackle manufacturers who make electronic water-temperature gauges have fostered the mistaken notion about bass preferring one range of water temperature over another. On their instruments they plaster guidelines stating that the preferred temperature for largemouths is from 68 to 75 degrees, that the range for smallmouths is from 63 to 68 degrees, and that spotted bass "like" water temperatures in the range of 65 to 70 degrees (they list the "preferred" temperatures for other gamefish and panfish as well).

I shudder at the fact that probably tens of thousands of anglers who purchase this equipment use it wrongly.

Fish do not favor one water temperature over another! Nor will they travel great distances, as some would lead us to believe, to find water temperatures which are supposedly preferred. If that were true, those locations in lakes or reservoirs near large metropolitan areas, where industries discharge warm water during the winter months, would contain every fish in the entire reservoir!

Fish of all species are cold-blooded, meaning that their bodies are always the same temperature as the water they are in. So all fish are perfectly "comfortable" all of the time, regardless of the temperature of the water surrounding them.

A bass does not leave 80-degree water and search out 65-degree water so he will be more comfortable. He is perfectly comfortable in any water temperature, be it 80 degrees, 65 degrees, or 40 degrees!

The various depths bass will descend to are never determined by existing water temperatures at those levels. Instead, the depths bass will go to are determined by a combination of other conditions such as existing light penetration, water stratification (when in evidence), and water oxygen.

Water temperature does have an influence upon bass, however, for it exerts an effect on the body metabolism of the various species. The guidelines accompanying water temperature gauges, therefore, should not list "preferred" temperatures, but rather temperature ranges within which the species can be expected to exhibit maximum activity. At temperatures below the range needed for maximum metabolic rates for any given bass species, the fish will not feed regularly nor actively, and lures or baits must therefore be presented at very slow speeds because the fish are somewhat lethargic. As the metabolic rates increase, spurred by increasing water temperatures, the fish require more frequent replenishment of food stores. They are now more active when they feed, too—in fact, they are more active in everything they do—and better results will necessarily be seen with much faster lure speeds.

Monitoring water temperatures, then, gives the angler some idea as to which types of lure presentation will prove most effective. If the underwater bar he is checking is twenty-five feet deep, and his temperature gauge says the water at that depth is only 55 degrees, he will know to use a very slow retrieve, or perhaps even switch to live baits which can be worked slower still. If the tip of a shoreline point he's checking lies in only ten feet of water, however, and the temperature at that level is 76 degrees, he can probably expect to see his best action by cranking in his lures as fast as he can turn the reel handle.

CHAPTER 6

Feeding Behavior and Live Baits

An angler who finds bass "biting" is very lucky indeed. The reason is that bass do not feed continually or at every opportunity. When the water is warm (above 55 degrees) the fish will probably feed three times a day, with each foraging session lasting anywhere from twenty minutes to about two hours. When the water is cold (below 55 degrees) the fish may feed only once a day, or once every other day, with the foraging session probably lasting less than an hour.

It therefore stands to reason that an angler who ventures upon his favorite lake or reservoir in the hopes that the bass are "biting" is faced with the odds significantly stacked against him. It will, perhaps, be better for him to forget completely about bass biting and concentrate instead upon trying to provoke striking responses—

which, as we will see, are entirely different from feeding responses.

Nevertheless, there are times when an angler will run into feeding bass, and he should know how to take command of the situation. So before we delve into the complexities of how bass strike we should first look very briefly at their feeding habits. This ties in very nicely with the previous chapter, in which we saw that water temperature is the single determinant of how often and how eagerly bass will stock up on groceries.

Any bass's diet may be as varied as the living conditions under which he may be found, though there is always one hard and fast rule governing his dining selectivity. He is a predator of Class-A rating and therefore will seldom show interest in potential food items unless they are exhibiting some sign of life. But except for this fetish he has a wide range of tastes. Any given feeding moment may see him foraging upon frogs and other amphibians, eels, small snakes, aquatic and terrestrial insects, and crustaceans—and even birds, mice, and baby muskrats. The favorite items on his menu, however, are nearly always crayfish and minnows (which may include baitfish species such as threadfin and gizzard shad, golden or emerald shiners, and the young of panfish or other gamefish, to name only a few).

It is interesting to note that none of the bass species feed by actually closing their mouths down upon their prey. Rather, they quickly open their mouths while simultaneously flaring their gill covers and expelling water through the gills. This creates a suction effect, allowing them literally to inhale their prey. Additionally, feeding bass are not likely to chase far after an escaping tidbit. This may be contrary to exciting reports in which some of our more romantic outdoor writers frequently describe a frantic "V-wake" rapidly closing in upon some surface lure from across the pond. Actually, the top speed of all bass is only about 12 MPH, and this speed can be achieved only in short bursts. As a result, a bass's feeding behavior is almost never a chase-and-catch affair. They have an instinctive method of "weighing" how much effort they must expend against the "energy value" of the potential food item.

I've spent countless hours watching bass feed on minnows in aquariums and in controlled lake situations. I've even donned scuba gear and gone underwater to observe the feeding habits of bass. Yet only in rare instances during the course of any of these observations have I witnessed chase scenes. Usually, just the opposite occurs. The bass and their forage seem to coexist, often hovering side by side and occasionally even brushing each other with swimming tails and fins. Then, in less time than it takes to read this sentence, some biological clock triggers a feeding desire and the nearest minnow disappears. No muss, no fuss, and little expenditure of precious reserve energy.

Similarly, one might, occasionally, see a bass bulldogging through a field of lily pads in hot pursuit of a skipping frog. But nine times in ten the frog will be placidly sitting on the edge of a pad and then suddenly, without warning of any kind, disappear in a ball of foam.

By the same token, a bass can expel a food item (or a lure) just as quickly as he can take it in, simply by reversing the suction process and blowing the item from his mouth. If he discovers or even slightly suspects he's been duped with a counterfeit, it's gone!

Glen Lau Productions, the people from Florida who film gamefish behavior around the world, have recently engaged in extensive underwater studies of bass-feeding habits. In order to provide insight for fishermen as well as biologists, most of the filming sessions were undertaken with anglers included in the action—specifically, sitting in a boat not far away and presenting a variety of lures to bass which had been located by a camera-equipped skindiver.

In many instances the frustrated diver would surface and exclaim to the angler in question, "Why the hell didn't you strike? A big bass had your lure entirely in his mouth and then finally blew it out!"

The incredulous reply was nearly always, "I didn't feel a thing!"

No better case could be made for any angler being intimately familiar with his tackle, as well as learning to maintain control and sensitive "feel" over whatever particular lures may be the order of the day. Usually, this is something which can be acquired only through experience, and even then he will probably still miss many fish, often never suspecting that some hawg may have had his lure and then rejected it.

We saw how water temperature regulates body metabolism, and how body metabolism in either accelerated or retarded states influences the regularity of feeding behavior. We know that when the water temperature is cold all bass species will be quite sluggish and lethargic. They'll feed now, to be sure, but the energy and enthusiasm with which that feeding behavior is carried out will be only marginal and infrequent. As a result, when the water temperature is cold, the angler knows he will have to work his lures very, very slowly.

Indeed, when the water temperature is below 55 degrees (50 degrees in the case of smallmouths), most artificial lures are very ineffective. The usual variety of plugs, spoons, spinners, and similar lures are designed to be "retrieved" and imparted with various types of "action." And most often these manipulations can be implemented or controlled only through the use of speed. Certainly, a proper definition of speed would have to include consideration of the very, very slowest speeds to those which are very, very fast. But the trouble with most lures is that at least minimal amounts of speed must be imparted. And under cold-water conditions, even the very, very slowest speeds may be much too fast to interest sluggish bass.

There are some lures, however, which do not fall in this category. And if the angler chooses to use artificials exclusively, he must consider only these types during cold-water conditions.

The lures we're talking about here are the soft polyvinyl-chloride baits such as plastic worms and salamanders, and the slow-action hard baits such as jigs which may be dressed with a plastic grub, plastic worm, some variation of pork rind, or perhaps a natural bait such as a minnow. These types of lures fulfill a number of prerequisites of cold-water fishing. First, they can most effectively be worked right on the bottom. This is important because we know that regardless of water depth or temperature, all bass will be on or near the bottom 90 percent of the time. These baits are generally weedless or snagless, or can be made so, and this makes them ideal for checking those breaks which are in the form of cover such as brush, rocks, and felled trees. And most important of all, these baits are at their best when worked at speeds ranging from dead-stop to ultra-slow.

A good rule of thumb for working the bottom-bumpers under cold water conditions is to cast beyond likely bottom structures, allowing the lure to sink all the way to the lake or reservoir floor. Then, reel in all of the slack line and with the sensitive rod tip moving vertically from the nine-o'clock to twelve-o'clock positions very slowly inch the lure along with a five-second pause after each movement or hopping motion you give the lure. Strikes won't be vicious now; just slight "bumps" or "taps"—and you'll have to set the hook quickly.

Under cold-water conditions, with lures being moved along slowly, a bass has ample time to inspect your offering at close range and if he's not convinced it's the real thing he'll totally ignore it. Any angler will therefore see his best success if he uses the lightest lines possible, minimal amounts of terminal tackle (such as snaps and swivels), and insures that his offering simulates real food. More on this later.

The second category of offerings ideally suited for cold-water fishing are the live baits. Nightcrawlers and live minnows are used the most, simply because they are easily obtainable. But crayfish, salamanders, and leeches will also account for their share of large-mouths, smallmouths, and spotted bass. Live baits likewise satisfy the prerequisites of cold-water fishing in that they, too, can be worked right on the bottom and are at their best when fished very slowly.

Almost any variation of live bait use could probably be traced back to the time of Dr. Henshall, and even earlier.

It should be noted, however, that each year an increasing number of anglers and fishing writers (to include this author) are coming to believe the practice of live-bait fishing to be unsporting, primarily because the great majority of fish that are caught on live bait take the bait so deeply they are gut-hooked, with severe damage to internal organs and therefore impossible to release, even if they are undersize. But for the sake of completeness in this book I would like to describe the most effective live-bait methods.

Bill Binkelman of Milwaukee, Wisconsin, and later Al Lindner of Brainerd, Minnesota, must be credited with substantially refining the use of live baits during the last several decades. Their methods have long since been the byword among modern anglers, so the techniques described here are ones they pioneered.

First, thread a light monofilament line through a slip-sinker. The line should test somewhere between six and ten pounds (much lighter lines can be used in cold-water fishing than warm-water fishing because the fish do not fight as hard—and because the much clearer water during this time of year requires them). The size of the slip-sinker is dependent upon the depth of the water you are fishing, of course, but also upon the amount of current or wind in evidence. With the line threaded through the slip-sinker, now tie on a very small swivel. To the swivel tie one end of a three-foot length of monofilament and to the other end of the line a size-8 long-shanked Aberdeen hook. The swivel prevents the sinker from sliding all the way down the line to the hook. And the center-hole in the slip-sinker allows the line to slip through easily. This is important because under cold-water conditions the bass are usually very spooky, and the slightest resistance on the line will cause them to drop the bait. Using a slip-sinker, a bass can inhale your offering and begin moving off with it without feeling any resistance.

In the case of nightcrawlers, hook them only once, right through the tip of the nose. This allows them to curl, uncurl, and gyrate as they are being worked across the bottom. In the case of minnows, hook them only once, right through the lips.

Using this type of rigging, the angler very slowly drifts across appropriate bottom structures that may at the time be holding straggler bass or that may have migrations of schooling bass. Or he may elect to use an electric motor or perhaps even his outboard for more precisely following some type of breakline (a change in the bottom contour such as a drop-off or the edge of a weedline). Since any type of motor may impart too much speed, Al Lindner has devised a workable system called "backtrolling." Basically, the motor is run in reverse, with the craft's broad transom headed into the waves and current to retard boat speed as much as possible. And even then, he frequently shifts into neutral to further slow the forward (actually, backward) movement of the craft. In order to prevent water from coming over the transom during rough weather conditions, he has bolted a homemade rubber splash-guard to his transom which sticks up to about the height of the outboard.

In backtrolling very carefully and slowly across a structure he is checking, the first indication of a "take" will be a very slight "bump," or perhaps no more than a peculiar resistance or barely detectable sideways jump in the line, whereupon Lindner immediately drops the rod tip and releases line to the fish.

Al likes to use an open-face spinning reel mounted upon a long, limber rod with a very sensitive tip. The fish is allowed to have the bait long enough to get the entire thing into his mouth. At that magic moment Al closes the bail on his reel, allows the slowly moving fish to take up the slack line until he feels a gentle resistance, and then quickly sets the hook. Sometimes he counts to five after the initial "bump" before setting the hook, and if he misses, it probably means he did not allow the fish sufficient time to take the bait. The next time he counts to eight, and so on until he has precisely determined how much time the fish need on any given day.

It was stated earlier that live baits are most effective when the water is cold and the bass are rather lethargic. This is usually the case during late fall, winter, and early spring. Live baits are also highly successful during midsummer or almost any other time when the fish are suspected to be on very deep structures. Beyond about twenty-five or thirty feet in depth, it is very difficult precisely to control either speed or the depth of artificials. But live baits, rigged with slip-sinkers, can be accurately controlled to depths of fifty feet!

The second situation in which live baits are highly effective is in angling for Florida bass. In the Sunshine State, anglers often use shad or other baitfish species, which may be as much as twelve inches in length and a full pound in weight, on a year-around basis. The popularity of this particular tactic has to do with the very nature of much of the Florida bass's habitat. His home predominantly consists of very shallow and expansive natural lakes (few manmade reservoirs exist in Florida) of the "flatland" type. Any depressions, holes, or other deep-water features existing in certain lake areas will be where the bass in that vicinity spend most of their time. But in many instances there are no variations in the bottom contour. Consequently, the structure the fish relate to often consists of the many variations of weeds and other vegetative growth which saturate the waterways. Frequently the weeds come up to within several feet of the surface throughout the entire waterway, making precise presentation of artificial lures all but impossible. The bass lie in the shaded potholes and other places where there are occasional breaks in the cover (substructure) rising now and then to pick off a free-swimming baitfish.

In these circumstances anglers most often use heavy-duty baitcasting rods with level-wind reels and lines testing as much as twenty-five or thirty pounds. Oversize shad, which are obtainable at most bait shops near popular Florida bass waters, are hooked either through the lips or the dorsal region. Just barely enough weight is added to the line to keep the baitfish from swimming to the surface, and a large float is positioned about three feet above the hook.

Next the angler motors to a lee shoreline, sets out perhaps two baits and then commences to drift very slowly with the wind across the impoundment to the other side (often a distance of several miles). Once the drift has been completed, he motors back to the lee shoreline and begins another, perhaps from a slightly different starting point to cover new water.

In this rare type of fishing he simply watches his floats, carefully feeding line when one or the other ducks under and then setting the hook with as much muscle as he can put into the rod. This angler is not searching for schooling bass on structure (that is another story which is discussed in the chapter on Florida bass) but for those impressive monarchs which are nearly always loners and frequently tip the scales at twelve pounds or better.

Fishing for Florida bass is discussed in more detail in Chapter 13.

CHAPTER 7

If Bass Won't Bite, Force Them to Strike!

We have just completed a brief look at a few of the feeding manner-isms characteristic of lake and reservoir bass, and in coming chap-ters we'll continue to shed still more light upon the subject.

But as we have emphasized before, bass do not feed often nor do they feed at every opportunity. With this in mind, most of the time most anglers will have far better success if instead of trying to locate feeding fish they concentrate upon what the fish will be doing for those other twenty-odd hours each day. From this section on, our angling philosophy can therefore be stated as follows:

If any species of bass is not in an active feeding stage and yet has ample opportunity to inspect a slow-moving live bait or artificial lure, chances are he will totally ignore it. Take any lure with which you can exercise precise depth and speed control, however, buzz it

*right past him very quickly, giving him only a fleeting glimpse, and
you can actually provoke him into striking. Nature has not endowed
him with the ability to reason the consequences of his responses. He
simply reacts to a stimulus—and as a pugnacious predator, hungry
or not, he absolutely must strike!*

George Pazik, the publisher of *Fishing Facts Magazine,* explains it another way with his "sleeping dog" analogy. "If you step
on a sleeping dog's tail he will probably snap at you. He is not hungry and he does not desire to eat you. From an inactive state he has
simply been forced to involuntarily respond to a stimulus over which
he has absolutely no control. It is all a matter of reflex behavior.
Come back at almost any other time and you can again provoke him
into snapping. Bass (and other gamefish) can be similarly provoked
into involuntarily responding to stimuli. When a fast-moving lure is
brought through a school of fish on structure, or even past the nose
of an individual fish, before there is even time to be wary he reacts
out of instinctive compulsion and strikes." How "fast" the lure has
to be moving to elicit this response depends again upon water temperature, as described in Chapter 5.

There are a number of ways in which anglers can force bass to
strike, but all are highly dependent upon speed and depth control of
lures. Depth is critically important because bass will not move great
distances to take any lure. If the water is fifteen feet deep and bass
are right on the bottom, a lure buzzed across the surface would
almost never see them rise to pick it off. Remember, the concept of
forcing fish to strike is based upon the presentation of the lure in
such a manner that the bass has no time to be wary, and in such a
manner that a spontaneous reflex behavior may be elicited.

The speed at which the lure is presented is as important as the
depth. If an extremely fast retrieve is used during those times when
the water is relatively cold, the fish will be lethargic and not as
reponsive as they would be to a much slower retrieve. According to
Buck Perry, all instances of successful or unsuccessful bassing can
be stated in terms of controlling the speed and depth of lures. Seldom, providing you are in the right place at the right time, do any
other factors exert influences as critical as these.

It follows then that since bass are nearly always on the bottom,
regardless of the depth of water, "depth control" will mean that the
angler's lures will necessarily have to be worked on or very near the
bottom. Surface lures, of course, might be effective at certain times
of year if the "bottom" the fish are lying on is only two or three feet

deep. And diving plugs which run at a depth of eight feet may be the order of the day if the fish are lying on structure which is nine feet deep.

Any angler's understanding of artificial lures, therefore, depends upon a combination of things. First, he must know the various depths at which certain lures in his tackle box are designed to run. Next, he must be aware of the speeds with which they are capable of being retrieved. Then he must use only those lures which are capable of running at the depth at which the bass are presumed to be, and he must use them at speeds varying in accordance with the water temperature at the depth he's fishing.

All of these component parts are interrelated, and the angler must "get it all together" if he is to succeed. If only one of the component parts is out of harmony with the existing conditions under which the bass are living, he will have little success. For example, the angler may be fishing at the right speed, but his lures may not be reaching the depth where the bass are. Or he may be controlling the depth precisely but be using lure speeds which are either too fast or too slow to provoke strikes.

FAN-CASTING THE CRANKBAITS

"Crankbaits" come in a variety of forms. But the one thing nearly all of them have in common is that they are best suited for shallow-water work, and they can be retrieved very rapidly, especially with the new high-gear-ratio reels. Crankbaits are just the ticket for flatland bodies of water where there is a preponderance of cover and where the water depth does not usually exceed six or eight feet. They are also ideal for use on other types of waters during those brief periods when the fish are in relatively shallow water. This is usually when the fish are moving toward their spawning grounds, when they are actually on their beds, or during their return movements to the edges of the depths. Another time they may be effective is during that brief period in the fall when the fish exhibit "false-spawn" tendencies or when any given bass school maintains a slightly shallower sanctuary and their migrations are consequently along shallower structures.

Examples of types of crankbaits are the popular "fat plugs" or "alphabet plugs" such as the Big-O, Big-N, and others, and the tight-wiggling slim-minnow plugs such as the Rapala, Rebel, and Bang-O-Lure. But also included in this category are those plugs which sport

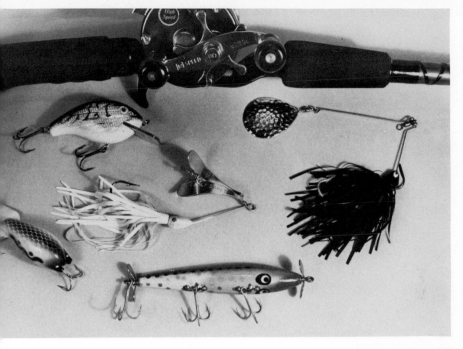

Crankbaits are designed to be retrieved as fast as you can turn the reel handle. Here are the most popular types.

a wide lip up front. They characteristically float at rest and then dive to various depths when retrieved at the faster speeds. Then there are the spinnerbaits. These have a safety-pin appearance with a molded leadhead on one wire shaft and one or two spinner blades on the opposing shaft. We could probably even include some types of surface baits in this grouping, too, especially those in a cigar shape with propellor blades fore and aft.

Since crankbaits are best suited for those brief times, mentioned earlier, when the bass are in shallow water, using them to force fish to strike is a relatively simple matter. While quietly maneuvering his craft with an electric motor, or perhaps even when wading, the angler saturates cover formations with fan-casts. "Fan-casting" means the angler's lures emanate from a pivot point like the spokes on a wheel. The pivot point is then moved and the fan-casting procedure repeated. This allows the angler to fish various cover formations from a number of different directions. He moves along methodically, pitching his lure into every pocket in the weeds, along the edges of brush from several different directions, or in or around other cover. The idea here is twofold: cover as much area during a day's fishing as possible; and bring the baits back at a variety of depths and speeds. In other words, try to establish a pattern the individual fish seem to be adhering to. When in the shallows they will probably be widely scattered but predominantly holding at similar depths and around similar types of cover.

Fan-casting the crankbaits is a popular pastime of tournament bass anglers. In most instances they are pressed for time and therefore cannot look for widely separated schools of bass on deeper structures. So they saturate the cover areas, searching for stragglers.

A rather stiff rod with a limber working tip is best for fan-casting the crankbaits, and watching the tournament pros at work is like observing the inner workings of a well-oiled machine. A fat-plug, for example, is cast several yards past a stump and then retrieved as close by the cover as possible. When the bait nears the rod tip, toward the end of the retrieve, it is quickly yanked from the water, an arc is simultaneously put into the rod and the bait is on its way to another likely-looking spot. The motion is often so fluid that it's difficult to ascertain exactly when the last retrieve was ended and the next cast begun. The angler who rapidly retrieves his bait past more potential fish lairs during the course of the day usually succeeds in eliciting the greatest number of aggressive responses. A bass lying in the shade of a felled tree or some other cover will nearly always hear the commotion of the approaching bait before he actually sees it. This alerts him. Suddenly, it brushes by his nose! There is no opportunity to take a lengthy look at it or to decide whether he's hungry or not. The entire matter takes place within a split second, with the fish having absolutely no choice as to behavioral response. He reacts and strikes. It is all that simple.

We know from previous chapters that bass often are shy and retiring, and when in the shallows they will seek heavy cover where they can hide and seek shade from the bright light. Let's say you have located an expansive weedbed which affords these conditions. The water is eight feet deep and the weeds come to within several inches of the surface. Since the weedbed lies on a direct route between a shallow bay (where you previously located spawning bass) and the deepest water in the area, you suspect large fish will be congregating here before moving all the way into the depths to resume schooling. Let's look at what would probably be the best way to fish the weeds thoroughly.

An angler fan-casting this particular weedbed (let's say it's rectangular in shape) with crankbaits would probably have several rods lying beside him in his boat, all of them prerigged with different types of lures. First, he would position his boat at one corner of the weedbed. Picking up one prerigged rod, a shallow-running fat-plug would be retrieved along the edges of the weedbed, using a moderately fast retrieve. Then the same bait would be cranked back along the same edges as fast as he could turn the reel handle. If this produces no results, he would reach for a second rod rigged with a deep-diving plug, bringing it back in the same manner. Still no go? Next, he'd probably reach for a rod with a spinnerbait tied on, pitching it far back into the midst of the weeds and skittering it across the surface and through any potholes that might exist. If this doesn't produce, he might move to an opposite corner of the weedbed and repeat all of his lure presentations.

By using several types of lures, and variations in the ways in which they are retrieved, he has thoroughly checked various depths and speeds.

We have maintained, until now, that bass will always be on or near the bottom. This has been to help us best understand how bass live and move on structure. But now we should probably modify that statement just slightly. Bass will always be on or near the bottom when the water is more than eight feet deep. Therefore, when working lures in water more than eight feet deep you should not fish the water but the bottom! If the water is less than eight feet deep and there is heavy cover present, such as felled trees, brush, or weeds, the bass may be at any depth. Therefore, when working lures in water less than eight feet deep, you must check not only the bottom but all intermediate depths as well! This is the reason why we made three types of lure presentations along the outside edge of our hypothetical weedbed. If you'll recall, we worked a fat-plug at a moderate speed (covering the water from the surface to about two feet deep). Then we cranked back the fat-plug as fast as we could turn the reel handle (to work depths ranging from about three to five feet). Finally, we switched to the diving plug to check the remaining depths (from six to eight feet deep). This is called "straining" the water.

If there were indeed bass in or around the weeds, as we suspected, one of these presentation attempts would almost certainly succeed in provoking strikes. If no fish are taken, it would be foolish to putter around any longer. The cover has been thoroughly checked, using different depth and speed controls, and we'll want to move on down the shoreline to the next likely-looking cover.

Fan-casting crankbaits later in the year, during the fall, will see a slightly different approach. The bass will be loosely schooled now, in smaller groups, and they are not likely to be around cover in very shallow water. But they will be on slightly shallower structures than they were using during the summer months, such as long points which jut out from the shoreline, bars, reefs, the vicinity of midlake islands, and around drop-offs and staircase ledges. Now, the spinnerbaits, surface plugs, and fat-plugs will probably be useless. The angler will be fan-casting the diving plugs instead. And now he will probably not need to strain the water by fishing all depths (this, however, is something you'll have to determine for yourself, depending upon the type of water you're fishing). Rather, he'll be concentrating upon fishing the bottom.

Chart 22 shows how he might choose to fan-cast a sloping shoreline point which continues underwater for some distance. We have shown the angler here beginning in close to the bank and progressively moving toward deeper water. But the point could be fished equally effectively by starting in deep water and working toward

Chart 22. Fan-casting a point continuing underwater

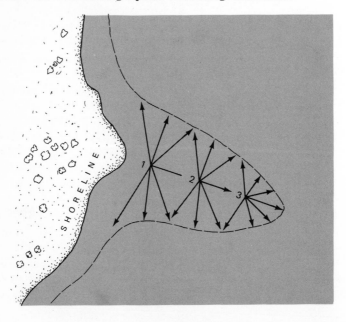

the shoreline, depending entirely on personal preference. If the fish seem to be coming predominantly into shallow water during their migrations, I would probably begin by fishing the deep water first so as not to spook any fish which might be tight in against the bank. This is often the case when the water is very dingy or murky. But if the water is very clear and you know the fish are not coming far into the shallows in their migrations, beginning close in to the bank and gradually working toward the depths will probably allow for better control over your lures.

The thing to remember in working the point shown in Chart 22 is that when the angler shifts his fan-casting pivot point from position 1 to position 2 to position 3 (or vice versa), he will also necessarily have to change lures. Each change of position will find him working different water depths, and he'll have to switch to progressively larger (or smaller) lures capable of running deeper (or shallower). At any time when the lures cannot be felt "ticking" the bottom during the retrieve, the angler can rest assured that he has lost his depth control and needs to correct the situation immediately (by retrieving the lure faster to make it run deeper, or as already mentioned, by switching to a lure of a different size).

SPEED-TROLLING

Not many anglers enjoy trolling for bass. This is probably because they feel that dragging lures behind the boat does not permit them to participate as actively in their sport as casting.

Nevertheless, I highly recommend that every angler learn speed-trolling. When upon any large body of water, speed-trolling is by far the most expedient method one can use to determine what type of structure the fish are predominantly using, how deep they are, and what lure speed is best for that particular day. Once the bass have been found, the angler can anchor quietly and cast to them if he prefers.

It should be emphasized that speed-trolling is not a technique to be used exclusively and with total disregard for all other methods. Rather, it is still another highly specialized tactic to be put into play as conditions dictate. In the previous section we saw how fan-casting the crankbaits was the best way to provoke strikes when bass are in and around heavy cover and in water less than about eight feet deep. Fan-casting crankbaits is therefore best suited for spring and perhaps fall bassing, or for use in those lakes and reservoirs which are extremely shallow and consequently have bass scattered through the cover rather than schooling in the depths.

Speed-trolling, on the other hand, is the most effective way to "check" intermediate-depth structures which may be holding either straggler bass or an entire school during the course of a migration. Since it is basically an open-water tactic, for use in situations in which depths may range from about six or eight to twenty-five or thirty feet, speed-trolling is best suited for use during the late spring, summer, and fall months.

In the next section we'll look at "bottom-jumping," which may be used during the summer, winter, or any other time when the bass have abandoned both shallow and intermediate depths for the very deepest water (twenty to fifty feet or more). We will then have a knowledge of three specialized techniques (fan-casting the crank-baits, speed-trolling, and bottom-jumping) which should enable us to venture upon any lake or reservoir during any month of the year with the assurance that we know how to find the bass and have the skills to catch them.

It was Buck Perry who refined speed-trolling to an art. And probably the most appropriate way to begin a discussion of it is by first examining his preferred tackle and lures.

Buck uses a rather short, stiff trolling rod upon which is mounted a level-wind trolling reel filled to capacity with monofilament line which has had all of the stretch removed. The stiff rod affords many benefits which a lighter or more "whippy" rod probably would not allow. First, when trolling at the slower speeds, the stiffer rod is more capable of transmitting to the angler everything the lure is doing. It is much easier to tell when the lure begins free-swimming (loses contact with bottom structure) or perhaps when it begins violently digging into the bottom (this means the wrong size lure is being used, the trolling speed is too fast, or too much line has been let out). With substantial amounts of line paid out behind the boat, as is usually the case in trolling, the stiffer rod also gives the angler more leverage in setting the hook.

The line Buck uses is twenty-pound-test No-Bo. "No-Bo" is a monofilament with all of the stretch removed, thereby making it very "wiry" and unsuitable for anything but trolling. Most other monofilament lines are elastic, which sometimes makes setting the hook difficult, but more importantly, a stretchy line may see greater amounts of "bowing" as water resistance exerts its influence. This results in loss of precise depth control over lures. If No-Bo mono-

It was Buck Perry who perfected speed-trolling. Here he works a break-line on a submerged, wooded point that juts out into a lake. (*Courtesy of Fishing Facts Magazine*)

filament line is not readily available in your region, you can obtain it by writing to Buck Perry, Hickory, North Carolina 28601. Or you can use braided Dacron line with a ten-foot terminal length of twenty-pound monofilament. What makes No-Bo even better than conventional trolling lines is that it is metered or dyed at various intervals, allowing the angler continually to monitor the amount of line he has let out. This is important because when an angler makes contact with the fish he will want to know exactly how far behind the boat the fish hit so he can return unerringly to that location.

It stands to reason, in all of this, that conventional spinning or baitcasting tackle is seldom suitable for use in speed-trolling. By the same token, once the fish have been located, trolling gear is unsuitable for casting to them. Therefore, Buck usually has two trolling outfits on board (one serving as a spare) and two other outfits for use in later casting to the fish.

Lures used in speed-trolling must fulfill two prerequisites. First, they must run "true" at a variety of trolling speeds (many lures are capable of running at only one speed and when trolled faster than that particular speed they flip over on their sides and slide to the surface). Second, they must be capable of maintaining a consistent depth, regardless of the trolling speed (many lures are not capable of this and will run either shallower or deeper as the trolling speed varies).

Today, there are many types of lures on the market which are adequate for speed-trolling. But that was not the case many years ago when Buck was developing the speed-trolling technique, so he decided to begin manufacturing his own lures (which are still available today). His creations, after countless hours of testing and redesigning, were dubbed "spoonplugs," and many anglers have affectionately described them as looking like shoehorns that have been stepped upon by a horse.

Spoonplugs come in a variety of sizes ranging from very small to large. Each size is intended to run at a specific depth, and they will precisely maintain their respective depths regardless of trolling speed. An additional feature of spoonplugs is that when they become fouled with bottom debris such as dead leaves or weeds, they immediately come to the surface. This allows the angler immediately to clear the bait of the debris so he can return to checking his structure. Some other lures do not do this and will continue to run at their prescribed depths with weeds trailing from their hooks, and this makes them very unproductive.

Other types of lures suitable for speed-trolling are the diving plugs. These are usually baits which float at rest and then descend to some depth determined by the size of the lure itself or the size of the wide lip built into its face. Examples of lures falling into this category are Hellbenders, Super-Rs, and Bombers. A quarter-ounce Bomber, for example, trolled at the fastest speed at which it will continue to run "true," will run about eight feet deep. Tie on a three-eighths ounce Bomber and at the same speed the lure will run about twelve feet deep. A jumbo half-ounce Bomber runs from fifteen to eighteen feet deep. And other lures, like the Magnum Hellbender, will run to depths of from twenty to thirty feet. It is possible to make lures dive deeper than they were intended to run by adding pinch-on weights to the line or by letting out substantially greater amounts of

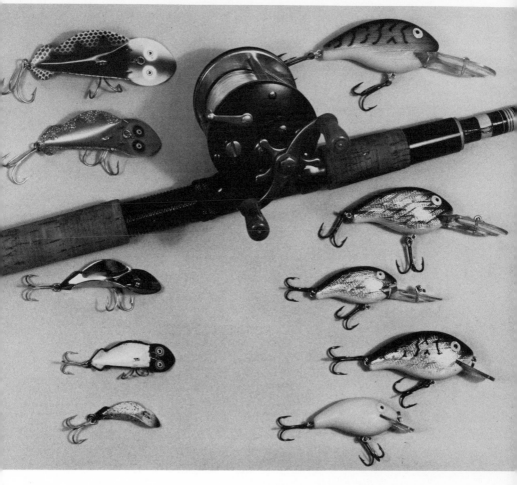

These two types of lures are favorites with speed-trollers. Note the progressive differences in sizes for working various water depths.

line. But this practice is not recommended unless there is no other possible choice, because the lure's action may be dampened, or there may be an increased tendency for the lure to snag on obstructions. It is much better to control lure depth by changing to a different size lure. If you are working a structure which lies eight feet deep and you want to begin checking structures at the twelve-foot level, switch to a larger lure designed to run at that deeper level.

Now, let's go speed-trolling! Assume a comfortable position in your boat, holding your trolling rod in your right hand if you are right-handed, or vice versa if you're a lefty. Rest your reel and the hand holding the rod in your lap if you prefer, and with the length of your rod lying on a horizontal plane, brace the butt section of the rod against your knee, allowing the opposite hand to be free for operating the motor. Plugs which dive deep exert quite a pull, which can be tiring if the rod isn't braced in some manner. I'll sit facing you, with my rod out the other side of the boat to reduce the possibility of our lures tangling with each other.

We'll say that it's late spring, the bass have completed their spawning activities, and they are now beginning to congregate in loose groups near the edges of the depths. We'll say we're on a highland type of reservoir located in Missouri. And our preliminary investigations concerning water coloration and associated light penetration, oxygen levels, and other factors have suggested we concentrate our efforts in a southwestern section of the reservoir. We know from our past study that the fish will be neither in very shallow nor very deep water but probably at depths ranging from eight to twenty-five feet and in association with on-structures (those which are in some way related or connected to the shoreline).

We've also examined a contour map and discovered there are a number of on-structures in the immediate vicinity. They consist mostly of shelves near the shoreline where the water progressively stair-steps into the depths. There are also occasional points jutting out from the shoreline which extend for some distance underwater before dropping off steeply into the depths at their tip ends.

According to the map two major breaklines (contour lines where there is a major change in depth) predominate in this area. One is located ten feet deep and the other eighteen feet deep. We know from our past experience that the largest numbers of large bass will be caught at breaks on breaklines, so we decided to begin checking them out.

Since the first breakline we'll be checking lies ten feet deep, we'll tie on a 200-series spoonplug (color isn't too important), which is designed to run about ten feet deep. How much line do we let out? Well, line length is always determined by the depth we're working; in shallow water minimal amounts of line are let out and in deep water a greater amount. As a general rule, *if you are trolling in water from six to twelve feet deep, let out from twenty to thirty-five yards of line. In water from twelve to twenty feet deep, let out from thirty-five to fifty yards of line. And in water from twenty to thirty feet deep, let out from fifty to eighty yards of line.*

Line length is very important, and that is why we have suggested the use of a metered line such as No-Bo, or some other type of nonstretchy monofilament which you have dyed various colors yourself.

Okay, our lines are out, about twenty-five yards behind the boat, and our lures are running ten feet deep. We turn the boat toward the shoreline so we can immediately get on the breakline. Just as the bow of the boat moves over the breakline we'll see a radical change in depth on the depth sounder. That is the time to begin steering gradually away from the shoreline to follow the course of the breakline from directly overhead. Moments later we'll feel our lures begin ticking bottom. The water temperature is 65 degrees, so keep the boat moving along at a moderate speed. We'll check slower and faster speeds later.

According to the map, this breakline or drop-off runs in a rather straight line for almost a mile, so we should have no trouble staying on course. We keep our eyes on the depth sounder. Suddenly we find ourselves over twenty feet of water! If we remain in that position, our lures will lose contact with the structure, so we gradually turn the boat back toward the shoreline until we're back on the breakline again.

Meanwhile, I'll check the map to see if I can find any breaks on this breakline. There are several! Just ahead, not more than fifty yards, is a pile of rocks. We should be over the top of them in a few seconds. And our lures will pass over them a few seconds after that. There! Feel your lure skipping and digging? Nothing.

That break really looked nice on the map, and since it is the only one in the immediate area, I think it's worth closer investigation. Let's troll it again, but this time from the opposite direction. Sometimes bass lie on structure facing in one direction and will strike only when the lure approaches from a certain angle.

We make another pass over the break, at the same speed, and again nothing happens. We have to turn the boat around in order to resume working down the same breakline, so while we're at it let's make one more pass over the rock pile, this time at a much faster speed.

We turn the boat toward midlake, swinging in a wide arc to get back on the breakline, increasing our speed. The boat passes over the break, a few seconds later our lures pass over it, and then BAM! You've got a fish on, and a good one! I throw a marker buoy overboard and you turn the boat toward midlake and then shift into neutral to play your fish. The chunky bass makes two long runs, causing your reel's drag to screech, but each time you slowly muscle it back, and minutes later it's ready for the net. It's a dark green and absolutely beautiful four-pound largemouth! Several weeks ago when she was on her spawning bed she probably weighed five and a half.

With your prize clipped securely on a stringer, we ease back to within casting distance of the rock pile. It should be about twenty-five yards to the left of where I threw the marker buoy. You carefully let down the anchor and then we both reach for our baitcasting rods. We'll use the same size lures we had on our trolling rods, and we'll have to cast beyond the rock pile and then really crank the lures in, because these fish seem to want a fast speed today.

We make ten casts apiece and feel our lures bumping the rocks each time, but receive no strikes. We try varying our speeds, and even change to different colors. Still nothing.

Let's try one more trolling pass over the break, from the same direction and at the same speed as before. As we're following the breakline I'll reach over and pick up the marker buoy.

We feel the rocks again but receive no strikes. Your bass was probably a straggler. Let's continue working down the breakline.

Several hundred yards ahead we find several stumps on the edge of the breakline, but several trolling passes from different directions and at different speeds produce no fish. We've worked this breakline now for quite a distance, checked it thoroughly and haven't had much luck. But we've only spent one hour of our time and we've eliminated a considerable amount of water. Now let's move deeper and check out the breakline lying at the eighteen-foot level.

You turn the boat toward midlake and then cut the engine so we can tie on large lures. If we tried to work the eighteen-foot breakline with the lures presently on our lines we wouldn't be able to reach the bottom. Those lures are designed only to work at ten feet deep. We'd be working our lures eight feet over the top of the bass!

Okay, our deeper-running lures are tied on and you swing the boat in the direction of the eighteen-foot breakline. Remember, we have to let out a little more line this time. About forty-five yards should do it. There! I felt my lure begin ticking bottom. We're on the eighteen-foot breakline. You already knew that because you saw the neon dial on the depth sounder indicate a change of depth.

I check the map again. This breakline is not nearly as long as the first one we trolled. It gradually tapers off to form a flat about one hundred yards farther down the shoreline. And there appears to be only one break on this breakline. It looks like some kind of indentation or sharp cut in the smooth contour of the drop-off. Even more important, it's not too far from the rock pile where you caught the first bass. We may have found a migration route the bass will be using in coming months when they occasionally move from the nearby deep water. There! I felt the break with my lure; it began free-swimming for a few seconds and then made contact with the structure again on the other side of the indentation.

Suddenly I feel the boat turn sharply toward midlake. I turn around in my seat and you have a deep bend in your rod again, and a grin on your face a mile wide! You damn rascal. You're skunking me today!

I toss the marker buoy overboard again. This is a good fish you have on. I can see that clearly because you don't seem to be able to budge him. He just keeps taking line!

About six minutes later I reach for the net again (this is getting monotonous). She's a dandy. I'll give her six pounds, easy.

With the fish flopping on the floor of the boat, you just sit there staring. The first fish brought aboard was your largest to date, and now you've just caught one still larger!

We clip your second bass onto the stringer and ease back to within casting distance of the break. This time it should be located exactly forty-five yards to the left of the marker buoy. We pick up our casting rods, remove the lures we had on before for working the ten-foot level, and tie on lures which will go eighteen-feet deep.

Bang! Now it's my turn to get in on the action! On my first cast I hook a fish and quickly crank him to the boat. He's only a three-pounder. I let him flop on the floorboards and send out another cast. Bang! Another fish, and this one feels like he'll go about five pounds. Then you have another fish on; another three-pounder. Man, what a string of fish we're collecting!

Then the action stops. It's early in the year and the school probably wasn't very large to begin with, and the fighting of those four bass probably spooked the others.

I quickly begin scanning the map. I'll mark all the locations I can find where there are breaklines in the form of drop-offs at the eighteen-foot level. There might be more fish, located elsewhere, under the same conditions. You begin heading us in the direction of the first one I've located.

We round a steep point jutting out into the lake and see another boat not far away coming out of a shallow cove. You recognize the guy in the boat as one of your regular fishing buddies, so we decide to stop and see how he's been doing.

He caught a few, just at dawn. The largest weighed a pound and a half. The big ones aren't "biting" today, he claims. The heck they're not, you answer! I ask your friend where he's been fishing. Back in the bays, he answers. Wherever there are lily pads or stumps along the shoreline. Really tore them up there three weeks ago. I can see the rods lying in his boat. The plugs he's tied on probably don't run much deeper than two feet. That is when you reach for your stringer. The five bass we've caught so far that day weigh close to twenty-five pounds, and that's almost a five-pound average!

How did you catch those monsters? your buddy drools. Easy, you say. We were simply fishing at the right depth, at the right speed, and in the right location. That's all there is to it!

The imaginary fishing trip we have just taken was not some exaggerated, once-in-a-lifetime experience. It's true that it often takes more careful scrutiny of a contour map to locate ideal structures, and an angler will often have to spend much more time working those structures before contact is made with the fish. Usually the fish will not average so large, but other times they may be even larger! Catches such as the one we just described do indeed take place on a very consistent basis for those who understand bass behavior and have invested long hours acquiring skills for use under different types of conditions.

The breaklines we were trolling were rather straight-line affairs. And it is wise to concentrate on these types at first until speed-trolling at various depths becomes something you are familiar with and feel comfortable doing. Then you can begin working those irregular breaklines such as the ones found on points, bars and similar structures.

In concluding this section there are a few things which should be reemphasized.

First, speed-trolling requires that your lures maintain continuous contact with the bottom structure you are working. If the lure begins violently digging into the bottom, it could mean one of two things. Either the lure is too large for the water-depth you're working, or you have strayed away from the breakline and too far into the shallows. Similarly, if the lure begins free-swimming, it could mean one of two things: either the lure is not large enough to get to the bottom, or you have strayed away from the breakline into much deeper water. The longer you are able to keep your lures in position or "right on the money," the sooner you'll contact bass. Remember that bass generally stay very close to their structure. And if a portion of any trolling pass wanders from the breakline and your lure misses making contact with a break by as little as five feet you may not succeed in provoking strikes.

Chart 23 shows how this very thing might happen. A nice point extends from the shoreline. The point possesses one major breakline at the fifteen-foot level before dropping off into the depths. The angler, in this case, has made three trolling passes, and we can easily see that he did not precisely follow the breakline but rather made straight-line trolling passes. If there are breaks holding bass and those breaks are located along sections of the breakline where his lures were out of position he probably would not receive any strikes. He has not thoroughly checked this structure.

Okay, now let's alter Chart 23 just a bit. Let's say the angler made the same trolling passes, but this time was careful to follow the breakline precisely. Under these conditions there could still be a

Chart 23. How to lose the breakline in speed-trolling!

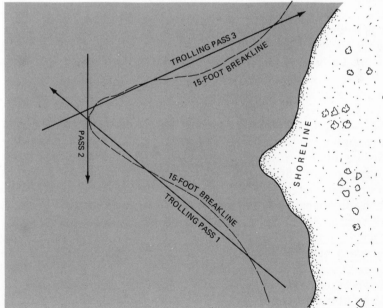

good chance that he would not succeed in provoking strikes. As we can see in Chart 23, our angler has made only three trolling passes. He still has not thoroughly checked this structure! He'll want to make several more trolling passes from the opposite direction. And then he'll want to make several more passes after that, running his lures at other speeds. Those additional passes executed, and our angler still having received no strikes, he can confidently say that the structure has been checked, there are no bass on the structure at that very moment, and it's time to move to the next likely location.

Another point to remember is to vary the speed of your lures in conjunction with the water temperature. When we took our imaginary fishing trip, we began trolling our lures at a moderately fast speed because we knew the water temperature at the depth we were fishing was 65 degrees. And even at that, we had to try a still faster speed before we were successful in provoking strikes. Had the water temperature been only 58 degrees, we would have begun the day using much slower trolling speeds. Conversely, if the water temperature was 75 degrees and we were using, say, a five-horsepower outboard, we might have had to run our lures with the throttle nearly wide open! All of this, however, is something you'll have to determine for yourself by experimenting. Just remember to troll faster when the water is warm, slower when it's cold.

In many bodies of water, midlake structures may be so immense that it is difficult to determine where the fish are likely to be. The largest number of big bass will still be at breaks on breaklines, of course, but there may be so many breaks that the angler has little choice but to speed-troll them all.

Chart 24 shows a stream channel on the floor of a flatland reservoir. As we can see, the flats are rather uniform in depth and the channel itself averages about one to three feet deeper. We can consider the channel to be the breakline in this case. And the breaks the fish may be adhering to might be scattered bushes or felled trees lying along the edge of the channel, a rock pile or number of stumps here or there, or perhaps even the bend in the channel itself. Since the depths do not vary tremendously, one lure could be used to check this entire structure. We've indicated a trolling pass configuration which would fairly well succeed in checking the structure. All the angler would have to do would be to run the trolling pass in the directions indicated at one speed and then run the pass again at another speed from the opposite direction. If fish were in the area he would probably succeed in provoking strikes. But if not, the use of

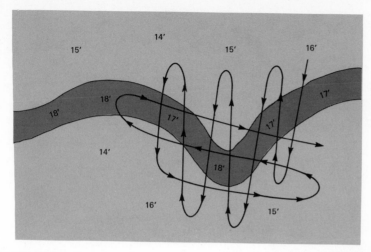

Chart 24. Speed-trolling a stream channel in a flatland reservoir

speed-trolling tactics would have enabled him to check this structure thoroughly in far less time than had he anchored and cast to the structure.

BOTTOM-JUMPING

Actually, bottom-jumping is not a single technique but consists rather of a number of speed- and depth-control variations any angler can use to force bass to strike when they are in moderate to very deep water. It is a valuable tool which can be used during mid-summer, during the winter months, or at any other time when bass are at depths beyond the reach of effective crankbait fan-casting and when the bottom is simultaneously so saturated with dense cover that speed-trolling is all but impossible.

The best lures for bottom-jumping are the leadhead tailspinners such as the Little George, jigging spoons such as the Hopkins, and especially leadhead jigs (which may be dressed with plastic grubs or pork rind) and plastic worms rigged with slip-sinkers.

Rods and reels that are best for bottom-jumping can be of the spinning, spin-casting, or baitcasting variety. But the rods should preferably be stiff and of wide diameter at the butt, gradually tapering to a limber tip. This design makes them ideal for "feeling" the lure over bottom structure (much in the same way a stiff trolling rod with a sensitive tip transmits to the angler everything a speed-trolled lure is doing). Stout rods, of course, also provide the angler with the

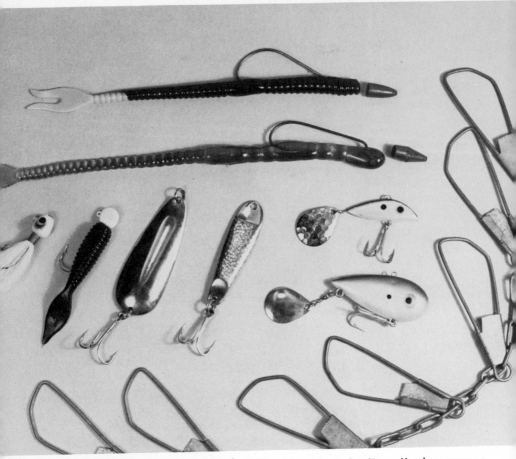

My favorite bottom-jumping lures. They include jigs, jigging spoons, plastic worms and leadhead tailspinners.

muscle or leverage he needs to pull hawgs out of tree-tops and brush piles. Reels should preferably be of the fast-retrieve or high-gear ratio variety. Line test should depend upon the degree of water clarity and the amount of cover in evidence. In some southern impoundment where the water is stained, the bottom cover is gosh-awful, and the fish likely to top the eight-pound mark upon occasion, twenty-five-pound line might be just the ticket. On the other hand, clear water and only marginal amounts of cover, with the fish averaging less than three pounds, might require lines as wispy as only six pounds test.

Bottom-jumping can be used to pluck straggler bass from deep bottom cover such as bushes, trees, and brush, or it can be used on schooling fish migrating from the depths to adjacent structures. But since both situations may have so much in the way of bottom cover or contour irregularities it is often difficult, especially on the larger structures, to determine which of many possible contact points or various breaks the fish may elect to use. In bottom-jumping, therefore, an angler usually fishes the entire structure, leaving no part of it unchecked. The most orderly and methodical way to go about this is by fan-casting (we're not talking about crankbaits now but about the bottom-jumping lures listed above).

Chart 25 illustrates a way in which fan-casting the bottom-jumping lures may be executed. Shown is a stream channel lying on the floor of a flatland reservoir. We know from our studies of flatland waters that the stream channels (or the main riverbed) usually offer the deepest water in the area and are therefore the home of the fish. Through a process of elimination we can see in Chart 25 that fan-casting crankbaits would be ineffective, simply because of the water depths in evidence. We can also see that speed-trolling would be difficult because the channel lies an average of ten feet deeper than the surrounding flats. Regardless of the direction of any trolling pass we might make, our lures would be "out of position" a good deal of time during each pass. We haven't mentioned what types of cover, if any, might be lining the edges of the channel, but that isn't really necessary because we can already see that bottom-jumping will probably be the most effective way to fish this varied-depth structure.

Any bass in the channel, either stragglers or school fish, will probably be congregated in the area of the sharp bend. The reasons for this are twofold: first, the bend in the channel possesses the deepest water in the area; second, the bend constitutes a break on a breakline (or substructure on structure).

Also shown in Chart 25 are the two recommended boat positions for fishing this structure, labeled A and B. It really wouldn't make much difference which position we decided to fish from first. The idea of working the structure from two different angles is simply to present the lure from different directions. I have seen many fishing situations almost identical to the one depicted in Chart 25, in which, for reasons known only to the bass, they would not strike at lures cast from position A. But work the same structure from position B, and BANG!

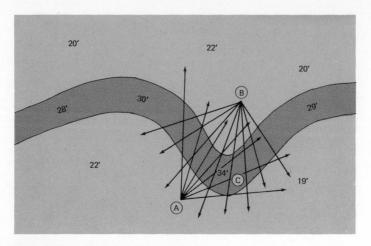

Chart 25. Boat positions for fan-casting a bend in a channel

Let's go fishing and see if we can determine the best way to check the stream channel structure shown in Chart 25, using bottom-jumping techniques.

First, using an electric motor, we should probably begin by quietly maneuvering to position C. There we would take a water-temperature reading. This is important because the water temperature will tell us what lure speeds we'll want to begin using (we'll say the area has already been diagnosed as ideal in regard to light penetration, oxygen saturation, and other variables). While at position C we might also drop overboard several marker buoys, especially if we are working this channel bend for the very first time and are not intimately familiar with its dimensions.

Next we would move to position A and quietly anchor, using the markers for a reference in beginning our series of fan-casts. Let's say the water temperature was found to be 60 degrees. That is somewhat below the largemouth's maximum metabolic range and would therefore probably eliminate from consideration those types of lures which are designed to be bumped along the bottom at rather fast speeds, such as the tailspinners. For starters, let's use jigs. You tie on a black quarter-ounce jig with a black pork-rind eel as a trailer. I'll tie on a yellow jig with a two-inch red grub as a trailer. I'm not

For precise lure presentation when bottom-jumping the deeper structures, use a marker buoy. Angler is Bill Weiss, on Kentucky Lake.

going to fish at first. I'll coach you, and if you get into 'em I'll join the action.

If for no other reason than to cover the water methodically, you should probably begin fan-casting in a clockwise direction. We're only about ten yards from this side of the channel, and about fifteen yards from the far side of the channel, but I want you to make very long casts substantially beyond the far side of the channel. I'll tell you why in a moment.

Now the moment the lure hits the water after you've made your cast, take up the slack line with a turn or two of your reel handle and allow the jig to free-fall on a tight line. This is important because bass will very frequently grab a jig "on the fall" and if the line isn't tight you'll never feel him. If he gently sucks it in you'll probably feel a barely perceptible "bump," and you'll have to strike quickly because it won't take him more than a split second to discover he's made a mistake. And when that happens he'll eject it just as quickly as he took it in. In fact, many times a bass will take a falling bait so lightly you'll never feel a thing. The only indication that he's taken the lure may be a small twitch in the line, or you may see the line jump sideways a bit. If you ever sense a strange "nothingness" at the end of your line, reel in the slack as fast as you can and strike! A bass has picked up your jig and is swimming toward the boat with it! Whenever you're fishing bottom-jumping baits, you have to be a constant line-watcher, especially when you're using jigs or plastic worms. It might even be a good idea to use fluorescent, colored line such as DuPont's "Stren" because of the sharp contrast it presents against the background of water (underwater it's invisible).

Okay, I said I would explain why I wanted you to cast far beyond the presumed location of the bottom structure. The reason is that we're working fairly deep water here. And tight-lining a lure after the cast does not permit it to sink straight down but instead causes it to swing in a pendulum-like arc back toward the boat. If you had not cast far beyond the structure, you'd actually find yourself short of it when the jig finally touched bottom.

You've made your cast and tight-lined the lure all the way to the bottom. The jig is now lying on the flat on the other side of the channel and you're about to begin working it back to the boat. But we have to make something very clear before you start retrieving the jig. Don't ever retrieve a bottom-jumping lure by turning the reel handle! Use only the rod tip. Remember at the very beginning of Chapter 6 how we saw the way a bass inhales a lure and how he can blow it out again in an instant without the angler ever being aware he had a hit? Well, that type of occurrence usually happens when an angler is reeling in his lure. When he begins reeling, he robs the rod tip of most of its sensitivity.

The way to maintain constant feel of your jig (or other bottom-jumper) while simultaneously retrieving it is first to point your rod tip toward the lure. This will probably see your rod tip pointed at about the nine-o'clock position. Now slowly reel in that little bit of slack line lying on the water and then stop the reel handle! Now, slowly raise the tip of the rod to the vertical or twelve-o'clock position. As you're doing this you can impart rod-tip manipulations if you wish to make the jig hop, skip, or whatever. Just remember that the only way you should bring the jig in is by raising the rod tip, and since the water is quite cool you should be performing this maneuver slowly.

With the rod tip now in the vertical or twelve-o'clock position, quickly lower it back to the nine-o'clock position while simultaneously taking several turns of the reel handle to absorb the slack you've allowed by dropping the rod tip. You're back at the starting position now, you've moved the jig toward you by about four feet and maintained continual feel over it all the while, and now it's time to begin raising the rod tip in the same manner as before. Feel the jig as it scratches the bottom cover and bumps along. Sometimes you'll mistake the bump of the jig hitting a stump or log for that of a fish. It takes some practice to be able to tell the difference between a bass and some types of cover, but if you're ever in doubt, go ahead and strike. Many times you'll drive the hook into a branch or tree trunk or log. But sometimes that "log" will start racing for the other side of the lake—and then just feel the old adrenalin pump!

Okay, you've worked the jig across the structure all the way back to the boat and now it's lying on the bottom directly below us. Don't reel it in yet. The next cast can wait a few more seconds. Take up any slack line you may have and slowly raise the rod tip vertically from about the eight-o'clock to the ten o'clock position. When you've reached the ten-o'clock position, begin lowering the rod tip, allowing the jig to flutter back down. Bass will often follow a jig or other lure all the way to the boat but refuse to strike, and this vertical pumping motion sometimes does the trick.

All right, we didn't take a fish on that first cast, so it's time to make another, this time slightly to the right of where the previous cast landed. Follow the same procedure as before. Feel the jig across the flat to the edge of the channel and then feel it tumble over the edge and sink on a tight line down the side of the channel's far wall. Now, work it across the floor of the channel, climb it up the other side of the channel wall and hop it back to the boat. Easy, huh?

If you want to, you can occasionally cast a different color jig. Sometimes it makes a difference. But most times it doesn't. Or if you find the cover is heavier than you suspected and you're hanging up on every cast with the jig, you might want to switch to a plastic worm rigged in some weedless fashion. But whatever the case, continue to work this first series of fan-casts at the same slow speed.

Let's say you've now completed the first series of fan-casts. Now it's time to start all over again, making the same clockwise series of casts, but this time substantially increase the speed with which you bring your lure in. We're controlling depth, since we're insuring that our lures stay on or very near the bottom. Now we have to determine what speed the fish want.

We'll say you completed this series of fan-casts and have still had no luck. Raise your anchor, use the electric motor to move your boat to position B, and begin presenting your lures from a different angle, insuring that you try at least two speed variations.

Still no strikes? Well, as Buck Perry says, "You may find structure with no fish, but you'll never find fish without structure." In any case, we can confidently say this structure has been thoroughly checked, and we've determined one of two things. Either this structure is not presently holding fish, for one reason or another, or the fish which are present are holding deep in the bend of the channel in a sanctuary state of inactivity. Let's not putter around any longer but go check some other structures, hoping to find a few stragglers or some sign of a major fish movement. If the fish aren't moving on the other structures either, they could be ready to migrate soon. And if that's the case this stream channel might be worth another look if we're still in the immediate vicinity. We already know the water temperature and the structure's basic configuration. Next time around it should take us only a few minutes to drop our markers and see if anything's doing.

We have been working a stream-channel bend on the floor of a flatland reservoir. We've been using the technique of bottom-jumping because the existing conditions (heavy cover and deep water) tell us this method should be more effective than other tactics we know of. Further, we've been working jigs (or plastic worms) because we determined the water temperature to be on the cool side

I show a string of four- to six-pound largemouths taken from Table Rock Lake in Missouri by "bottom-jumping." Johnny Morris, owner of the Bass Pro Shops, helped with the catching, which saw us bring aboard sixty-two bass in two days. All but these few were released.

and we know this state of affairs always necessitates slower speed controls.

Let's look again at the same stream channel shown in Chart 25, but this time let's alter the conditions slightly. Let's say it's late summer, we've dropped our markers and taken a water-temperature reading and found the water on the flats to be almost 80 degrees.

The water in the channel is 75 degrees. Under these conditions we know our jigs might not be very effective because they are designed to be worked at the slower speeds. With the water much warmer now, we know that any success in provoking strikes will probably depend upon our being able to work our lures substantially faster.

A good choice would probably be leadhead tailspinners. These lures cast like bullets, sink quickly, and are at their best when re-trieved from moderate to very fast speeds.

Moving to position A, we begin our series of fan-casts again, radiating them in a clockwise direction. Again we cast far beyond the structure, allow the lures to sink on tight lines all the way to the bottom, and then begin working them back by raising our rod tips from the horizontal to vertical positions. This time, however, we bring them back at a faster clip, occasionally stopping our retrieves dead and allowing the lures to flutter back to the bottom on tight lines (to maintain our depth controls).

After completing the last cast of our fan-cast series, we begin over again. And this time we really begin ripping those rascals back. They touch down on the bottom after the cast, we extend the rod tips as far as we can reach in their direction, take all of the slack out of the line and then quickly sweep the rod tips far back over our heads. And again, we quickly lower the rod tips, take in the slack line we've generated with this action, allow the lures to sink to the bottom on tight lines, and sweep them off the bottom still again.

WHAM! You've got a fish. Hey, I've got one too! Mine's a small one, only about two and one-half pounds. I quickly horse my fish to the boat but I don't lift him in. The hook is in his upper lip so I can safely grab him by the lower jaw. That temporarily immobilizes the fish so I can free the hook and turn him loose. Playing fish longer than necessary often exhausts them to the point of being unable to recover. And if they flop on the floorboards of the boat, much of their protective body slime is removed. When that happens and the fish is released, bacteria in the water attack the unprotected area on the skin and soon kill the fish. Next I grab for the landing net. Your fish is a whopper!

Hold your rod tip high. Make him pull against the bend in the rod because that will tire him more quickly. Sure, I know that if you hold the rod tip high he might jump. But so what? Sure, there's a chance he might throw the hook. But look at that son-of-a-gun cart-wheel through the air and tail-walk on the surface and shake his head! Savor every minute of it, pal. You're learning what bassing is all about.

Okay, I'm ready with the net. I'll tell you what I'm going to do. I'm going to hold the bag of the net very quietly just below the surface of the water on the opposite side of the boat. That way the fish won't see me jabbing the net into the water and spook and maybe break your line. When you think he's ready to be landed, reel him to within about six feet of your rod tip and then release the drag on your reel. Press your thumb against the reel spool and that will hold him. That way if he's still got some spunk and suddenly takes off you won't have to worry about the tight drag causing the hooks to pull out. Just feed him line as he runs and then bring him back again. Now, very slowly lead him around the bow of the boat. I'm waiting for you. Now, gently lead him head-first into the bag of the net. Just as his head enters the net I'll scoop forward. Don't worry. He can't swim backward out of the net.

There! What a prize! I'll give him nine pounds, and I'll slap your back for a job well done.

We've been using an inundated stream channel in describing the bottom-jumping technique of forcing fish to strike in deep water. But keep in mind that bottom-jumping can be used in all deep-water structure situations which, because of existing conditions, might not permit the use of speed-trolling strategies.

Tom Mann, the tournament pro and tackle manufacturer from Eufaula, Alabama, uses bottom-jumping techniques on the deep riprap foundations of dams and causeways (riprap is any manmade, steeply sloping structure made of large chunks of crumbled rock). In fact, it was he who perfected the warm-water "ripping" method just described with which you caught your big fish.

Billy Westmoreland, the smallmouth king from Celina, Tennessee, uses bottom-jumping in the form of inching jigs down Dale Hollow Reservoir's steep shale slides and gravel points.

Bill Dance and Roland Martin, the top favorites in almost every national bass tourney, use bottom-jumping techniques for working sunken islands, bars, holes, and other deep-water structures which are laced with heavy obstructions.

The only other bottom-jumping technique yet to be discussed is also commonly referred to as "doodle-socking" or "yo-yoing." Lures used in this type of bassing are usually the leadhead tailspinners, jigging spoons, jigs, and certain types of heavier spinnerbaits.

This technique is used to take straggler fish or those bass which are grouping loosely in small numbers in the very heaviest brush, felled trees, or standing timber.

Let's say there is an expansive flat on the floor of a flatland reservoir and the water depth over the flat is approximately twenty-five feet. In the middle of the flat there is a small grove of about a dozen standing willow trees—a natural attraction for bass which may have somehow become separated from their schools. The tops or crowns of the trees come up to within about two feet of the surface. Bass in this situation may not always be right on the bottom. Instead, they may choose to suspend themselves at some arbitrary depth right in the middle of the branches.

Obviously this is a case in which neither casting nor trolling techniques would be very successful. In order to snake bass out of the tangled tree branches, the angler must position his boat directly over the trees and then lower a lure right down through the branches. It's a great way to bankrupt yourself with plenty of lost lures, but it's also a way in which some of the largest bass of the season are derricked aboard.

Even in this situation, speed and depth control over lures is critical, and the angler will have to "cover all bases" in order to determine what the winning combination may be for any given day.

The most preferred method of fishing such a structure is to begin by lowering the jigging spoon or other lure all the way to the bottom. This may take some fancy rod-tip manipulations as the lure sinks, bounces off branches, becomes wedged, is jiggled free, and then sinks some more.

With the lure resting on the bottom, the angler reels in any slack line which may have developed and with the rod tip begins a vertical jigging motion, raising the lure about three feet and then allowing it to flutter back down. Again, a bass that hits will usually take the lure "on the fall" or just as it is being raised. And of course, cooler water temperatures will necessitate a much slower jigging motion than what would be used under warm-water conditions.

If the angler doesn't receive a strike with the lure working near the bottom, he raises it about five feet and begins anew, trying to determine the level the bass are suspending at. One day he may doodle-sock all of his fish at eighteen feet deep and the next day find fish in the same trees suspending at the twelve-foot level. The day after that they may be right on the bottom, twenty-five feet deep. After one tree-top has been thoroughly "checked" the angler moves on to the next, hoping to pick up a fish here and another there.

I have known anglers to use fifty-pound line while yo-yoing. That may seem absolutely preposterous. But try doodle-socking sometime. Hook a big fish, with perhaps fifteen feet or more of tangled branches between the two of you, and the reasoning behind overly heavy line might not seem so outlandish after all.

Finally, now that we've described what I believe to be the three most effective bass-fishing techniques, and the seasons and water conditions under which each is most effective, keep in mind that there is always a certain degree of overlap in which, perhaps, more than one technique could be put into play under existing conditions.

In certain circumstances, you may find that either speed-trolling or bottom-jumping could be used, or perhaps speed-trolling or fan-casting crankbaits. Determining which technique to use, when more than one could be implemented at any given time, depends upon three things. Which technique will allow you to make contact with the fish in the shortest amount of time? Which technique are you best at? Which technique gives you the most enjoyment?

TRY TO ESTABLISH A PATTERN

One interesting phenomenon of lakes and reservoirs is that straggler fish and bass schools can often be found under identical conditions prevailing at different locations in the same body of water.

Let's say you've categorized a certain reservoir as being of the flatland variety. You've taken into account the season of the year (it's midsummer). You know which general areas of the reservoir possess ideal water coloration and oxygen conditions. And now you are examining a contour map to ascertain the locations of structure which may be holding bass.

The fishing trip is to last several days while you're on vacation and you decide a good place to begin your search is the edge of the main riverbed. What you'll be fishing, of course, will be the breaks or substructure along the edge of the channel, and they will probably be in the form of deltas (ridges along the edge of the channel) or perhaps brush, trees, and rocks lining the channel's banks.

During the first morning on the water you fish ten different riverbed locations. None of the locations where felled trees or deltas are in evidence, however, produce fish. But two locations where there is heavy brush over a clay bottom yield fish! The thing to do now would be to note carefully the exact features of the locations where the fish were taken. Let's say your fish came from exactly eighteen feet deep (we know there is clay and brush) and the water is murky. If you can duplicate these conditions elsewhere along the main riverbed, chances are excellent that most such areas will contain fish!

Every large body of water is likely to see bass adhering to numerous patterns on any given day (patterns may change, however, from day to day and week to week). And the more patterns you are able to deduce, the heavier your stringer will grow. Let's say that after thoroughly working several delta situations, you discover bass are clinging only to those deltas where the water is exactly twenty-two feet deep and where the crests of the deltas are covered with rocks. The thing to do, then, would be to examine your contour map and mark every location you can find in which identical conditions prevail. Very likely a high percentage of those locations will contain bass, while other deltas not adhering to the pattern may be entirely barren. Fishing patterns is an ideal way to find straggler bass during the spring and again during the fall when the fish are not adhering to schooling dispositions but instead are somewhat scattered about.

You can also pattern schooling bass at other times of year. Let's say that in a large highland reservoir you make contact with a school of bass migrating upon a steep rock point which juts out from the shoreline. The water is murky-green, the surface is windswept, and you're catching bass at exactly twenty feet deep. Suddenly, while you're fighting a fish, the school spooks and vanishes into the depths. No use spending any more time there. You quickly check your contour map and note that there are a dozen additional shoreline points within a half mile of your present location. Eight of those points are rocky, steep, and possess murky-green water (the others are sandy, shallow, and the water is calm and gin-clear). It's a good bet at least half of those eight points, where identical conditions exist, will also be presently witnessing a bass migration with the fish coming to the twenty-foot level. The other points, which don't adhere to the pattern, probably wouldn't be worth the effort of a single cast.

It's a frequent occurrence on many bodies of water to see anglers buzzing back and forth in their bassboats in seemingly random directions. A certain percentage, to be sure, probably aren't dedicated fishermen but people who would rather ride boats. But the experts on the water that day are probably checking patterns. A pair of anglers in one boat may that day have found straggler bass clinging to submerged islands where the bottom is sandy at twenty-five feet deep, other anglers may be working every felled cypress tree they can find where the water is stained and the depth is twelve feet. Still other anglers may be working school fish on steep shale slides.

Establishing a pattern is one of the surest ways to fill the boat with good numbers of fish in short order, though you'll probably want to release the majority of them. Take, for example, a recent fishing outing I had with my friend Johnny Morris. Johnny is a noted tournament pro and also the honcho of the Bass Pro Shops, perhaps the world's largest mail-order supply house for bass-fishing gear. We were fishing Table Rock Lake in Missouri during the late spring of 1975 and the fish had just completed their spawning and were beginning to congregate along the edges of the depths.

The first morning we fished a wide variety of structure adjacent to the depths with various types of lures. We weren't having much success. Then, suddenly, we picked up six bass in rapid succession. They came from a wind-lashed shoreline where steep rock ledges plummeted off into the depths. All of the fish were taken about ten feet deep by casting deep-diving crankbaits. We then tried spinnerbaits and plastic worms, fishing the spinners four feet deep and the plastic worms fifteen. Nothing. Then back to the diving plugs, retrieving them at the ten-foot level, and BAM! Another fish on. We'd established a pattern!

For the remainder of the day, and all of the next, we fished only those steep rock shorelines which were exposed to high winds (the water was quite rough). And in a total of twelve hours over the two-day period, we boated sixty-two bass. Thirteen of them were over three pounds! Other steep rock shorelines which were of identical configuration but were not exposed to the wind failed to produce a fish. So did those shorelines which were windswept but only gradually sloped away with sandy bottoms.

One characteristic of all expert bass anglers is they are very observant, and they have very good memories. They never catch a single bass, anywhere, without noting the exact conditions under which that fish was living. Remember we said at the beginning of this book that 90 percent of the water is usually barren of fish because only 10 percent, at any given time, possesses those ideal characteristics which bass are seeking under the existing weather and water conditions. Therefore, if conditions are right for one bass they are right for others of the same species. Noting the conditions under which one fish is caught, then, can give you a good idea as to the conditions under which you will probably find others.

JUMP-FISHING

The angling technique called "jump-fishing" or "fishing the jumps" can provide the most exciting bass action any angler could hope to experience. The best times of day for jump-fishing are early in the morning, late in the afternoon, or at almost any other time when the surface is glassy calm. Anglers slowly motor about mid-lake areas, searching for signs of surface activity. First there will be only a dimple or slight splash on the water, and then another, and then still another. Suddenly, as much as an entire square acre of midlake water erupts in frothy frenzy as the bass which have suspended themselves at some arbitrary middle depth suddenly rise to the surface to slash into schools of baitfish (usually gizzard or threadfin shad).

Anglers witnessing such surface disturbances must push the throttle all the way forward and rush to the scene under full power, because the action will usually last less than two or three minutes. Upon approaching to within about fifty yards, the throttle is pulled back. Skirting the melee from a cautious casting distance away, either under the power of an electric motor or with the outboard running at very slow speed, they then throw shad-imitating plugs and other lures into the action and are usually immediately hooked up. I have seen anglers so excited by the action that they failed to set the hook properly when the first fish hit, only to take a few turns of the reel handle and have yet another bass on. A lucky angler will manage to get in about six casts and boat six fish (throw the fish on the floor of the boat and quickly send out another cast; you can string your catch later). But then, just as suddenly, the action subsides and the anglers have to resume searching quiet waters for other impending surface carnage.

It has long been a puzzle to anglers why a school of bass, with thousands of free-swimming baitfish about, could or would single out an angler's lure.

I think the reason for this is because baitfish, for protection, school very tightly. And as they move about they present themselves to the predators as only a shifting mass. In order to score, the bass must first charge the school to break it up and then isolate and run down individual baitfish. Usually they are unsuccessful in their attempts to scatter the shad. Liken it, if you will, to thrusting your hand into a pail of water. The instant you extract your hand, the hole or void instantaneously fills itself. The same thing happens when bass charge a highly concentrated mass of small fish.

An angler's lure retrieved through and then out of the baitfish school, however, gives the appearance of a baitfish which has somehow become separated from the school, and any marauding bass nearby will seize the opportunity to nail it. In fact, it is very common to catch two bass on the same plug!

Jump-fishing affords unforgettable action with light tackle. And if you like to see bass hit on top, now is an ideal time to use surface baits. Those with propellers fore and aft, skittered rapidly across the surface, will get the dickens knocked out of them.

There are a number of tips you may want to keep in mind regarding jump-fishing. First, look for the greatest amount of surface activity in those lake or reservoir areas directly over the old riverbed. Around midlake islands or places where humps or bars jut up from the bottom are also prime locations to try. Many anglers even make use of binoculars, checking distant areas for signs of surface activity or for numbers of gulls or other water birds. High-flying gulls nearly always are signaling the locations of baitfish below them. There may be bass near the baitfish, or there may not. If the gulls begin to dive, however, get over there fast! They are swooping down to pick up bits and pieces of mauled baitfish, and that is a sure indication that bass are working the area.

Additionally, when retrieving your lures through the baitfish school, allow every other cast or so to sink much deeper than usual (from eight to fifteen feet). Then, as you work the lure in, cause it to dart and struggle slowly. The reason for this is that a number of much larger bass may be lurking directly beneath the smaller ones charging the baitfish. These larger fish seem reluctant to come right to the top, preferring instead to lie deep and leisurely pick up injured baitfish sinking down through the water from the on-going commotion above.

Finally, when the surface activity subsides, don't immediately give up on the area. It's relatively easy to keep tabs on the baitfish, and you can be almost certain the bass, even though now at their suspended depth (from ten to twenty-five feet deep), will also remain within close proximity of the forage. With an electronic depth

Popular jump-fishing lures are those which resemble shad. Those that run deep will probably take larger fish.

sounder, the school of baitfish will show up as a solid band of red on the scope, from the surface to about five feet deep. Larger, individual lines or spikes on the scope, at various depths below the baitfish, are the bass. If you switch now to heavy spoons, jigs, and leadhead tailspinners, pumping them up and down directly beneath the boat at the level of the bass, you may succeed in taking several more.

CHAPTER 8

The Secret of Lure Selection

The majority of anglers in this country have very peculiar notions about lures, but mostly because they have been brainwashed. They go to the store and buy a bunch of lures in chartreuse colors. Or perhaps the fluorescent pink ones which are supposed to be the latest rage. Or they hear that the bassblastit lures now have a special tail fin which shimmies with a revolutionary new action which is supposed to really turn bass on, so they buy some of those. Or some outdoor writer publishes an article called "Use Big Lures for Big Bass" and so they run out and buy big lures, but they catch no more bass than before. The next month another writer publishes "I Catch Big Bass on Little Lures." That must be the answer, they figure, so they run out and this time buy a bunch of little lures.

The truth of the matter is that action, size, and color, compared to other variables, do not usually constitute critical influences upon the bass-catching effectiveness of any particular lure (the only exception to this might be in the case of lure size, which often but not always determines how deep the lure will run on the retrieve).

All of this, of course, may infuriate certain lure manufacturers, because success in making this year's profit margin exceed last year's often depends upon the manufacturer's coming out with new colors, new actions, new designs and different sizes of former lures. But what I'm concerned with is helping you to catch more and larger bass.

I have emphasized many times that proper depth and speed control over your lures is what determines whether you will be able to elicit feeding responses or provoke strikes. It won't matter one iota whether you are fan-casting or speed-trolling a green, yellow, red, or any other color lure if you are free-swimming that bait six feet deep and the bass are twenty-five feet deep. You won't catch any fish. It won't matter whether the lure is very small, medium size, or extra large if that lure is being fished on the surface and the fish are eighteen feet deep on the bottom. You won't catch any bass. It won't mattr whether the lure is vibrating, shimmying, or wobbling if the water is warm and the lure is not moving fast enough to provoke a strike. You won't catch any fish. I don't care how many tournament professionals have "endorsed" a particular lure. If you're reeling that lure in very fast and the water temperature is 50 degrees and the bass are sluggish, you won't catch any fish.

You should never lose sight of the fact that the depth at which you fish your lures and the speed at which you run them are the two primary determinants as to whether you'll see success. Lure color, size, action, and other variables are only aids which enter the picture later and, depending upon existing conditions, may or may not have a marginal influence upon the effectiveness of any given lure. For example, if you find bass on a submerged bar at twenty-two feet deep and you're catching a good fish on every fifth cast by ripping the lure back as fast as you can, then perhaps you can "up" your catch-percentage to a fish on every other cast if you switch from a blue lure to a yellow one. But change the speed of the lure to very slow, or retrieve it at ten feet deep instead of twenty-two feet deep, and you'll discover the fish suddenly seem to have stopped biting.

It should therefore stand to reason that the advanced bass-

Here's a wide variety of lure types, sizes, colors and actions. But the one thing the lures in each respective tray have in common is that they are designed to be worked at the same depth and the same speed.

angler's tackle box should be systematically arranged with "categories" of lures. In one cantilever tray might be an assortment of lures designed to run six feet deep at slow speeds. Another tray might contain lures which run fifteen feet deep at slow speeds. And still another might contain lures which run at some other depth or some other speed. In any given tray there may be a variety of different brand-name lures, in different colors, sizes and actions. But the one thing every lure in each tray has in common is that each runs at the same depth and the same speed.

Whenever you purchase new lures, ask yourself several questions. For what purpose do I intend to use these lures? At what speeds should they be retrieved or trolled, and at what depths do they run? If you're able to ascertain from the directions on the boxes that the lures run six feet deep on the retrieve and are recommended for very fast speeds, and you know you need some lures for that kind of work, you can be confident that your purchase is a wise one.

Concerning the influence of depth and speed controls over lures, consider two recent experiences of mine.

Jerry Bartlett and I were at Kentucky Lake, which straddles the Kentucky-Tennessee border. We were fishing for fall bass in about eight feet of water on a long bar adjacent to a rocky shoreline. The fish had migrated to the bar from twenty-two feet of water, following stair-step ledges. Jerry and I were throwing almost identical lures. They were leadhead tailspinners of the same size and action, and we were rapidly buzzing them up the side of the bar. Jerry's tailspinner lure, however, was green and mine was white.

About every third cast Jerry got an arm-jolting strike. He'd already landed four bass which averaged three pounds. I'd made just as many casts but hadn't received a strike.

Finally, in exasperation, as he lifted still another fish into the boat, I said "Gimme that lure," and we switched. Jerry continued to catch bass, on the lure I had been unsuccessfully using. I caught nothing, using the same lure he'd just been slaying them with!

I wracked my brain, trying to solve the problem. Then I discovered what was happening! I was using an Ambassadeur 5000 baitcasting reel with a 3-to-1 gear ratio. He was using an Ambassadeur 5500-C reel with a 5-to-1 gear ratio. With each turn of the reel handle his lure was being retrieved almost twice as fast as mine! Quickly, I reached for another rod with a high-speed reel mounted on it, tied on a tailspinner, and three casts later socked the hook into a four-pounder.

In a similar situation, with Nick Ansely, I was permitted to play the winning hand and Nick was fuming, trying to evaluate his problem. We were fishing Santee-Cooper in South Carolina. A school of bass had been located along the edge of the old Santee River bed, at about fifteen feet deep. I was throwing leadhead tailspinners again, and so was Nick. Both lures were of the same size, the same color, and the same action. So far I had put six fish into the boat, averaging about 2½ pounds. Nick hadn't received a strike. I suspected he was about to bounce his leadhead tailspinner off my forehead if these goings-on continued, so I coughed up some answers.

After each cast Nick was retrieving his lure at the same speed as I, but he was doing so the very instant the bait hit the water! I was allowing my lure to sink all the way to the bottom before beginning my retrieve. I was catching the bass for no other reason than because I was fishing fifteen feet deeper. He didn't clout me after all, but he did begin letting his lure sink to the bottom. Soon he was into good bass, too.

I am hoping—I am confident—that you now possess enough knowledge of bass behavior so that you will never again purchase any lure *solely* because of its color, size, action, or any other feature not directly related to its depth and speed capabilities.

Lure colors and other "aids" do indeed have their influence from time to time, as we shall see in coming sections of this chapter. But you should consider these influences only *after* you have located the fish or the probable locations where they should be in accordance with existing weather and water conditions, and *after* proper lure-speed and lure-depth determinations have been made.

HOW BASS SEE YOUR LURE

We know bass are sensitive to light and will seek to avoid bright light by hiding in the shaded seclusion of heavy cover or by retreating into the depths. Since "color" is really only a combination of various wave-lengths of light, and since certain wave-lengths are able to penetrate only to certain depths (depending mostly upon water clarity), it should stand to reason that bass are able to see certain colors better than others under certain water conditions in which light intensity varies.

According to numerous scientific studies, bass can distinguish a wide range of color hues in clear water, but they do not perceive colors in exactly the same way we do. To simulate how bass see colors, look through a light yellow filter such as the kind used for photographic purposes. Or look through a piece of light yellow cellophane such as the kind used to wrap candy or fruit. Also realize that with various wave-lengths of light penetrating only to certain depths, a certain color lure held in your hand may appear entirely different when fished on the bottom at random depths.

For example, the various wave-lengths of light which combine to make the color red are the first to be absorbed as light intensity diminishes as a lure is lowered into the depths. Even in relatively clear water, a lure or plastic worm which appears to be red near the surface will gradually appear to turn gray as it descends into deeper water. Then it will appear to turn black and then, at a depth of about twenty feet, it will actually become indistinguishable. In muddy water the color red may seem to disappear from sight only five feet below the surface! Actually, the lure is not really disappearing, but the light-waves which combine to make the color are absorbed by the water, preventing their further penetration into the depths. So in certain instances the lure you select from your tackle box may not be the same color you are actually fishing when you ply your efforts during the hours of dawn or dusk, when you move into very deep water, or when you fish water which is muddy, murky, or stained. The irony here is that an angler who caught a good bass on the bottom at fifteen feet deep with a fast retrieve and an all-red lure may think to himself, "Man, these red lures are really hot stuff." Actually, he has a lot to learn. First, it was almost

Chart 26. Various colors and their "visibility" at different depths

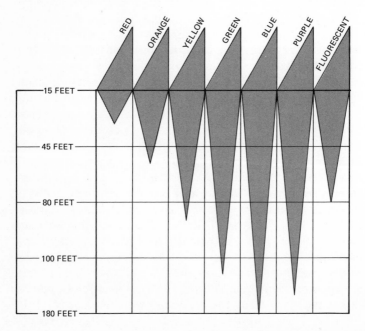

entirely the depth and speed control he was employing which accounted for the bass. And secondly, the lure color he was fishing at that depth, according to the way the bass perceived it, was not red at all but black!

Down deep it is a dimly lit world of dark blues, greens, and blacks (technically, black isn't a color). And the colors at this end of the spectrum not only can be ascertained most easily but retain their original appearance in deeper or darker waters. In fact, scientists claim (I don't know how they discovered this) that if it were possible for a bass to live in extremely deep water, he could accurately distinguish dark blue colors at a depth of 180 feet!

In all of this, the question which immediately comes to mind is "do bass prefer, or are they more responsive to, one color as compared to another?"

Even though there have been controlled experiments in which bass have shown a decided preference for red in clear, shallow water, many scientists believe we'll never, conclusively, have the answer to that question until we are able to teach bass to talk. But still others believe that certain other variables often enter the picture and in so doing may offer plausible explanations as to why bass often seem to "take" certain colors more readily than others. All of us have probably at one time or another had the experience of throwing, say, a blue plastic worm and seeing good success. As an experiment we tie on an orange worm or some other color, implement the same speed and depth controls, and draw a blank. But then tie on the blue worm again, and BAM!

A nationwide survey has revealed that anglers overwhelmingly prefer black, blue, purple, green, and red plastic worms. And that they use the blacks, blues, purples, and dark greens when fishing deep, dark waters or under conditions of low light, reserving the pale green worms and translucent reds for shallow or clear-water work. This would seem to substantiate our previous words about bass being able to see certain colors better at certain depths.

Additionally, there may be one more facet to this business of color preferences among anglers. I, for one, firmly believe a good deal of success in fishing certain colors has to do with the faith an angler has in his lure (after, of course, he has attended to the matter of speed and depth control). This may sound entirely unscientific, but the truth of the matter is that anglers place varying degrees of confidence in various colors (even in certain "types" of lures as they rummage through their tackle boxes looking for "old faithful"). Perhaps the color they prefer was first recommended to them by some fishing authority whom they respect. Or maybe the angler coincidentally took a nice string of bass on that particular color one day. Whatever the case, he comes to "believe" in that color. Actually, the color of the lure may be of little importance under the conditions he's fishing. But if he "believes" in the certain color he tends to fish that particular color (or lure type) more precisely, methodically, and carefully than some other lure or color he has less confidence in. Attitude has always played an important role in successful bassing.

Along these same lines my friend Dick Kotis, of the Arbogast Bait Company in Akron, Ohio, has recently conducted a number of interesting experiments. Arbogast has long been a leader in researching gamefish behavior and how fish react to colors, sounds, and other variables frequently incorporated into lures.

Dick discovered that dark colors tended to spook bass in clear water while the fish were not at all alarmed by more subtle hues. In fact, completely transparent lures produced best of all under conditions of extreme water clarity. As a result, Dick began marketing clear plastic lures. They didn't sell. Despite claimed bass-catching results (which usually sells any lure), there was something about a lure you could see through that turned anglers off.

As a possible solution to the problem, Dick then began making the very first chrome-colored plugs ever to be seen by anglers. Chrome is a good substitute for clear, because when fished in transparent waters where bass are spooky it has the same unobtrusive effect. Since anglers could not see through a chrome lure they began buying the plugs and now, in transparent waters at the right speed and depth, they are catching more bass than ever! As mankind continues to evolve, we discover he is often just as finicky as the bass he pursues.

An angler's goal in selecting the proper lure color should be twofold. He must evaluate the water conditions and select a lure color which the bass can readily see. At the same time, he must insure that that particular color does not radically contrast with its surroundings, because this will probably spook the fish.

We can deduce two practical rules, then, regarding lure color. Under conditions of darkness (stained water, muddy water, deep water, or after dark) use the darker-colored lures such as the blacks, blues, purples, and so on. Under conditions of bright light (clear or shallow water) use the lighter-colored lures such as the whites, yellows, translucent reds, and pale greens.

Silver and gold colors, by the way, such as those found on metal lures which have been plated, are classified as neutral colors. They can be readily seen at most depths, yet they do not seem to cause an "alarm" effect in clear water conditions. Therefore, they can be used almost any time.

The eyes of both man and bass possess what the biologists call rods and cones. Rods are light-intensity receptors. Cones are the color receptors. We possess a large number of cones, thus enjoy precise color discrimination (but only under conditions of bright light). We possess far fewer rods, and this is why our visual acuity begins to fail as the amount of light intensity recedes. As dusk yields to full darkness, our depth of field (how far we can see) rapidly diminishes and our once-sharp object-definition begins to blur. Since we always need light in order to have color, with the transformation of dusk into full darkness, colors change to shades of gray and then black.

Bass possess fewer cones than man, and this explains why their color perception is not quite as advanced as ours.

However, bass possess five times as many rods in their eyes as man, thus enabling them to feed or strike very easily when in deep water or after full dark. But while bass can easily see under conditions of darkness, they are quite myopic. The lenses of our eyes are flat and we can adjust them for either long-range or short-range vision. Bass possess nonadjustable, round eyes, making them very nearsighted. But this is usually of little consequence to them, since water that possesses any degree of color or turbidity has a tendency to retard long-range visual capabilities anyway.

This makes another case in favor of precise lure presentation when working various types of structures. When bass are actively feeding, they simply may not be able to see your lure if it is some distance away. And if you are attempting to provoke a strike, it must be closer still! The farther away the lure is presented, while still within his visual range, the more time the fish has to evaluate it, and a basic tenet of provoking a bass into striking is *not* to allow him this opportunity.

In the chapter dealing with light penetration we said that bass have fixed-pupil eyes which are incapable of adjusting or accommodating to various light intensities. And that in order to adjust to the light they must therefore change their locations.

We should probably note at this time, however, that there is one kind of light adjustment bass can make without changing their locations, and that has to do with what we call "acquiring night vision."

Man can acquire a certain degree of night vision by simply subjecting his eyes to pitch darkness for lengthy periods. But this night vision can be destroyed instantaneously by the presentation of a bright light. For example, if you are walking outside after dark for an hour and then somebody flips on a bright spotlight it immediately blinds you.

Bass acquire a similar type of night vision over lengthy time periods. As dusk falls, the acquisition process begins and continues through the night hours. Then in the morning as daylight begins to appear the fish lose their night vision and acquire day vision. This is important for anglers to keep in mind. Let's say an angler is casting plugs to a gravel bar after dark. For some reason he needs a bit of light—let's say, to tie on a new lure—and he inadvertently sweeps the beam across the water. This has exactly the same effect as if someone shone the spotlight in your eyes after you'd acquired your night vision during your evening walk. The introduction of the light into the water will temporarily blind the fish as well, and when this happens they will turn themselves inside out trying to leave the area. So if you are ever fishing after dark, or during other low-light periods such as the evening hours or just before dawn, and require a light for some reason, use only a dim penlight and only for brief periods. You'll avoid spooking any fish in the area, and you'll also avoid having your own night vision completely destroyed.

I think fishing after dark has been grossly overrated in recent years. You can catch good fish, to be sure, but you can similarly catch good fish during the daytime hours—and without the hassle of not being able to see, pestiferous insects nipping at your flesh, and whatnot. The reason why many anglers go in for after-dark fishing is very simple. They are basically shoreline pluggers with little knowledge of deep-water structure-fishing tactics, and the after-dark hours are when there are most likely to be more fish scattered about the shallows.

Now I am not saying I never fish after dark. Each body of water has a personality all its own, with the fish in some waters being more active in the morning, the fish in others being more active during the afternoon or early evening, and the bass in still others being more active after full dark. Additionally, after dark is an ideal time to enjoy explosive surface action with topwater baits.

If you would like to get into the business of nighttime bassing, let me offer two suggestions. First, use heavier lines. With your depth perception impaired, many baits will catch in bushes and trees as you over-cast your shoreline targets. With light lines and whippy rods, all you'll succeed in doing in such cases is giving the cover a good shake-job, and then you'll either lose your lure or have to move in to the bank to recover it from the branches. But with heavier tackle you can often jerk yourself free of the cover, and thus not disturb the water you plan to fish. Secondly, use dark-colored lures such as the blacks, purples, browns, and so on. After dark, as we have seen, bass can see darker-colored lures better than light-colored lures. According to the scientists, darker lures offer a greater contrast with their surroundings than light-colored ones; a bass looking up at your lure from beneath will actually see a darker lure against the night sky better, because the lure's silhouette is more pronounced. Whatever the explanation, it's pretty well accepted that in fishing after dark black lures will out-produce those of other colors by about ten to one.

A similar situation can occur in very muddy or stained water. The particles in the water scatter the light and block its passage, much in the same way that smoke obscures our vision through air. I have seen bass hit black lures very well in muddy water, but I've also seen them hit light-colored lures. Since there are many degrees of water clarity, the best thing to do is to experiment with a variety of lure colors to see which fare best under the existing conditions. Many anglers like to switch to those types of lures which have some kind of spinner blades on them, believing what little underwater light exists will be reflected off the blades. Other anglers switch to those baits which vibrate or rattle, allowing a bass to use his sense of hearing in addition to his vision to home in upon a lure. The concept of underwater sound is discussed more thoroughly later in this chapter.

In this section dealing with how bass see lures, we should briefly look into the matter of lure sizes. Size is still another variable which should be considered only after the fish have been located and proper depth and speed controls implemented.

A popular fallacy perpetuated over the years in regard to lure sizes has been, "Little lures catch little fish and big lures catch big fish." I say, "Bunk!"

If, for example, 90 percent of the diet of bass in a particular lake is comprised of 2½-inch threadfin shad, a lure which most closely represents this forage will likely prove most successful as compared with a lure which may be only one inch long and another which may be six inches long. So in addition to evaluating water color, oxygen saturation levels, and a host of other variables, it's wise to try to determine what the bass primarily feed upon in any given body of water. Personnel around marinas can probably tell you, you can observe forage in clear, shallow water areas, and when you clean bass you can examine stomach contents. If the majority of bass seem to have two-inch crayfish in their bellies, you'll probably have better success with two-inch bottom-jumping lures in a brown color than, for example, yellow six-inch surface lures.

The problem encountered in deciding which size lure to use is that often you'll have no choice! This is especially true in speed-trolling, in which you sometimes simply have to use very large lures in order to get down to the depth you wish.

Probably the best advice regarding lure sizes is to experiment. Many times you'll have to use larger lures as you move into deeper waters, and there is no getting around this. But use no larger a lure than is necessary to accomplish your depth-control task. Similarly, shallow waters often require very small lures, and again there is no getting around this. Whatever the situation, completely forget the garbage about little lures catching little fish and big lures catching big fish.

Lure action falls in the same category. Naturally, a lure which is three or four inches long and of the wobbling type will appear to have more action in the water than another wobbler which is only an inch long. But whatever the size of the lure, remember that "action" is not "speed." To prove this to yourself, tie a wobbling plug to your line and lower it into the rushing current of a river, holding it in a stationary position. Without retrieving the lure, you'll notice that it still has action.

Anglers who fish very shallow water, as during the spring, or from the shore, should keep a very low profile so as not to spook nearby bass.

Of the many considerations which enter into successful bass fishing, lure action is probably by far the least important and yet, curiously, one of the features most promoted by tackle manufacturers.

Finally, we should briefly talk about light refraction. This has to do with how the surface of the water distorts light and thereby causes objects above the water, when seen from below, or below the water when seen from above, to appear to be positioned at unreal angles. To understand how light refraction works, stick a pencil into a glass of water and you'll see that it appears to be broken or bent at an unreal angle. Because of this phenomenon, when in shallow water, bass can easily see an angler standing in a boat or on the shoreline, but only if the fisherman is within the angle of refraction.

If you've spent much time around the shorelines of lakes and other waters, you've probably seen plenty of small bass. And you may have noted that they don't always immediately dart away. Rather, they frequently only move a short distance away and then stop. They aren't spooked, yet. What they are doing, very simply, is backing away slightly to increase or expand the angle of refraction so they can have a "better look." Then, just watch them scat!

So when fishing shallow waters from a boat, as for instance during the spring spawn, stay seated and make long casts. That way you'll be out of the refraction angle. And when fishing from the shore, as in the case of farm ponds, don't tramp down to the very edge of the water and stand at your full height. Ease up only to within a few yards of the water and in a crouched position, or perhaps even on hands and knees, and break up your outline by partially concealing yourself behind a tree or bush.

SHOULD YOUR LURES SMELL GOOD?

When Tom Mann introduced his now famous line of "Jelly Worms" in a multitude of fruity flavors, he caused a curious stir in bass-fishing circles. Anglers immediately divided themselves into two camps. There were those who threw blueberry-, watermelon-, and peach-flavored worms (among others) with confidence, but usually with the brims of their hats pulled down over their eyes to conceal their identities. And there were those who simply sat on the sidelines, scoffing and hee-hawing over the circus antics.

These angling skeptics may be enjoying the first laugh, but it's becoming more and more apparent they won't relish the last.

Obviously, no bass that ever finned a migration route ever had an insatiable craving for apple-, grape-, or lime-flavored worms. And I can't ever remember having dressed a bass and discovered his belly full of blueberries or persimmons. Yet such flavors impregnated into plastic worms, and still other flavors added to various other lures, have been conclusively proven to be more effective in catching bass than identical but unscented worms or lures fished at the same speed, the same depth, and in the same location.

It must be remembered that bass spend most of their time in a dark, shadowy world (in the depths or in cover) where they must depend upon the efficiency of all of their senses to locate food or detect sources of potential danger. Vision plays a very important role in this survival, but when their vision is retarded because of conditions such as muddy water, the fish begin relying heavily upon their smell, taste, and hearing.

Bass possess nostrils (sometimes called "nares"), but these are not the only means by which they are able to smell or taste. They also possess taste and smell receptors on their gill-rakers and along the sides of their bodies, enabling them continually to monitor the water about them. In fact, the senses of taste and smell are so refined in bass that they are able to detect substances in the water about them in such minute concentrations as a few parts per million.

Actually, we are not positive which tastes and smells, if any, attract bass or "turn them on." But from various scientific studies we do know there are certain tastes and smells which are unpleasant to bass and will repel them.

Man-scent has long been considered a noxious odor to fish, and also to many animal species, as deer hunters well know. In the case of bass it's the acid (known as "serine") in your hands, which is present in greater quantity in some people than others, that is most frequently responsible for repelling the fish. Other noxious smells or tastes include those of gasoline, motor oil, battery acid, insect repellent, and deodorant. Traces of all these substances, and perhaps many others as well which we do not yet know about, may find their way to anglers' hands and then onto lures.

Plastic worms and other lures, then, need not necessarily smell or taste good to bass, but they certainly should not smell or taste bad. The reason for impregnating such lures with various flavors is to mask any noxious substances which the angler may inadvertently transfer to the lures he's using.

We should mention, however, that masking your lures with various flavors or scents is really necessary only when using certain types of artificials. In the case of hard lures such as spoons, plugs, spinners, and similar baits, masking is not necessary. The nature of the materials these lures are made of prevents them from absorbing noxious odors. And since these lures are designed to be retrieved through the water at relatively high speeds, they undergo a continual washing process. Soft lures, however, such as plastic worms, salamanders, grubs, and pork rinds, are quite porous and will easily absorb noxious odors. This even includes lures such as jigs which may have bucktail or marabou dressings. These types of lures, in addition to being porous, are designed to be worked at speeds ranging from slow to dead-stop. And if they reek of some noxious odor it will dissipate into the water around the lure. It is believed that if this is detected by bass in the area, they will respond to it as dangerous, perhaps before they even see the lure.

Many manufacturers, for reasons of their own (cost is one), do not impregnate their soft plastic or porous lures with any type of flavoring. In such cases I always rub a drop or two of anise oil onto my lures before fishing them and every half-hour thereafter. Or you can use vanilla extract or sassafras, clove or cedar oils. These should be available at almost every grocery store or pharmacy. Just be sure you use no more than two drops on any given lure at one time. Too much of the flavoring can create a noxious smell itself.

In my tackle box, in addition to a small vial of some type of masking scent, you'll also find a small tube of liquid soap. This can be nothing more than concentrated dish-washing detergent. Or you may prefer one of the special "fishing" or "sportsman's" soaps now on the market. Each time I handle my electric motor battery, switch my outboard's fuel lines from one tank to another, or rub some bug dope on my neck, I give my hands a thorough scrubbing to insure that I do not transfer any noxious odors to the lures I'm using.

In the case of live baits I would not recommend using any type of scent because their natural odors should not be camouflaged. But do be sure you handle such baits only minimally.

There is one final matter regarding scents that we should investigate before moving on to the next section. Not many anglers are aware of it, but bass which are injured when returned to the water, such as those which have been foul-hooked or mishandled by an angler, secrete their own type of danger scent into the water, and this will nearly always have an adverse affect upon nearby fish.

In one study, skindivers located a school of bass on a deep rock bar. From a safe distance they started movie cameras whirring as a boat containing two anglers carefully moved in and began presenting lures. They immediately began catching bass, one right after another, and each fish was tenderly unhooked and released back into the water. Upon release, each bass made a beeline back for the safety of the school.

Then, as an experiment, one of the fish was purposely injured before being returned to the water by making a small knife-slice in the side of the fish. The school would not accept this fish but began moving away from him. Individual members of the school even tried to ward off the intruder. Finally, the injured bass went off on his own and buried his head in a clump of weeds, trying to hide. The interesting thing about this experiment is that the moment the injured bass was released into the water, the remaining members of the school stopped hitting.

If you get into numbers of good bass, be very careful handling the ones to be released.

GIVE THEM AN EARFUL

While bass use all of their senses in combination, their sense of hearing is another which comes into greater use when the bass's vision is impaired. Very dark water, such as that which is extremely muddy, may even force bass to rely almost entirely upon the detection of underwater sounds in their feeding behavior. At close range (from two to five feet) a bass can pinpoint the exact location of a lure or baitfish and unerringly seize it without ever using its eyes at all! It therefore stands to reason that under certain water conditions, sound may be an important variable for the angler to consider.

Bass possess ears, but they actually hear with three internal hearing systems which work in support of one another. Their ears are buried deep in their heads and are not open to the outside water. Bass hear by detecting vibrations which are transmitted indirectly from the water through the skin, flesh, and bone of the head to the ear. As we have seen, bass, like other fish species, also possess a "lateral line." This is a series of very sensitive nerve endings just below the skin and similarly have the function of detecting vibrations. In all fish the line runs from the head to the tail, and in some species such as the bass it can even be discerned as a distinct black line that looks almost like a pencil mark. The third hearing system doesn't really detect vibrations but consists of a gas-filled tube running from the swim-bladder to the ear. This organ amplifies those sounds which are picked up by the other hearing systems and transmits them to an ear proper. There, the vibrations are amplified still further by a series of hollow bones before being sent to the brain, where they are classified and interpreted. It all happens within a split second.

Due to the unique silhouettes of various aquatic creatures and their methods of displacing water (locomotion), each emits his own characteristic type of vibration. For example, a baitfish swimming at some middle depth, such as a threadfin shad, would send out different vibes from those of a crayfish scratching along the bottom. Bass become familiar with these sounds, recognizing some as meaning food, others danger, and so on.

All of this means that a lure which is not producing strikes may be giving off a vibration like nothing a bass recognizes. And if he cannot see the lure, to aid in his classification of it, he may spook and dart for the depths.

Biologists have ascertained that bass can discern sounds ranging from 20 to about 2,000 cycles per second (CPS), but they are most attracted to vibrations of between 65 to 75 CPS. With this information, George Perrin of Fort Smith, Arkansas, began studying sounds emitted by various types of lures. Perrin is top boss at the Plastics Research and Development Corporation, which is a leading manufacturer of fishing lures under the Rebel name. Using a 36,000-gallon test tank, a frequency generator, an oscilloscope, and various types of graph-recorders, he made an interesting discovery. The ten most popular lures currently on the market, while differing markedly in size, shape, action, and materials, all had one thing in common. They were all very similar in the types of sounds and vibration patterns they emitted. Plastics Research markets a number of artificial lures of different sizes and shapes, but it is understandable why Perrin insists that all emit vibration patterns in the 65 to 75 CPS range.

Every serious bass-angler probably owns scads of lures put out by many different manufacturers. And it would not be practical for every angler to rig a test tank and monitor the sounds emitted by various types of lures. But he should realize that sound plays an important role in gamefish behavior. And if one particular type of lure seldom pays off, when presented properly, he should not hesitate to switch to another.

While the shape and action of any given lure will play a major role in determining what vibrations it will emit, many manufacturers have begun adding other types of sound features to lures. Most often these are produced by hollow chambers inside the lures which contain free-floating weights. When the lure is retrieved rapidly, these weights create a very noticeable rattling noise. Time and again, though we are not sure why, these lures have proven successful in out-fishing similar lures which did not emit such sounds.

One possible explanation is that bass are continually on the

Lures that "sound off" have rattle-chambers inside, or are designed to buzz or vibrate on the retrieve.

alert for distress vibrations emitted by various types of forage. Such vibes are not the ones customarily given off by free-swimming forage, but rather signal that some fish or other creature has been injured. Such sounds are often responsible for triggering some predatory response in bass, many times transforming them almost instantaneously from an inactive state to one of frenzied feeding and striking. Perhaps this rattling sound in some way imitates these distress vibrations.

Still other types of lures such as the spinnerbaits and the leadhead tailspinners "sound off" through the use of whirling Colorado blades. Underwater, these lures thump and vibrate. When buzzed across the surface, the blades cup air and force it underwater where it is then released, creating a gurgling sound.

Even lures which have traditionally been thought of as being quiet are now known to yield considerable amounts of sound underwater. We're talking here about plastic worms, plastic salamanders, and jigs. The noise these lures make is a peculiar rubbing or rasping sound. And they can be made even noisier by using special slip-sinkers which are designed to rattle.

We still need plenty of investigative work in the matter of underwater sound and how it influences bass behavior. Until then, continue to use a wide variety of lures when underwater visibility is poor. Then, if the bass seem to be showing a decided preference for one type of lure, stick with it.

A few words should also be said about sounds emitted by an angler during the course of his day's fishing. I remember how, when I was a boy, my father would insist that conversation be held to a minimum when fishing. He believed the sound of our voices would scare the fish. We now know, however, that this does not happen.

The surface of any body of water acts like a shield, blocking out 99 percent of all above-surface sounds. While aboard boats, anglers can talk as much as they like with no concern as to whether they will be spooking the fish.

However, don't bang oars against the side of your boat, don't scrape your tackle box along the floor of the boat, and don't carelessly throw your anchor overboard. Actions such as these, and others, will allow alarming vibrations to penetrate the surface layer of water, sending bass out of the area as though their tails were on fire.

The Mercury outboard people have determined that electric

motors do not spook bass even in shallow water, while gasoline outboards do not alarm the fish when they are at depths of twelve feet or more.

TACKLE TIPS

The modern bass-angler who consistently succeeds in making good catches may do so using a wide variety of tackle. It may not always be the most expensive obtainable, but it is always in excellent repair. There is nothing more irritating than to put into play an advanced knowledge of bass behavior, hook Old Calijah, and then have a reel malfunction or a line break. Things like this will happen to even the most tackle-conscious angler on occasion, but during a lifetime of fishing they will happen to him far less frequently than to some other angler who neglects his gear.

I disassemble each of my bass reels several times a year to clean and lubricate them thoroughly. Now is also an excellent time to check for weak springs or worn gears which may presently be operative but may fail in the very near future. They cost only pennies to replace.

At this time I also very carefully inspect each of my rods. Hair-line cracks in the fiberglass can happen for a variety of reasons and they may go entirely unnoticed until heavy strain is placed upon the rod by a big fish. Give your suspect rods to your kids to use in fishing for smaller bass or panfish. If the fiberglass appears to be in good condition, next check each of the guides for signs of "grooving" or other unusual wear. Monofilament line, actually, is a very hard material and it may in time cut into the guides. When this happens, rough edges occur and these will cause extreme line-wear. Pay special attention to the tip guide because this one seems to show signs of wear first. Replace any guides which are suspect, and do so at once, following the instructions the manufacturers include with the guides.

By the way, in regard to guides, those manufactured of aluminum-oxide are believed to be the hardest known and therefore are the most durable and similarly least harmful to fishing lines. Next best are guides made of carboloy.

Tackle boxes should be neatly arranged. This enables one to locate any lure on a moment's notice and it also eliminates fussing with the box and shuffling it around, which may send alarming vibrations into the water. Carpeting on the floor of your boat will further help to dampen inadvertently caused noises or vibrations.

Lures should be given very careful consideration. And the prime area of neglect is their hooks, which many anglers allow to become dull, rusted, or bent out of shape. Hooks should always be needle-sharp, and they can be sharpened in almost no time with a small abrasive sharpening stone or a triangle-file. And while you're at it, check other parts of the lure as well. Is the line-tie loose? If so it may fall out when you have a heavy fish on. The same applies for hook-hangers.

Your fishing line is the only link between you and your fish; it probably constitutes a minimal investment compared to other bassing expenditures, and yet it is the one tackle item on which too many anglers scrimp. There is no economy in purchasing a line which will not cast or troll properly or one which easily deteriorates.

I purchase my line in bulk spools containing about 1,200 yards each. And I buy only premium quality line, which costs only pennies more than the cheap stuff. By purchasing line in bulk spools, rather than fifty or a hundred yards at a time, a saving of about 30 percent can be realized.

Simply purchasing quality line is not enough, though. You must also take care of it. Store your line in a cool, dark place, because it will deteriorate rapidly when exposed to heat or sunlight. I have seen anglers keep the same line on their reels for as long as three years and then curse it when it breaks under the strain of a fish. The lines spooled onto my reels are used for twenty hours of fishing (about two days on the water) and are then removed and new line spooled on. Use the old line for "backing," on your reels, wind it onto the kids' panfish rods, or throw it into a trash can. But don't throw it into the lake! Line discarded into the water will not deteriorate. And in addition to looking like hell, it wll foul other anglers' outboard props and may even cause birds or other wildlife to become enmeshed and die.

During the day's fishing, I clip six feet of line from the terminal end every half hour. The end of your line frequently comes in contact with weeds, rocks, stumps, logs, sand, and other bottom cover and consequently suffers rapid abrasion. A fifteen-pound-test line dragged over such cover for only a few minutes may well be worn to the point of now yielding only four or six pounds of holding power.

Knots are important, too, and paper flyers showing how to tie various knots usually come in boxes of new line. The DuPont line

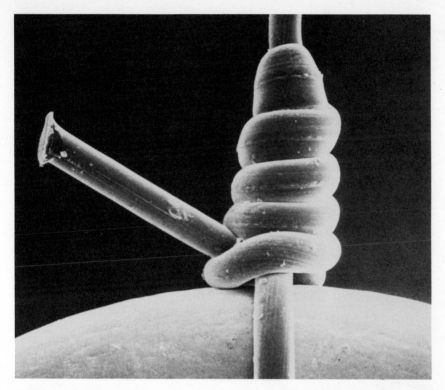

Of all knots for freshwater fishermen, the improved-clinch is one of the best. Tying knots slowly and carefully is important: a poorly tied knot can reduce line strength by 50 percent. (*Courtesy of DuPont Line Company*)

people have conducted numerous tests and have determined that the improved-clinch, Palomar and Uni-knots are the best for freshwater fishing because they do not drastically reduce line strength. A simple overhand knot may reduce the line's strength by as much as 50 percent!

In tying a fresh knot, first spit on the line. This will lubricate it so a minimal amount of abrasion or cutting occurs when the knot is carefully snugged up. Then test the knot with a strong pull. If it breaks, consider yourself lucky. That knot, which was probably improperly tied, might have cost you the bass of a lifetime.

USE THE RIGHT BOAT

An angler who is fussy about the type of boat he bass-fishes from will see the odds of successful bassing stacked in his favor.

There are two problems at hand, however. First, there is no single boat design which is best for all types of bass fishing. In fact, a versatile angler fishing many types of waters and using many techniques through the various seasons could probably find a justifiable use for a minimum of six different boats. The second problem is that not many of us can afford to own a number of different boats, each to be put into use as individual situations dictate. Most of us are financially restricted to a maximum of one boat. Yet an angler who fishes exclusively from only one type of boat will be unable to fish many types of waters. He will also be unable to put into use all of the tactics we have discussed so far.

So let's take a very brief look at the boating picture and see which types of boats are best for various types of bassing adventures.

First consider the bassboats. These are generally of tri-hull or high-performance hull design, averaging in length from about fourteen to eighteen feet. Big engines make them perfect for racing across some expanse of midlake water to throw lures at bass in the "jumps" before they quickly go back down. Comfortable, contoured seats with back-rests, and bow-mounted electric motors, make them ideal for long hours of quietly sneaking through swamp cover searching for spring bass. (As a word of caution, however, don't sit in the high pedestal seats when the craft is under way; this makes the craft top-heavy and difficult to maneuver, which could cause a needless accident.) Bassboats are also just the ticket for maneuvering around cover during later weeks to fan-cast the crankbaits. And still later they can be used while bottom-jumping your lures in deep water.

But when it comes to speed-trolling, the bassboat is an abomination. Even though the art has been dubbed "speed"-trolling, the slowest speeds offered by some of the larger bassboat mills may be too fast. It's true that with a depth sounder and a foot-controlled electric motor, an angler perched in the bow of a bassboat can easily pinpoint the location of lone structures. But following a structure such as a breakline for a long distance in search of breaks is a precarious venture at best. Due to their mortar-box designs, bassboats are highly susceptible to breezes or currents, and quick course changes with an electric motor or outboard are almost impossible. Yet that is exactly what a speed-troller needs to accomplish with his chosen boat as he bird-dogs along some winding bottom contour.

For speed-trolling and other meticulous bottom contour work required of a moving boat, the best possible craft is a fourteen-foot aluminum V-bottom equipped with an outboard of from five to eighteen horsepower and an auxiliary electric motor. With this rig an angler can turn on a dime, even in the face of strong winds. Also, if the weather turns a bit rough he can usually stay on the water. Not so with bassboats. They are usually incapable of coping with swells, high winds, and other rough-water conditions. No angler, obviously, should stay out if the weather is so bad that continued fishing could be dangerous. But the point I'm making here is that we have to expect upon occasion to encounter a certain amount of wind and wave action, and certain types of craft under these conditions will allow you to continue to present your lures in a precise manner while other craft will just wander all over the place.

As a side note, I recommend that every angler wear a life-preserver whenever the weather gets rough or whenever the craft is being used for high-speed transportation from one location to another. Sure, life-preservers look silly as the dickens, and certain types may be uncomfortable to wear. But if a sudden mishap occurs (all accidents happen without warning) they'll save your life, so color me silly and uncomfortable.

An angler who wants to fish a shallow river which possesses many riffles and sand bars may find neither a bassboat nor a fourteen-foot V-bottom to be suitable. What he'll need, probably, is a twelve-foot shallow-draft johnboat equipped with an outboard in the three- to ten-horsepower range, with an electric motor as an auxiliary.

In the case of streams or perhaps even farm ponds, a canoe or ten-foot johnboat, with only an electric, may be the very tool needed to get the job done. On the swift western rivers that possess hidden and very dangerous rocks just below the surface, an inflatable neoprene raft could be the answer.

It is imperative, then, that any bass angler match the boat he is going to use with the type of water he will be on and the fishing techniques he will be using.

Sit down and make a list of every bass trip you can remember taking during the last three years. Now, make a second list showing the types of waters and types of fishing techniques you honestly plan to be concentrating upon during the coming three fishing seasons. With the two lists completed, you should be able to make an accurate evaluation of the type of fishing you enjoy most and most frequently engage in. If you can afford only one boat, get the kind which will enable you to pursue your sport most effectively and efficiently.

This may mean buying a brand-new boat and it may mean selling the boat you presently own. Either of those are major decisions to think about. But consider this, also. If your boat does not help you catch bass, or if it hinders you, it's worthless.

If scanning over your two lists reveals that 95 percent of your fishing takes place on small natural lakes where there are regulations restricting you from using more than 10-horsepower outboards, and you've just purchased a bassboat with a 150-horsepower monster hanging on the transom, then you purchased the boat for some reason other than bass fishing. Conversely, if you presently own a johnboat with a 6-horsepower outboard, and 95 percent of your bassing is on a sixty-mile-long flatland reservoir, then perhaps a bassboat would be well worth the investment (but if possible, keep the johnboat too, for back-trolling and speed-trolling).

Even with a boat geared to the type of fishing you do most, there will still be occasions when you'll be trying other types of bassing for which your craft may be unsuitable.

In those situations, try to rent a boat at the waterfront. Or try to borrow one from a friend who knows he can trust your good judgment and care in using his craft.

Another suggestion, which we'll follow up in greater detail in Chapter 15, is to join a fishing club in your region. The individual members will almost certainly own a wide variety of boats. You and some other member can then team up to fish local waters more effectively.

CHAPTER 9

A Look at River and Stream Bass

The heaviest bass-angling pressure these days is exerted upon the larger lakes and reservoirs, especially those impoundments which are manmade. Second on the list of popular bass waters are the smaller natural lakes and the farm ponds.

Many rivers and streams that lace the countryside, however, go entirely unnoticed and unfished, and this is unfortunate. Those flowing waterways that have not been subjected to the ravages of industrial pollution or acid drainage from strip mines often provide excellent opportunities for catching largemouth and smallmouth bass. South of the Mason-Dixon line, spotted bass show up regularly on anglers' stringers, and in the deep South some of the very best angling for Florida bass may be had in rivers.

As in lakes and reservoirs, bass in rivers and streams use

structure for resting and moving. But there is one additional condition found in such waterways which is seldom found in lakes and reservoirs, and this is current.

Current is a flowing-water phenomenon which has unique characteristics, regardless of where in the country the river or stream is located. For one, current is nearly always stronger near a dam and for a few miles downstream of it, until it gradually begins to diminish in velocity. Also, any flow of moving water is prone to take the easiest route, which is usually a straight line, until some land feature diverts it. In the process of being diverted a bend is created, with the current washing out and undercutting the outside bend and thereby making the water much deeper. Conversely, the inside of the bend possesses a quieter flow of water, allowing sand, gravel, and sediment to sift to the bottom and create a bar or shoal. In flatland areas, a river or stream may be straight as an arrow for mile after mile. But in highland regions, or places where there are mixtures of very soft and very hard ground, look for the river to take on a serpentine form.

As a general rule the current of any flowing waterway will usually be much stronger toward the surface and toward the middle of the flow. Lesser current velocities are usually found along the floor of the river or stream and close to the banks. Bass frequently take advantage of this situation by resting in depressions scooped out of the bottom while fast water gurgles above them. Or they may rest behind the protection of midstream boulders or along the shoreline where cover formations create quiet pockets of less turbulent water.

One rule to keep in mind when fishing most rivers and streams, then, is that bass will seldom be found in the swifter flows. They prefer instead to rest in quieter currents directly adjacent to the main flow. And they will always face into the current, as this allows them to maintain their positions with the least expenditure of energy. It also allows them to keep on the watch for food which the rushing current may bring their way. They may have to dart out momentarily into the fast water to capitalize upon the free eats, but very shortly they will return to their holding stations in the quieter edge waters.

Finally, bass populations inhabiting rivers and streams are extremely sensitive to changing water levels. During the early months of the year, spring rains and run-off water may cause smaller rivers and streams to run over their banks. When this happens, and the water is rising slowly, the fishing can be fantastic around shoreline bushes, brush, and cover. There are two reasons. First, the bass have a natural tendency to move shallower in order to get out of the main flow, which may be extremely turbulent. But also, rising water floods the shallow banks, and tremendous quantities of food is either exposed or washed into the water. The bass may have come to feed upon insects, earthworms, and other tidbits, or they may be there to dine upon baitfish and panfish that are also looking for an easy meal. Later during the year, the water level will probably begin to recede, gradually forcing the fish away from the shallow banks and back to their normal holding stations. Fishing can also be excellent under these conditions. But if the water begins to fall rapidly, look for most angling action to terminate. Unusual drops in the water level send bass hurrying into the depths until conditions stabilize.

In all of this it should be evident that current and water levels have an important influence upon where bass will be found in any river or stream. As in lakes or reservoirs, locating the fish or the locations where they should be is the first order of business. Then, as we already know from our study of lakes and reservoirs we'll have to implement proper depth and speed controls over our lures to entice the fish into biting or provoke them into striking. The current will play a major role in presentation of lures in rivers and streams. And since flowing waters are nearly always murky, muddy, or a bit cloudy, we'll also have to consider aids such as sight, sound, and smell.

HOW TO FISH THE LARGER RIVERS

The larger rivers can often be fished using the same strategies you would probably put into play when searching for bass in highland lakes and reservoirs. There will be current to contend with, to be sure. But there will also be similar depths and bottom structures, and bass will be using them.

Nevertheless, still other types of structure which may be fish-magnets of the first order in smaller rivers and streams may be inconsequential in the case of larger rivers. A good example is where a rushing current is diverted, causing a bend. In a small river this could very well be a hot spot for almost any species of bass. But in a much larger river, the bend may well be a half-mile long and several hundred yards wide!

During the spring, bass in the larger rivers may spawn right .on the banks of the main river channel, wherever there are suitable bottom materials. But because the current has a tendency continually to layer the bottom with sediment in these areas, the fish are even more likely to leave the main channel completely, migrating up smaller rivers, feeder tributaries, and streams. The water is usually quieter in these tributaries and there is greater likelihood of there being small pockets, coves, bars, shoals, and similar features which protect the beds. If there is evidence of brush, stick-ups, felled trees, or stumps on shallow flats adjacent to the main flow of the feeder tributary, these too make for ideal spawning conditions.

The mouths of feeder tributaries, where they empty into the main river, play important roles during the spring months. The deep pools and associated bars and points in these regions will be the early-spring holding stations where the bass will wait for just the right water temperature for spawning before moving farther upstream in search of bedding sites. These areas will also be the locations where spawn-spent bass begin gathering in loose groups before returning to the depths of the main channel to resume schooling activity.

After the spawning is ended and the majority of the larger fish have reentered the main river, look for them to seek sanctuary and migrate in association with on-structures (those in some way related to the shoreline). Examples are numerous; they include long points jutting out from the shoreline and at their tip ends dropping off steeply into deep water, stair-step ledge formations leading from the depths to the shallows, trees that have toppled into the water, steep banks where land-slippage has scattered boulders into the water, and long gravel bars. Near dams, the fish may select temporary holding stations near the concrete aprons of the manmade structures, in the quiet water behind wing-dams, and below the dams in the quiet eddy waters adjacent to tail-races. But as the season progresses, the fish may gradually switch to deeper off-structures (those not related to the shoreline). These may consist of the shoals associated with midriver islands, deep bars, humps sticking up from the bottom, underwater ridges, rock piles, and so on. This transition, as you may recall, is characteristic of the bass populations and their movements in highland lakes and reservoirs. Chart 27 shows a large river channel with a feeder tributary and several types of typical on- and off-structures.

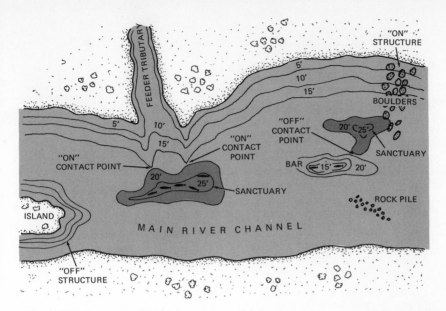

Chart 27. On- and off-structures in a river

It is not likely that you will be able to find bottom-contour maps for use in fishing the larger rivers. But local engineering offices, departments of natural resources, and inland Coast Guard detachments may be able to supply you with navigation charts which indicate average depths and the locations of static structures such as midriver islands, dams, feeder tributaries, and other river features which do not customarily change with time. It is not practical for various government map agencies to attempt to chart bottom contours, such as breaklines, points, bars, and similar conformations, because the current continually rearranges river banks and floors. Swift currents during spring high-water periods may easily erase sandbars overnight, undercut banks, or perhaps even wash away layers of mud in certain areas to expose hard bottoms or rock piles. Conversely, slower currents during midsummer may deposit sand and gravel to form new bottom structures.

In fishing the larger rivers, then, the sanctuary areas will remain pretty much the same. They will be in or near the deepest water any given area has to offer. But the migration routes may change from time to time as certain bottom structures are obliterated by the current and new structures formed.

With little available in the way of bottom-contour maps, you'll have to spend plenty of time with your eyes glued to the dial of a depth sounder. I turn my depth sounder on the moment I leave the dock in the morning and it stays on until I'm ready to quit later in the day. Many times in randomly glancing at the scope during the day's fishing I've discovered productive bars or drop-offs, structures which often did not exist in that location only a few weeks before! Similarly, I've caught good bass on a deep sandbar, been forced off the water for several days because of heavy rains and swift currents, returned when the weather stabilized, and discovered the bar gone!

Regardless of the water depth the bass will be adhering to (which depends upon the season of the year, the amount of light penetration, and the existing current), they will always be on or very near the bottom. The water may be five, ten, or thirty-five feet deep, but the bass will always be hugging some type of bottom structure out of the main current. If, for example, the current is coursing swiftly along the shoreline but meets a steep point which juts out into the water and is therefore diverted toward the middle of the river, the bass will be on the back or down-current side of the point (if they are using it). If there is a midriver island, the approaching current will be split or pushed wide to both sides of the island. In the process, shoals will frequently build up along the sides of the island or on the island's down-current side, with the bass resting on the protected sides of the shoals.

When the fish are in relatively shallow water during the prespawn, spawn, and postspawn periods (as they are traveling to and from their bedding sites), fan-casting crankbaits is an effective way to take them. Crankbaits, as we know, are tight-wiggling plugs which run shallow on the retrieve, spinnerbaits, surface lures, and plugs which float at rest and then dive on the retrieve. And fancasting, as you will recall, is a method whereby the angler saturates the area with casts, hitting every likely piece of cover. The bass are scattered now and you'll have to pick them up one at a time and wherever you can find them. But keep a few things in mind. First, this is a time of year when the water may be very muddy. Therefore, those crankbaits which rattle, vibrate, buzz, or kick up a surface disturbance will probably get more strikes. Plastic-worm fishing is also highly effective when the bass are spawning in the quiet tributaries. But as the fish move back toward the main river channel, plastic worms often lose much of their effectiveness. It is simply too difficult to detect the faint tap . . . tap . . . tap of a bass inhaling your worm when swift currents are tumbling it along.

When fan-casting the crankbaits, the angler must carefully

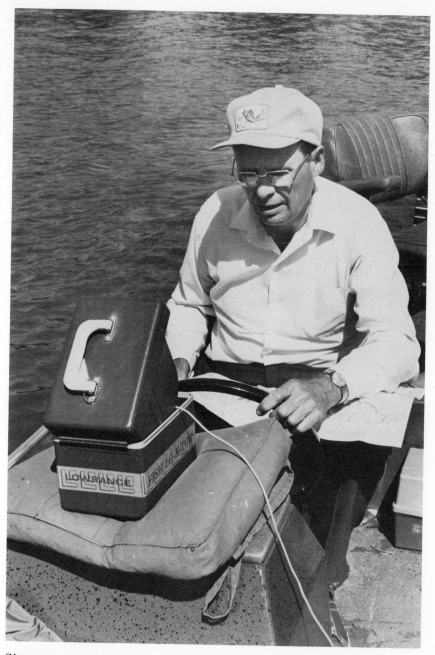

Since current continually rearranges the bottom contours, the river angler has to make frequent use of a depth sounder. Bill Weiss checks on the location of a deep bar.

control the speed of his lures. Traditionally, the best way to work crankbaits in attempting to provoke strikes is by reeling them in as fast as possible. This tactic may work as well in the larger rivers as in lake and reservoirs. But other times too much speed may have just the opposite effect. River bass gear their lifestyles to the velocity of the current, and those food items which are most likely to be taken are ones which are moving along at the same speed as the flow of water. Baits or lures moving along considerably slower than the current, or faster, often come off as phony, and the bass make a danger classification and refuse to strike.

The best strategy to employ when fan-casting the crankbaits is to experiment with your retrieves, trying to "pattern" the fish. Some days a fast retrieve will take them; other days they'll want the lure barely twitching and struggling as it is carried along with the current. But whatever the case, insure that you concentrate on those locations where quiet water lies adjacent to the main flow.

As the season wears on and the fish move deeper on shoreline-related structures, speed-trolling is effective. With some type of current always in evidence, lures which are cast and allowed ample time to sink may be far out of position before the retrieve is even begun. Through boat control, however, you can keep your lures continually in position, just ticking the bottom, as you work the deeper down-current breaklines of various structures. When speed-trolling in the larger rivers, it's always wise to work into the current. Working with the current will nearly always reduce your control over your lure's depth and speed.

When the bass make their transitions from on-structures to off-structures later in the season, either speed-trolling or bottom-jumping may be effective, depending upon the depth the fish are holding at and the velocity of the current. If given the choice, I would always opt in favor of speed-trolling. But if the water is too deep for this and bottom-jumping is the only alternative, it's best to mark the structure with a buoy, anchor both the bow and stern of your craft, and use heavier lures which will sink quickly before the current has a chance to carry them out of position.

We said before that regardless of time of year or the depth at which you may have been catching your bass, rises in water levels with associated increases in current velocity will see the bass move considerably shallower to forage and also to avoid the turbulence of the midriver flow. In the Ohio River I have followed the gradual movements of bass from the shallows to the depths and from on-structures to off-structures as the season progressed. By midsummer I may eventually be catching them on the quiet side of bars lying in thirty feet of water. But if two or three days of torrential rains fall, I immediately leave the depths and begin fan-casting crankbaits around shallow water cover lying against the main river's banks. Often the bass will move into the heaviest brush and felled trees, on their down-current sides, where the water is only one or two feet deep! But I know, too, that this is only a temporary change of home; after the weather stabilizes and the water level begins receding, the fish will drift back to their former holding stations.

As winter approaches, most bass fishing, with the exception of marginal smallmouth action, all but ceases in the northern states. The fish will move to their deep winter homes, which are usually quiet depressions on the river floor. With their body metabolisms severely retarded, they engage in little moving or feeding. But as far north as the Tennessee Valley region, the winter season will see some of the largest smallmouths of the year brought aboard. Largemouth action may be good, too. The spotted-bass fishing will be rather slow, however, unless the angler ventures still farther south. Throughout the Gulf States, angling for all of the bass species usually remains superb through the winter months.

We've been talking about rivers which may be as much as several hundred yards wide and in places fifty feet deep or more. Now let's shift gears and look at how bass live and move and feed in other flowing waterways.

SMALL-RIVER AND STREAM SAVVY

Generally, smaller rivers and streams (both north and south) which have some type of current harbor smallmouth bass as the dominant species, with largemouths or perhaps spotted bass in evidence in quiet sections or deep pools. Frequently, in waterways containing all three species, you can flip a cast in varied directions and before even seeing the fish, accurately predict which species has struck your lure. The bass found in such meandering waterways, however, seldom run as large as their counterparts found in the larger rivers, lakes, and reservoirs. A three-pound largemouth or a two-pound smallmouth taken from a small river is a real dandy; from a stream, fish of only half those sizes would be good catches.

Fishing the smaller rivers and streams can be both very easy and agonizingly difficult at times. In such smaller waterways, the bass are confined to much smaller areas, seldom having a deep-water sanctuary available for resting or retreat. This often makes it ridiculously easy to determine exactly where the fish should be. But by the same token the water is usually very clear and an angler's careless approach may cause the fish to spook and scatter, sometimes visibly skipping over shallow riffles in an attempt to place as much distance as possible between themselves and the intruders.

Because of the very nature of shallow waters, the inhabiting bass populations do not exhibit much schooling behavior. There may be exceptions in which widely separated deep pools hold loose groupings of fish during the midsummer and winter months. But in the great majority of cases the shoreline cover, the presence of midstream obstructions, and the way the current rushes by these structures will determine where the fish will be. In many instances the spring, summer, fall, and winter homes of the fish will be one and the same. But the fish can be predictably counted upon to alter their holding stations slightly around such structures as light penetration changes during the day or current velocity increases or decreases with changing weather conditions.

In my experience, nothing is better suited to small-river and stream bassing than light spinning tackle, for several reasons. For one, with the fish not running as large as in other waters, there simply is no need for heavy-duty baitcasting reels with their smooth-running drags and big crank handles. Also, much of any stream or riverbank is lined with trees and overhanging branches, which give the waterway a tunnel appearance. To work shoreline or midstream obstructions effectively, the angler often must cast from rather unorthodox positions, making use of underhand or sidearm throws. In these situations, spinning gear is usually easier to handle. For the same reasons, flyrodding is almost entirely out of the question.

There may be times, however, when largemouths have to be horsed out of heavy cover. And when such is the case the four- and six-pound lines used for smallmouths and spotted bass may not suffice. So I usually take along two outfits, the second being a slightly heavier spinning rig loaded with ten- or twelve-pound line.

In the lure department, you won't require as wide a selection of offerings as are often required in fan-casting, speed-trolling, or bottom-jumping in larger waters. An ample supply of flashy spinners measuring about two inches in length and in gold and silver will take smallmouths and spotted bass in most rivers and streams. For largemouths it's difficult to recommend anything more productive than slim-minnow plugs in both floating and sinking designs. They should weigh about one-quarter ounce, measure about 2½ inches in length, and be in shad, mullet, or silver colors. If very heavy lily pads, brush, or felled trees are present, small spinnerbaits, weedless spoons, or six-inch plastic worms may come in handy.

In the live-bait category, smallmouths and spotted bass hurry to the dinner table when crayfish, hellgrammites, or spring lizards are on the menu. Largemouths dote upon crayfish, nightcrawlers, various minnow species, and small frogs. Often, many types of baits can be gathered while actually fishing by taking a break from the action and kicking over rocks in midstream while a partner holds a seine net several yards downstream.

The best way to fish live baits in the smaller rivers and streams is to hook them only once very lightly, add a single buckshot to the line to keep the bait near the bottom, and allow the gentle current to nudge the bait along as it tumbles slowly downstream around structural conformations on a tight line.

We know that all bass are extremely sound-conscious. And the rasping and grating of a canoe or johnboat hull scraping sand or gravel in shallow water will easily spook any fish in the area.

To eliminate the sounds incurred in navigating any kind of shallow-draft boat through occasional riffles and other shallow-water areas, successful anglers are often those who disembark and wade quietly. In quieter sections of water you can sling the craft's bow rope over your shoulder and the boat will follow behind as you wade, enabling you to sneak unobtrusively to within casting range of suspected bass lairs. If the water has any current, though, this tactic can cause endless frustration. The craft will continually prod your backside or try to get ahead of you. In such cases, I often beach my canoe temporarily and hike along some gravel bar in a crouched position, casting into shoreline pockets and around various midstream obstructions. After the water has been thoroughly fished, I retrieve my craft and venture on downstream to the next likely location.

In the smaller rivers and streams, as in the larger rivers, bass of all the species will be facing into the current, and they will be in those quieter sections adjacent to the main flow. An immediate decision will have to be made as to whether the waterway should be fished upstream or down. Positive or negative results may be seen with either method, and the debate as to which ploy is the most effective often causes butting of heads among the most serious anglers.

Too much ruckus upstream on your part, when fishing in a downstream direction, is likely to have one of two effects. If you dislodge gravel, silt, and other debris in wading or carelessly maneuvering the craft, and this tumbles downstream through locations you intend to fish next, the bass may spook. Other times, though, just the opposite may occur. You may inadvertently kick up crustaceans, nymphs, and other tasty tidbits and cause otherwise nonfeeding bass to start taking an interest in potential food items coming their way.

Many times you'll have no choice in the matter. But whenever the option presents itself I like to fish upstream, occasionally making use of a small outboard or perhaps an electric motor if the current is just a bit too fast for comfortable paddling. The main reason is because bass are always on the lookout for food coming with the current. And the best way to simulate natural food is to cast upstream, allowing the flow of water to bring your bait or lure in the direction expected by bass.

If fishing downstream is the only practical way to work the river or stream of your choice, I would make two suggestions. First, stay in your craft as much as possible. If shallow water occasionally makes it necessary to disembark, anticipate those areas ahead of you which are likely to contain fish and give them a wide berth. And rather than casting directly downstream, hug one bank or the other and try to cast quartering upstream.

For all species of bass, it is important to be able to "read the water." Each pool in a river or stream presents an entirely different personality which must be carefully evaluated. The current may slide from one side to the other, submerged rocks or logs with water rushing over the tops may have caused deep midstream depressions to form, or perhaps some grain field on a nearby hill may supply one particular pool with locusts or grasshoppers while leaving the other pools farther up or downstream untouched.

It was mentioned earlier that in the case of bass found in lakes and reservoirs, the fish do not feed continually nor at every opportunity. But in smaller rivers and streams that may not be true at all. Food is not usually abundant in the smaller flowing waterways. And because the current requires bass continually to expend energy, their replenishment of food stores is an on-going process.

Bass use structure in every type of water they inhabit. In smaller rivers and streams, wherever there is the slightest change in bottom conformation, you may find bass. A single midstream boulder on an otherwise barren flat may be the home of several fish. A single root mass near an otherwise uninteresting bank will probably have several bass nearby. In nearly all cases the fish will be found on the down-current sides of the structures.

One hot spot for smallmouths is where two rivers join or where a smaller feeder tributary enters the main flow. Fresh water gushing into the main channel, especially after summer showers, acts like a tonic, and if you're there with anything resembling eats you're in business. These locations, at any time of year, often present a divided appearance where the clouded or murky water rushing in from the feeder stream yields to the clear waters of the main channel. This "edge" is a type of structure, and bass will adhere to it as religiously as they might to a drop-off, point, or gravel bar. Smallmouths will also move into those areas where a main current divides around a very large midstream obstruction and forms a foam-flecked eddy on the backside. The surface water here is often turbulent which serves to refract penetrating sunlight, but just below, at the base of the obstruction, the water is usually calm and makes for a good holding station.

Largemouths will nearly always be in the quieter stretches. They'll hang around the perimeters of deep pools if there are any. But look for them more often along undercut banks, in brush piles, in the branches of felled trees, or under matted vegetation in close to the banks.

Spotted bass in small rivers and streams are sometimes unpredictable, and unless you reside to the south of the Ohio Valley tributaries, they will probably constitute only "bonus" fish occasionally taken while fishing for largemouths or smallmouths. The reason why they are sometimes difficult to pattern is that at any given time they may adopt the same behavior mannerisms of either largemouths or smallmouths inhabiting that particular waterway. Sometimes they seem to favor moving water and will be mingled with smallmouths wherever there is current rushing by sand, gravel, or rock structures. Other times they will be with the largemouths in the branches of felled trees and under the weedbeds.

Florida bass, when found to be inhabiting rivers, exhibit behavior similar to that of largemouths.

CHAPTER 10

Farm Ponds Are Special

In the East and Midwest they are called "farm ponds." In Texas, anglers refer to them as "tanks." And throughout the desert region of the Southwest their Mexican-derived moniker is *resata*. But whatever the name, bodies of water ranging in size from one to about fifty acres are extremely popular with North American bass-chasers.

The reasoning is probably very easy to understand. First, farm ponds are quite numerous and accessible. At last count there were about three million of them dotting the countryside, and state departments of natural resources, in cooperation with state and federal agricultural extension agencies and the U.S. Soil Conservation Service, are helping to build and stock more each year. Presently, the state you reside in probably has somewhere between fifty and sixty thousand ponds. Many are created for the purposes of watering livestock, others to supply drinking or irrigation water, and still others strictly for recreation.

The great majority of such ponds are located on private property. But a courteous request for permission to fish, plus the guarantee that you'll close all gates behind you and leave no litter, will usually get you in.

A second plus in favor of farm ponds is that they annually satisfy the angling appetites of millions of fishermen who just don't have full days available for working the larger impoundments and the necessary travel time required for getting back and forth. With knowledge of four or five ponds in his area, any angler can fish virtually every day of the week. All that's needed is a bit of time in the morning before heading for work or a few hours of free time after dinner in the evening. If water or other conditions are not favorable at one pond (you might find the landowner's kids swimming, for example), it's usually just a few minutes' drive to another.

Just as important as all of these reasons, though, is the fact that the bass in most farm ponds grow fat and belligerent. In fact, it's not at all uncommon for pond bass, even in the northern states, to reach weights in excess of eight pounds.

Farm ponds provide excellent laboratories for learning and practicing the art of deep-water structure fishing. Because such ponds are far smaller than lakes and reservoirs, there will not be as many productive structures, and the fish will often be relatively easy to locate. Migration routes will usually be compacted (not as long or complicated), allowing the angler to get a real "feel" for how bass live and move on structure. An angler can even play make-believe, envisioning the pond he is fishing as only a small segment of some larger lake or reservoir. A number of successful fish-locating-and-catching sessions under such conditions should make him more than able to venture upon expansive waters, isolate certain regions, and fish them effectively.

It may be difficult to obtain maps showing the bottom contours of the various manmade ponds you plan to fish. If maps can be had, they will probably be topographic maps from the U.S. Geological Survey (address given earlier), which show the land contours before the pond was built. But since many ponds are created for special purposes, bulldozers may have obliterated the former land contours and in the process formed new structures.

One good source of information as to the bottom contours of

any pond is the landowner himself. With a pencil stub and small notebook tucked away in your fishing vest, you can ask questions and as you receive answers begin drawing a rough chart of the pond. Where is the deepest water in the pond? Is there a feeder stream channel or perhaps several of them running along the floor of the pond, or is the pond fed by natural springs? Is the bottom of the pond muddy or hard? Are there any radical bottom structures such as bars, drop-offs, or brush piles? What is usually the predominant water color, and does it change when it rains? When other anglers fish this pond, where do they catch their bass, and how? Answers to these questions, along with the map you have been drawing all the while, will save plenty of hours of random exploration.

But if the landowner is not able to provide answers to the questions you ask (the pond may have already been there when he bought the property), you'll have to begin mapping and interpreting on your own. The first task should be a careful evaluation of the terrain surrounding the pond, because such land contours often hint what the bottom of the pond looks like. Is the surrounding terrain hilly, or is it flat? The answer to that question may determine whether you should use highland or flatland strategies. Do you see any land features such as high rock bluffs? They may drop off into the water and form stair-step ledges with major breaklines. What about ridges or points extending down to the edge of the water? If these are present, they probably continue underwater for some distance, and they may be used by bass during a migration.

FISHING THE LARGER PONDS

A pond of more than ten acres in size and with depths of perhaps fifteen feet or more is most effectively fished with some type of boat. Usually a light car-topper such as a V-bottom, pram, canoe, or perhaps even an inflatable neoprene raft may be the best bet. An electric motor will aid in quiet yet precise boat control, but if you have any choice in the matter, use one of the high-thrust models because there may be times when you want to speed-troll.

You should have a small, battery-operated, portable depth sounder. And other typical big-lake equipment such as a light-penetration meter and styrofoam marker buoys may come in handy. The types of rods and reels you make use of will probably depend upon the water clarity, existing cover, and the size of the bass the pond is reputed to contain.

The best place to start is to determine whether the pond possesses flatland or highland characteristics. If it is a flatland pond, and if there is a stream channel winding across the bottom, we know for certain this will be the home of the pond's largest bass. During the spring they will sometimes migrate upstream along the channel, searching for spawning sites in the feeder creek arms and shallow flats wherever there is suitable bottom composition. But the largest bass seem to like to stay downstream, toward the dam. They'll leave the stream channel at the point where it loops in close to the shoreline or wherever there are signposts of some type to show them the way into the shallows. Then they'll select bedding sites at the bases of stumps and standing timber, and sometimes under overhanging bushes and cutbanks. I think the reason for the largest fish not going all the way upstream to the creek arms is that those areas are not only very shallow but usually very narrow. Add to this the fact that there's no deep water nearby and the big fish feel boxed in. The spawning areas farther downstream, while seemingly identical, offer one major advantage. They are very near to deep water, and if anything spooks the big fish they know their retreat is handy.

The postspawn period will see the bass begin drifting back toward the stream channel, and through the warmest and brightest midsummer periods, and again during the winter, the fish will probably spend most of their time in the channel. Further, they will be where the channel is deepest, which is usually near the dam. From the channel, as in typical flatland reservoirs, they can be counted upon to migrate toward the shallows several times a day (less often during the cold-water months). Now is when you should begin surveying the channel with your depth sounder, using marker buoys if necessary, to determine the locations where the fish can probably be expected to leave the channel and the probable routes they will take.

Since most farm ponds have abundant weed growth during the spring, summer, and fall, and since the weeds frequently extend all the way to the edge of the channel, the migration may consist of no more than rising out of the channel to scatter along the edge of the weedline. This constitutes a very short migration with some location along the edge of the weedline serving as the contact point, breakline, and scatterpoint all in one.

If the pond is relatively large, however, the weedline may extend for several hundred yards and you'll have to determine where, exactly, the fish will make contact with the shallows when they do migrate from the depths. Since the weedline/stream channel edge is the breakline, you'll have to look for a break on that breakline. As you will recall, a break is any noticeable change in the bottom contour or a place where some structural feature such as a stump interrupts the normal continuity of the breakline. Two very productive breaks along typical weedlines are where a slight finger of weeds reaches out just a bit further into the main body of water or where there is a well-defined change in the bottom composition, such as a long stretch of muddy bottom yielding to coarse sand or hard clay.

Working parallel to the weedline, I'd begin fan-casting crankbaits, beginning with shallow-running plugs and then switching to deep-diving plugs to check other depths. Remember, bass will nearly always be right on the bottom, except when the water is less than eight feet deep. If there are pockets back in the weeds, you may want to check them with spinnerbaits or plastic worms.

If you fail to find fish along the edge cover (breakline), it could be that the fish have not migrated or that the water is simply too shallow for them to come all the way into the weeds during the daylight hours. The best bet, in this case, would be to locate deeper structures associated with the stream channel. Any sharp bends in the channel should probably be checked out first. The bass could be in the outside bend where the water is deepest, or they could occasionally move to the inside bend where a shoal or bar has been created. You may also want to check the other side of the channel (the side opposite the weedbed). The other channel edge is still another breakline, and there may be stumps, rocks, felled trees, deep weeds, or almost anything else along the channel that the fish may be hanging about.

Using marker buoys, begin speed-trolling these structures, being especially careful that your lures are continually in position. Keep in mind that the water you are now working is very likely more than eight feet deep, so now you'll have to begin working your lures right on the bottom. It's also wise to use a variety of lure speeds to determine which is best on any given day. You must establish a pattern or a common depth the largest fish are migrating to and a common lure speed which most effectively provokes them into striking.

On very bright days, with the sun high overhead and no wind to ruffle the surface, the fish will stay much deeper, perhaps migrating only from the depths of the channel to the edges of the channel, or from the depths of the channel to some related off-structure. But on cloudy or rainy days the fish may "go all the way," at least as far as the signposts will permit.

Water clarity will have a crucial effect upon the sunlight penetration and consequently upon the migration behavior of the fish. When they migrate in a very clear pond you may not be able to catch them any shallower than fifteen feet, unless you wish to come back and fish the pond after dark. But travel a short distance away to fish another pond which is almost identical in structural conformation but has muddy water, and the fish may be found in pockets in the weeds very close to the bank where the water is only two feet deep!

We should mention one final characteristic of flatland farm ponds. If there is good deep water structure (the stream channel), shallow water fishing is usually not good. Bass always prefer the depths to the shallows, even though there may be plenty of cover in the form of weeds or felled trees. But if the pond is dishpan shaped, with almost no deep-water structure, shallow-water fishing can be excellent.

Now let's consider highland ponds. They are formed like high-land lakes and reservoirs, but seldom are they as deep. And if there is a stream channel running along the floor of such a pond, it may very well be the home of the fish. As in all highland waters, though, there are certain to be other fish-attracting structures, too, such as long steep points, bars, humps which stick up from the bottom, and so on.

In the case of highland farm ponds, then, we can set down two general rules. During the spring, early summer, and fall months, concentrate upon the shoreline-connected structures such as the points and bars. But during late summer, and also in the winter, the fish will be in or near the stream channel and they will be more prone, when they migrate, to use off-structures such as underwater ridges, humps, and so on.

We have not spent a great deal of time "talking structure" in this section. The reason is that most of what we said in earlier chapters about bass movements can be readily applied to fishing the larger ponds, because they are really only scaled-down versions of highland or flatland lakes and reservoirs.

Remember that the stream channel will play an important role in any farm pond, the migration routes will probably be compacted, the water clarity will determine how shallow the fish will move, and that locating good structure and then controlling depth and speed of lures is just as important here as elsewhere, and you should have no trouble.

WHAT'S DIFFERENT ABOUT MINI-PONDS?

Small ponds (less than ten acres) may contain some of the very largest bass. One reason is that so many anglers overlook them, wrongly deducing that "big waters mean big fish."

I know of one such pond in Illinois, on the property of a rancher who raises chickens. This pond is so small that you can cast a lure from one bank and almost reach the other side. For a number of years, however, not a single angler bothered with this piece of water, electing instead to fish the much larger twenty-two-acre sister pond located several hundred yards away.

One morning my friend Bill Murphy decided to work the larger body of water, but upon arriving discovered two other anglers there ahead of him. Rather than intrude, he hiked to the small pond, more with the intention of passing time than anything else. Within only fifteen minutes he had strung a pair of seven-pounders! And since that time, almost two years ago, the pond has yielded an additional seven-pounder and half a dozen in the four- to five-pound class. As you might expect, all anglers now visiting the chicken ranch fish the small pond first, moving over to the larger body of water only as their second choice.

In a majority of cases small ponds are best fished by walking the banks. Attempting to launch a boat is usually impractical. But even though the bass populations in such small waters are very much confined, do not assume they are pushovers. Again, the angler will have to determine whether the pond is of the flatland or highland variety. In the flatland type, the stream channel will be the home of the fish, and in the highland type either a stream channel or perhaps simply a deep hole will serve as the sanctuary. Regardless of the type of bottom contour, however, the angler will have to ascertain the locations where the bass are likely to be, and then he'll have to fish his lures at the proper depth and the right speed, all the while standing on the bank.

It is very unlikely, in a smaller pond, that the fish will be schooling much. But they may be gathered in loose groups wherever ideal structural conditions exist. And since these conditions may often be found very close to the banks, the angler should make his approach in a very cautious, unobtrusive manner. I wear very light-colored clothing and I often sneak to within ten feet of the water's edge on hands and knees, casting from behind a bush or tree. An angler who carelessly tramps down to the water's edge will send sound vibrations into the water and this will spook the fish. And an angler who stands straight and tall with his silhouette looming against the skyline will send nearby bass into a frenzy, and in their attempt to escape from the area they may well spook still other fish farther down the shoreline.

Pulling on hip-boots or chest waders is often a good bet in fishing the smaller ponds. For one, the angler's silhouette will be much closer to the water, reducing the angle of refraction. Also, wading may help an angler to reach certain structures with his casts which might be out of range when working from the banks. Whatever the reason for deciding to wade, be sure you do so very carefully and quietly and make long casts.

Once a smaller pond has been classified as being of either the highland or flatland variety, the angler can immediately begin checking various structures. But he will want to keep in mind that the depth he works his lures at, and the speed with which he retrieves them, will probably determine whether he'll be able to make contact with the fish.

In the smaller ponds, the very slightest deviation in bottom contour, such as a one-foot drop-off, may be the best structure the pond has to offer and consequently have every large bass clinging to it. A single felled tree, in a pond which is otherwise cover-free, may be the home of the fish.

Since the entire pond area can often be covered in a relatively short time, the most systematic approach to use is fan-casting. I cover various sectors of water in a clockwise direction, first casting toward the shoreline to my left and then radiating each succeeding cast around the clock. Various types of spinners are ideal for establishing both depth and speed patterns when working from the shoreline, because they can be worked slow or fast, near the surface or down deep. The first clockwise series of casts are fished just below the surface, with every other cast being retrieved at a different speed. Then I fish the same water over again, but this time allow the spinner to sink in a few feet before beginning the retrieve. If you count "one thousand and one, one thousand and two," and so on you can precisely work various depths and return to those same depths whenever you catch a fish. With each count of "one thousand . . ." approximately one second passes, with the lure sinking about one foot.

After having fan-cast one area, covering all depths and trying different speeds, move down the shoreline to where your first cast ended and begin over again. Soon you'll probably start catching fish. And after noting the "pattern of the day," you can work your lures exclusively at whatever depth and speed seem to be paying off.

When visible structures exist, such as weedbeds, stumps, and other cover, the fish may be holding in certain positions and want a lure presented from a certain direction. So in fan-casting, I may throw a lure several times at a stump from the right of it, see no action, and move down the shoreline and cast to the stump again from a position to the left of the cover to see if anything is doing.

Chart 28 shows a mini-pond. We'll say it's about five acres and of the flatland variety. An angler working the pond places himself at the various "X" positions and begins fan-casting. It's not difficult to evaluate this pond and the most likely structures. And we can see that the angler's fan-casting is systematic, allowing him to "check"

Chart 28. Fan-casting in a mini-pond

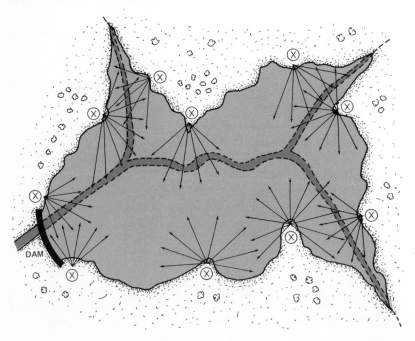

the water thoroughly. In three situations he has even worked the same structure from different positions. If he is working his lures at a variety of depths and speeds, I'll bet money he's catching bass. An angler who chose to wade this particular pond might have even better results, because he would be able to work more of the stream channel.

The very smallest ponds can easily be thrown out of balance by anglers who remove too many bass. So unless an occasional bass is a real sockdolager, or unless I know the landowner would like a few fish for dinner, I return most of my catch to the water, knowing they'll still be there for some other day's enjoyment.

STRIP-MINE AND QUARRY PONDS

In certain regions of the country, especially through the Appalachian range and in many Midwestern and Western states, strip-mine and quarry ponds can produce big bass.

As evidence of this, Ohio's present record bass came from a strip-mine pond (a previous state record came from a farm pond). The fish weighed almost eleven pounds!

Strip-mine and quarry ponds are created incidentally when coal, ore, or rock companies gouge long, rectangular trenches in the earth. A hard-packed road nearly always leads into the pit's inner recesses, from which mammoth trucks hauled out the sought-after deposits. When the contractors left the area, the pit filled quickly through natural seepage and rainwater accumulation. And in the process of "reclaiming" the land, state departments of natural resources, or even the contracting company, may stock the newly formed ponds, usually with bass and panfish.

Fishing strip-mine ponds and quarries, in my opinion, presents anglers with one of the toughest angling situations imaginable. The water is nearly always crystal clear, very deep, and devoid of any kind of cover or vegetation. The bass stay very deep, they are unbelievably spooky, and their migrations seldom bring them near the shallows except after dark and during other low-light periods. The angler has somewhat of an edge, however, in that he can nearly always count upon the fish using the old roadbed as their primary migration route. Since it is a hard-bottom structure which extends all the way from the shallows to the depths, and since the remainder of the pond probably consists of nothing other than sheer walls, any angler can expect to catch his large fish on the road.

The key to fishing such waters is fourfold. Use very light lines (four-pound test if necessary). Fish on the bottom and on the road-bed. Try a variety of lure speeds. And concentrate the bulk of your efforts during low-light periods (dawn, dusk, or after full dark).

Even after all of these tactics have been put into play, fishing success will probably only be marginal. Few anglers ever hike away from a strip-mine pit or quarry pond with a full stringer. But occasionally such waters yield bass big enough to make your eyes bulge.

CHAPTER 11

Strategy for Smallmouths

Powerful runs, consecutive leaps clear of the water, head-shaking, gill-rattling, tail-walking—they're all part of the game when an angler does battle with smallmouths.

But while the smallmouth, of all the bass species, is without question a most worthy gladiator on hook and line, his physiological shortcomings make him a weakling in many other respects. And this has made it very difficult for fishery scientists to extend his natural range, as they have admirably accomplished with largemouths.

One trait of smallmouths which is in their favor is that the species can survive in water having low oxygen-saturation levels. Largemouths and spotted bass require at least 5 parts per million of dissolved oxygen and prefer a range of 8 to 12 PPM, while small-mouths, according to Dr. Martin Venneman, who has researched the matter, can survive upon only 3 PPM. But the smallmouth is not nearly as adaptable as the other basses in his tolerance for water turbidity or various ranges of water temperature. Any minor degrading of smallmouth habitat, such as an insignificant rise in pollution levels, which other basses would probably take in stride, usually results in drastic lowerings of smallmouth populations. Smallmouths are very selective in their dining habits too, at least when compared to the "eat anything that moves" habits of their cousins. Finally, a good majority of soft bottom conditions, which may be tolerated or even favored by the other basses, just won't do in the case of smallmouths. The "brownies" are usually quite averse, for example, to mud, muck, mire, loose soil, silt, and abundance of vegetative forms such as heavily matted weeds and lily pads.

So the often-held belief that the smallmouth is a hardy and tenacious species is really very far from the truth.

Originally, the species was confined to the Great Lakes, the St. Lawrence, the upper Mississippi and the river systems of Ohio and Tennessee. In recent decades its range has been considerably expanded, though many attempts at this have failed. Smallmouth populations run especially high throughout New England, the southern regions of certain Canadian provinces (notably Quebec, Ontario, and Manitoba), most of the northern border states east of the Rocky Mountains, and Lake Erie. But the very largest fish which are brought to net each year come from none of these waters but rather from the large reservoirs and associated rivers of the east-central states and as far south as northern Alabama.

An ideal smallmouth lake or reservoir is usually one which is rather expansive, possessing depths of at least twenty-five feet and preferably more. It may be either natural or manmade and in the great majority of cases it will be of the highland variety.

The most productive smallmouth lakes and reservoirs are those possessing only modest fertility levels, meaning that the bottom composition is low in nutrients, so that plant life and vegetation will be sparse. The floor of the body of water and its many associated structures will probably be composed of sand, gravel, rock, hard-packed clay, marl (a mixture of clay and limestone), shale, or a combination of those substances. The water temperature must reach a minimum of 60 degrees during the spring months for spawning purposes and should preferably not exceed about 72 degrees at any other time during the year (though smallmouths are active and can be caught in water temperatures ranging from 48 to about 78 degrees). If there is a bit of current, in the form of either feeder tributaries or "density flows" (a result of active springs or wind and wave action), all the better.

Since the most productive smallmouth lakes and reservoirs are those with minimal levels of fertility, the water tends to be unusually clear. There will be exceptions to the rule, of course, but the water usually ranges from crystal clear to only very slightly green, blue, or brown.

Spawning behavior of smallmouths is generally about the same as that of the largemouths, but with three exceptions. First, the smallmouths will move onto their beds slightly earlier, usually when the water temperature is from 58 to 63 degrees, while the most purposeful largemouth spawning takes place when the temperature is from 65 to 70 degrees. Secondly, while largemouths will usually fan out their nests in water averaging from two to six feet deep, the smallmouths may bed considerably deeper. Their nests, while frequently in water ranging from four to eight feet deep, may often be as deep as fifteen feet or more. Milton Trautman, a highly respected fish scientist, has found smallmouth eggs hatching at twenty-two feet deep in Whitmore Lake in Michigan. Thirdly, male smallmouths in any body of water usually abandon the nests immediately after they have fertilized the eggs. Unlike largemouths, which are very protective of the eggs and newly hatched fry, male smallmouths leave the nests to whatever destruction may be wrought by the elements, panfish, crayfish, or turtles. Smallmouth mortality rates in the egg and fry stages are always exceedingly high.

Catching bedding smallmouths is very similar to spring angling for largemouths, but there are a few differences that should be kept in mind. Generally, smallmouths are not nearly as vulnerable to plastic-worm offerings as largemouths, usually preferring instead some type of "hardware." Additionally, topwater lures and many types of shallow-running crankbaits, which many times murder spawning largemouths, are seldom effective for spring smallmouths. While the angler may well be able to implement variations in speed control over these lures, to determine what is best for any given day, he is usually unable to probe deeper waters. And smallmouths which are bedding in water much deeper than five or six feet, which is very often the case, simply will not come up to take a look at some offering presented high over their heads.

The best approach, when smallmouths have been determined to be bedding quite deep, is to switch to deep-diving crankbaits, bottom-jumping lures (such as jigs, leadhead tailspinners, or spoons), or perhaps some variation of sinking plug or spinner. All of this, however, is something the angler will have to find out for himself while on location.

Smallmouths seem to be much more spooky than largemouths and perhaps the predominantly clear water is responsible for this. But whatever the reason for their habitual shyness, an unobtrusive approach, while keeping a low profile and making long casts, will result in far more strikes.

Very light tackle can and should be used. There may be occasional signs of brush, jagged rock formations, and perhaps even sparse weed growth where the fish are spawning, but this is usually of little significance. Largemouths characteristically make a beeline for cover when hooked, in an attempt to do a "wrap job" with the angler's line and break off. But the unusual nature of smallmouths is nearly always to make a frantic rush *away* from the shallow shoreline cover and into the depths. In many instances at Dale Hollow Reservoir in Tennessee I've found smallmouths bedding far back in the creek arms where there was brush and other cover, and have had no trouble using lines as light as six- and even four-pound test. Nine out of ten fish hooked in the tangles charted nonstop courses away from the cover and into the depths of the nearby creek channel, allowing me to leisurely slug it out with them in open water with little fear of losing the fish to cover. An exception to this behavior is when the smallmouths are bedding in locations where they have no immediate access to the depths. Then they will dive for whatever obstructions they can find.

As in the case of largemouths, the postspawn period will see smallmouths gradually drifting away from the shallows to resume schooling in the depths. How deep they will go, and how shallow they will move on structure during the course of their periodic migrations, is nearly always dependent upon existing amounts of light penetration. We know that smallmouth lakes and reservoirs are predominantly clear, at least compared to the slightly murky or stained waters most frequently inhabited by largemouths, and this means light penetration will be far greater. Consequently, smallmouths seldom move as shallow as the largemouths. Even in bodies of water such as Dale Hollow, which contains both species, the smallmouths are much more depth-oriented than their largemouth cousins.

At Dale Hollow I've caught good numbers of oversize large-

During midsummer, smallmouths such as this four-pounder may be taken as deep as forty feet. (*Courtesy of Bing McClellan*)

mouths as well as smallmouths. And during migrations the large-mouths have frequently been taken as shallow as six or seven feet deep. But to date not a smallmouth over three pounds has been taken from less than twelve feet of water. The largest ones have nearly always come from depths of from fifteen to twenty-five feet, though I know of several anglers who take them upon occasion as deep as forty-five feet! The only exceptions to this are during the spring spawn or when fishing after dark, during the winter months when the water takes on a slate-gray color and the fish move onto the steep points, or at other times when water or weather conditions severely retard light penetration.

Movements of smallmouths on structure are very similar to those of largemouths in that the fish will make contact with the shallows at some break on a breakline and they will follow other breaks or signposts to the scatterpoint. They will also predominantly use on-structures during the earlier part of the year, gradually shifting to deeper off-structures as the sun shifts higher in the sky. Later in the year, during the fall and winter months, they may continue to use off-structures or they may move back to the on-structures. Much of the very finest smallmouth angling at Dale Hollow and similar waters is during the dead of winter when the fish move onto the steep gravel points and shale slides. It seems that in waters located north of the Kentucky and Tennessee region, the fish use off-structures in deep water as their winter homes, but in waters located south of the Tennessee region they predominantly use on-structures. This is probably because waters located farther south do not become nearly as cold during the winter and the fish can still engage in regular migrations.

During midsummer, look for the fish to use off-structures. Here, Sam Piatt bottom-jumps lures on a deep breakline at Dale Hollow Reservoir in Tennessee.

As the season progresses an angler can switch from fan-casting crankbaits to speed-trolling to bottom-jumping, depending upon how deep the fish are. Bottom-jumping lures, such as jigs dressed with plastic grubs or pork rind, are all-purpose baits! The reason for this is that after the spring spawn the largest fish will live and move quite deep. And the water temperatures during the seasons may vary considerably. Bottom-jumping lures can be used at almost any depth, and they can be retrieved at almost any speed.

This is not to belittle the importance of knowing how to speed-troll, for that can be a valuable tactic whenever the water shows coloration. But in the very clear impoundments, the heavier lines required in speed-trolling, due to the strong pull many speed-trolling lures exert as they kick into the bottom, will usually spook the fish. All of these strategies, as you will recall, we outlined in Chapter 7.

When fishing on-structures such as the steep gravel points and shale slides, or the stair-step rocky ledges, I like to cast as close to the shoreline as possible and "walk" a jig slowly down the structure. This is accomplished by slowly raising the rod tip, lowering it quickly while reeling in the slack, and allowing the jig to fall on a tight line to the next depth level. The jig can be worked down to depths of about forty feet, keeping it right on the bottom. I accomplish speed control by using jigs of different sizes, designs and even by altering certain jigs. Large jigs, by comparison, sink faster than smaller jigs and round-head jigs, such as the Doll-Fly, fall quite fast, compared to other shapes. Flat-head jigs, such as the Hoss-Fly, sink much more slowly. The speed with which your jig sinks can also be varied by trimming the soft leaden jig head with a pen-knife. The parts of the jig which should be trimmed if the jig is meant to sink faster are the sides of the lure (so there will be less water resistance against the jig). If the lure is meant to sink more slowly, the bottom should be trimmed from round to flat to increase water resistance. Another way speed can be varied has to do with the way the dressing is attached to the lure. A grub, for example, impaled on the jig's hook with the thin tail riding in a vertical position would make the lure sink faster. With the tail in the horizontal position there is more water resistance and the jig falls more slowly.

Whatever the fishing strategy, smallmouths seem consistently to prefer smaller lures than those which might be used for large-mouths.

For any river or stream to sustain a healthy smallmouth population, it must have a gradient or "pitch" of no less than four feet

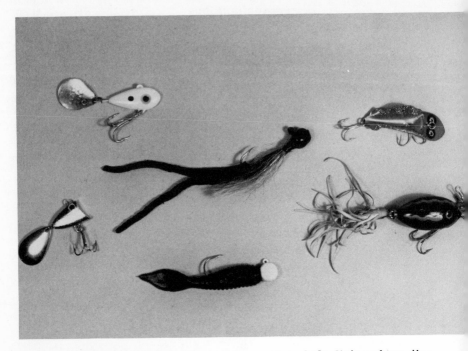

Popular smallmouth lures for deep-water work include diving plugs, jigs, speed-trolling lures and tailspinners. Except in rare cases, these fish don't usually go for plastic worms.

per mile and no more than twenty feet per mile. Intermittent, shallow riffles with bottoms composed of sand, gravel, and small rocks should separate long glides which contain occasional deep pools. The bass will use the quiet eddy waters adjacent to the riffles for spawning during the spring if there are no nearby feeder tributaries for upstream migrations. And when the spawn is completed, the fish will move back to their holding stations in gently moving waters adjacent to the flow of more turbulent currents.

When fishing rivers such as the Tennessee, which can be wide and quite fast in places, I usually watch for leaves, flotsom, foam, or twigs drifting downstream on the surface, because the way in which the debris moves with the water often tells me what lies below the surface. If the debris remains almost stationary in places for long moments, before finally being swept away again with the current, there may be a quiet-water section behind a deep boulder or log. If the debris flows in a circular pattern, some structural formation below has created an eddy. If debris traveling in a rather straight line suddenly changes direction and swings far to one side or the other, something on the bottom, such as a bar or shoal, is diverting the water. All of these occurrences, and more, may give the observant angler a hint as to where fish may be lying. Remember that they will usually be in less turbulent water adjacent to the main flow, that they will always be facing into the current, and that the most successful bait or lure is usually that which travels neither faster nor slower than the current but at the same speed.

These are my "tools" for catching smallmouths in the smaller rivers and streams. They include jigs, spinners and slim-minnow plugs, which I throw with light spinning tackle.

In general, the ways in which smallmouths live and move through the depths are, with only slight variations, very much the same as the behavior patterns of largemouths. Therefore, much of what we've said about fishing for largemouths in lakes, reservoirs, rivers, and streams can be applied to smallmouth fishing. The major variations to keep in mind are that smallmouth waters are usually infertile and consequently very clear, necessitating the use of light tackle. The species themselves nearly always live and move and feed at substantially deeper levels than largemouths; smaller lures are usually more effective; and the fish will be considerably more active than largemouths when the water is cool.

CHAPTER 12

Spotted-Bass Tactics

There is no question, in my friend Bill Henderson's mind, that the spotted bass is an ideal adversary, for it combines the power of the largemouth with the fighting stamina of the smallmouth. And while not every angler, obviously, stands a great deal of chance of breaking the world's spotted-bass record, which Bill currently holds, it is indeed possible to stack the odds of successful spotted-bass fishing at least slightly in one's favor by planning ahead.

The spotted bass, *Micropterus punctulatus*, exhibits some living habits characteristic of both largemouths and smallmouths, plus some which neither is known for. Variously known as a "spot," "spotted bass," "Kentucky," or "Kentucky spotted bass," the species was first identified in Kentucky in 1927. For many years it was believed that the bass was native only to that particular state; hence the moniker "Kentucky bass," which still prevails in most fishing circles despite subsequent investigation that showed that the species lived in a number of other states as well. Ichthyologists of the American Fisheries Society refer to the species as "spotted bass," in accordance with its Latin title.

Unlike those of his largemouth and smallmouth cousins, the range of the spotted bass is not widespread, and as a general rule the farther south one goes the more plentiful is the species. Draw a line from the southwest corner of Pennsylvania to central Kansas. Now vertically drop each end of the line directly south to the Gulf of Mexico and you have an almost perfectly defined region to which the spotted bass is confined.

Alabama leads all other states in the number of large spotted bass taken each year, and there the species is to be found in every major river, stream or large impoundment which has not yet been affected by modern man's thoughtless pollutants. But regardless of where the angler plies his efforts, spots are more often than not caught only incidentally while angling for either largemouths or smallmouths. An exception to this rule is Allatoona Lake in northwestern Georgia, where 90 percent of all bass caught are "spots."

Within its range area, the largest spotted bass consistently come from highland lakes and reservoirs; seldom do they grow to appreciable size in flatland bodies of water unless there are substantial depths. And almost never do the species exceed more than two pounds in weight in the flowing waters of rivers and streams.

A spotted-bass lake or reservoir is usually one which lies south of the Tennessee Valley region, is rather expansive, and has depths to at least 25 feet. The shorline will probably include high rock bluffs, ledges, shale slides, or outcroppings, which frequently drop off very steeply at the water's edge. The bottom should be rather hard and consist of rocks, gravel, sand, clay, crumbled shale, or hard-packed soil. In a great majority of cases there will also be standing or felled timber and brush on the bottom with underwater structure consisting of points, bars, ridges, humps, and similar conformations characteristic of all highland bodies of water. In addition there may be feeder tributaries gushing into the lake or reservoir. Sometimes these are only short, narrow, and rather steep cuts along the shoreline. But more often they are in the form of rather long, wide creek arms.

Spring spawning habits of the fish are similar to those of largemouths and smallmouths in that spotted bass seem to move upstream

The most productive spotted-bass reservoirs are very large and very deep. And they possess cover and bottom conditions favored by both largemouths and smallmouths. (*Courtesy of Kentucky Dept. of Tourism*)

from their winter homes toward the feeder tributaries. Also like largemouths and smallmouths, they will spawn along the banks of the main body of the lake or reservoir wherever there is suitable bottom composition. Look for underwater rock outcroppings or wide shelves layered with sand or light gravel. Or try the down-wind or down-current sides of shallow points and bars extending far out into the water from the shoreline. If there are stick-ups or light brush present, all the better.

The spawning instincts of spotted bass are triggered when the water temperature reaches the 62- to 65-degree range. In those impoundments which contain all three species of bass, then, the spotted bass will begin moving onto their beds just after the smallmouths and just before the largemouths. There have been exceptions to the rule, but most of the spotted-bass spawning activities I have noted have been in water averaging from about six to twelve feet deep, which means they tend to family matters slightly deeper than the largemouths but often shallower than the smallmouths.

After the spring spawn, the remainder of the year will find lake and reservoir spotted bass living and moving on structure in large schools. But their behavior varies in some respects from the basic habits of largemouths and smallmouths. First, they will often go to extreme depths—sometimes to one hundred feet or more. The fish also like to suspend or hold at some arbitrary medium depth in association with structure such as a deep-water rock ledge or shelf or perhaps even a sheer underwater rock wall. Chart 29 shows an example of this suspension characteristic.

Spots also seem to exhibit a greater tendency toward nomadic behavior than the other basses, gathering in schools and methodically working back and forth along long stretches of steep shoreline. Also, midday seems to produce much better catches, in contrast to the dawn and dusk activity frequently engaged in by the other basses, though like largemouths and smallmouths, the spotted bass is very active after full dark.

As regards the average depths at which spotted bass are found through the various seasons of the year, absolutely nothing is certain. But if pinned down, my general guidelines would be as follows: before and after the spring spawn, look for the fish to be associated with on-structures from six to twenty feet deep; through the summer months look for them to be associated with either on- or off-structures from ten to forty feet deep; and during the fall and winter, look for them to be associated with either on- or off-struc-

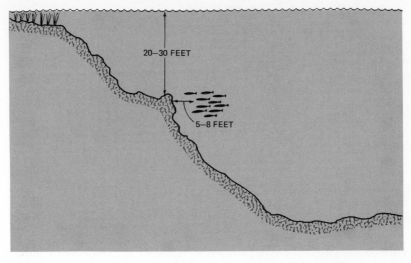

Chart 29. Spotted bass suspending near a mid-depth structure

tures, again at the six-to-twenty-foot level. As we have already noted, any time of year may see the fish go much, much deeper than this. But that is really of little concern because the prospective spotted-bass angler—indeed, any angler—will have great difficulty in attempting to maintain precise speed and depth control over his lures when trolling deeper than about twenty-five or thirty feet. By the same token he will find similar difficulties when bottom-jumping deeper than forty or forty-five feet.

It should stand to reason that topwater baits and shallow-running lures are only rarely effective for spotted bass. The only time these lures could possibly be considered for use might be during the spring spawn when fish have been located in the creek arms.

During the late spring, early summer, and again in the fall—or for that matter any time the fish are suspected to be at slightly shallower depths, ranging from ten to twenty-five feet—speed-trolling will account for the largest number of spots. The same speed-trolling tactics which were described in Chapter 7 can be put into play, but there are a few slight variations which should be considered. First, a top-notch spotted-bass lake or reservoir often possesses characteristics of ideal smallmouth water and largemouth water. It will often be very clear, with a preponderance of rocks, shale, and sand. But there will probably also be plenty of felled or standing timber on the bottom in certain locations and brush in others. Clear water screams for light tackle and light lines, but heavy cover demands stout tackle if the angler has any hopes of boating large fish. The only thing to do is to take the middle ground, and that will probably consist of a baitcasting or trolling rod with a level-wind reel filled to capacity with line testing from twelve to fifteen pounds.

We know that in speed-trolling for largemouths or small-mouths, the fish will always be on or near the bottom and that our lures must continually be kept in proper position on structure. "Proper position" means they should not be permitted to leave the structure and "swim free" but should continually bump or tick the bottom. The same holds true when speed-trolling for spotted bass whenever the conditions permit, such as trolling a point, bar, submerged island, or other structure. But keep in mind the nature of spotted-bass lakes and reservoirs and how they often have sheer rock bluffs adjacent to the shoreline. At Lewis-Smith Reservoir, which is typical of quality spotted-bass waters and where Bill Henderson caught his eight-pound-plus world record, the depth may drop from five feet to three hundred feet within only scant yards of the shoreline. And as we have already mentioned, spotted bass often like to suspend at some arbitrary middle depth along these sheer walls. Here is a situation, then, in which speed-trolling does not mean that the lures are continually bumping bottom. *The fish are still adhering to structure, of course, but the structure (the steep wall) is now on a vertical rather than a horizontal plane.* In order to speed-troll such structures effectively, the angler will have to keep his boat as close to the wall as possible without banging into it (and creating noise) and he will have to *stack* his lures. This means that he will make one pass down the lengthy shoreline with his lure running at a depth of, say, ten feet. At the end of the trolling pass he'll remove that lure from his line and tie on another which is capable of running at fifteen feet deep. Then he'll make still another pass with his lure running at twenty feet deep, and so on until he has determined the depth the fish are holding at. A variety of lure speeds will also be used with successive trolling passes.

As we mentioned earlier, spotted bass are at times quite nomadic. But at the other extreme, there are certain locations in any spotted-bass lake or reservoir which are likely to contain good

Expert angler Sam Piatt likes to wade when fishing for "spots" in small rivers and streams. Here he works a section of Tygart Creek in eastern Kentucky while float-tripping with the author.

numbers of fish on almost a year-around basis. One is a shoreline bar or point which enters the water and continues on for some distance before dropping off steeply at its tip end. If the bar or point is saturated with standing or felled timber or brush, if its tip end lies in at least fifteen feet of water, and if it drops off into at least fifty feet of water, you should be able to catch spotted bass there any month of the year. The fish may be schooling by size in this situation, or they may not be schooling but constitute stragglers of mixed sizes which have been attracted to the cover and structure. Whatever the reason for their presence, any smaller fish on the point will probably be located farther up the point toward the shallows and the larger fish will be hugging the tip of the point, directly adjacent to the depths.

Another year-around holding station which seems always to contain at least a few spotted bass is a "hogback" or underwater ridge which connects two midlake structures such as islands, bars, or points. And still another is a hump or submerged island that juts up from the floor of the lake or reservoir. If the top of the hump is brush-covered and lies in about twenty feet of water, and there is much deeper water surrounding the hump on all sides, it can attract spotted bass as bones attract dogs.

In rivers and streams, spotted bass will usually be found only in those areas where certain conditions exist. The species can tolerate cooler and swifter water than largemouths, but they do not usually prefer the low water temperatures and current favored by smallmouths. So if you chance upon a location which doesn't seem "just right" for either largemouths or smallmouths, it may be perfect for spots.

Although spotted bass differ in these preferences from largemouths and smallmouths, they like the structure and bottom composition sought out by both cousins. Look for them over clean, hard bottom materials wherever there are brush, felled trees, stick-ups, or standing timber. They are not often caught in the weeds, unless other, preferred types of cover are not available. And like their counterparts found in larger rivers, they seem to be very depth-oriented.

Spotted bass in the larger rivers, curiously, do not grow to much beyond two pounds. In smaller rivers and streams, even under ideal circumstances, they are certain to be smaller still. In waterways which average twenty yards wide, with depths ranging from two to six feet, the great majority of spotted bass will tip the bal-

If you're in the right place at the right time, "Kentuckies" will take almost anything you throw at them. But here are the favorites I rely upon when on most rivers and streams.

ance at only half a pound. All bass in these types of waters are products of their spartan habitat, feeding continually in order to replenish lost body energy, yet never getting quite enough to eat.

Light spinning tackle is the best bet for spotted bass in rivers and streams, however large or small those waterways may be. And the artificial lures or live baits which customarily are effective for either largemouths or smallmouths will do nicely as far as spots are concerned. If you want to try exclusively for the water's largest spotted bass (you'll probably never get one more than fifteen inches in length, and he should be considered a trophy well earned) ply your efforts in the scattered, deep pools.

CHAPTER 13

The Amazing Florida Bass

The Florida bass is a recognized subspecies of the largemouth. Physiologically, he differs from his bigmouth cousin only in scale count and a genetic predisposition toward attaining larger proportions, though in many instances he also takes on a darker color due to the nature of his abundantly fertile habitat.

The thing which makes the Florida bass so exciting to anglers is the impressive size the subspecies attains. While a nine-pound largemouth caught in some northern reservoir might well stand as a new state record to be envied by all, a nine-pound Florida bass yanked from some cypress tangle is seldom likely to raise eyebrows among locals. There, you'll have to con a member of the resident lunker population which tips the balance at better than twelve or thirteen pounds in order to find yourself the proud recipient of accolades and admiration. And if you're strictly a trophy hound bent upon establishing a new Florida state record, you'll have to slip the meshes around a fish weighing better than 19½ pounds.

The reason bass attain such large proportions in Florida (and select regions of other states containing the Florida subspecies) has to do not only with their unique genetic potential for oversize growth, but also the year-around climates which allow them to realize that potential. To understand this better, let's briefly examine the growing characteristics of both largemouths and the Florida subspecies.

In Ohio, which is typical as regards largemouth growth patterns in the North, bass enjoy a growing season of only about seven months each year. Body length steadily increases, to a point, and at a rate which is slightly less than that of Florida bass, but increases in real body weight are very slow-paced. This is because a large percentage of fat stores accumulated during the warm-water months are slowly consumed during the cold-water months of winter, when the fish fall into a type of semi-dormancy. The very low water temperatures severely retard body metabolism, and feeding or other activity almost ceases. But any living organism, however inactive during dormant periods, must still have access to energy stores in order to maintain whatever minimal metabolism is required to keep the organism alive. In the case of bass during the cold winter months, internal systems are satisfied with energy derived from the assimilation of fat stores rather than from the intake of large quantities of food during the warm-water months.

It is true that spring bass in Ohio and other northern states are the largest (heaviest) of the season. But much of this appearance is deceiving and constitutes only "false weight" in the form of roe sacks which have been continually maturing in the female's body, giving her a pot-bellied look. After she has dropped the majority of her eggs, one could not find a more haggard, shallow-looking fish specimen. Regular feeding activities will take place during the coming summer and fall months, with enormous quantities of food being consumed. But most of the weight accumulated during this growing period is stored in still more fat layers to see the fish through still another upcoming period of semi-dormancy. The entire affair might be likened to a person who gorges himself at every meal four days a week and then fasts the remaining three days. He will probably continue to gain weight, but it will be only in marginal increments.

As one moves progressively further south, of course, the period of semi-dormancy becomes shorter and shorter. Consequently, there is a progressive increase in the accumulated fat stores, which are gradually transformed into "real" body weight. In fact, in the southernmost states there may be almost no dormancy period at all, and the largemouth will realize his genetic growth potential. But still, due to their genetic growth limitations, the fish are not likely ultimately to equal those growth proportions exhibited by the Florida subspecies.

A noteworthy example of oversize bass growth has recently been seen in southern California. But the fish attaining impressive sizes there are not true largemouths. They are the Florida subspecies, which have been transplanted by joint effort between California and Florida fishery officials. In southern California, year-around air and water temperatures approximate those of Florida, and for other reasons that will be discussed shortly, the aliens have been putting on weight like Fat Albert at a pie-eating contest.

For decades fishery biologists, anglers, and fishing writers stalwartly claimed that George Perry's world record twenty-two-pound-plus Northern largemouth bass, caught in 1932, would never be bested. But when large numbers of California transplants in the fifteen-to-eighteen-pound range began showing up on anglers' stringers between 1970 and 1972, anxious stirrings among fishermen suggested the record might soon tumble. The fishery biologists, however, were still not so sure; after all, fifteen-to-eighteen-pound bass had been showing up in Florida for years.

Then during the summer of 1973, an angler by the name of Dave Zimmerlee boated a monster at Lake Miramar that weighed almost twenty-one pounds. At about the same time there began reported sightings of fish in the twenty-four-to-twenty-six-pound range cruising certain waters. The fishery biologists are whistling a different tune now! And I strongly suspect the record will probably be broken sometime during the next few years. By the time you read this, the event may have already transpired.

A necklace of thirteen San Diego City Lakes are currently in the limelight as far as regularly producing these whopper bass, though the Florida subspecies has been introduced into a total of twenty-seven California waters. Many fishery scientists believe it all has to do with a different style of fish-management being practiced in California, though no studies or data exist either to confirm or to deny the opinion. The San Diego City Lake managers impose a number of restrictions upon anglers. For one, most of the lakes are open to fishing only for six months, and then they are closed for six months, which allows more big bass to survive to the next season. Secondly, night fishing is not permitted on the waters. This can have an important influence, because record books in other states show some of their largest bass of the season are taken while stars are winking overhead. This is in line with what we said in Chapter 1 about the largest bass in any body of water being very reluctant to leave the depths except during those times when light levels are lowest. Angling pressure on the San Diego City Lakes is still further reduced by allowing fishing only on certain days of the week, such as Tuesday, Thursday, and Saturday. What the California people are doing, then, is carefully regulating the annual bass harvest, so larger numbers of lunker bass are permitted to continue growing.

Catching the transplanted Florida subspecies of largemouth in California does not differ markedly from catching largemouths anywhere. Many California-based anglers claim the largemouths there are much easier to catch than the supposedly wary Florida transplants. Others claim just the opposite is true. Whatever the case, and I believe there is little difference, an angler should have success with both basses if he approaches his fishing methodically and scientifically. This means evaluating water and weather conditions, locating bottom structure the fish might be using during the various seasons of the year, and then using whatever techniques are required under existing conditions to implement speed and depth control over lures.

I would be remiss, however, if I failed to relate the circumstances surrounding Dave Zimmerlee's recent catch at Lake Miramar. Zimmerlee, only an occasional angler by his own admission, began the day fishing from the shoreline. Around noon he rented a light skiff and caught a few small bass in various locations. It was only by accident that he suddenly noticed a very large bass finning near the surface. When he approached the fish for a closer look, however, it dove down to about five feet below the surface. Zimmerlee positioned his boat almost directly above the fish, hung a nightcrawler on a large treble hook and then dangled the bait in front of the bass's nose. It took the bait! But then things started to go wrong. Zimmerlee was using a rather inexpensive spin-casting reel which broke when he tried to crank in the fish. With no other alternative, Zimmerlee threw his rod aside, grabbed the line in his hands, and slowly pulled the fish in.

All of this goes to prove that bass fishing is as unpredictable as it is exciting, and every angler, regardless of how he plies his efforts, stands at least a certain remote chance of boating the fish of a lifetime. While experienced bassmen are working from expensive bassboats with sophisticated electronic equipment and contour maps, it could be a frail, tennis shoe-clad grandmother fishing from the bank with a length of stout cane who captures the next world record. And wouldn't that shatter plenty of egos across the country!

But I would also be remiss if I did not pointedly make it clear that trophy catches made by inexperienced anglers armed with crude gear are not regular occurrences when the bass-fishing picture is viewed in its entirety. No doubt occasional big fish will continue to be logged that way in the future. But an angler who combines the use of quality gear with an intimate knowledge of bass habits will consistently see far greater success with large numbers of big fish.

Catching Florida bass in that state calls for slightly different techniques than we have discussed so far. Like bass anywhere, the fish will of course always live and move in relation to some type of structure. They will spend most of their time in deep water, if they can find any. And they can be either tempted into biting or provoked into striking. But due to the consistently warmer air and water temperatures, an angler can expect to encounter a certain percentage of the Florida bass population on spawning beds during any month of the year (this is also true of largemouths in a few other deep South states).

Another thing about Florida bass fishing has to do with the waterways, which are practically always very shallow. As a result, though the fish will occasionally group together in small numbers, there will seldom be the schooling activity involving larger fish that one might encounter in some deep, expansive reservoir.

When we looked at the other bass species, we divided their habitats into four categories: larger lakes and reservoirs (which can be further broken down into highland and flatland varieties); larger river systems; smaller rivers and streams; and various types of ponds. There is really little need to do this in the case of the Florida bass subspecies, because their habitats are so consistent. In fact, many of the existing lakes in Florida are really nothing more than a place where some sluggish river expansively widens. An example is the Kissimmee River which, going north, widens in places to form Lakes Hatchineha, Cypress, West Tohopekaliga, and East Tohopekaliga.

Some may argue that since many such waters are fed by their own tributaries or springs, they are separate lakes in their own rights. But actually, much of Florida is nothing more than an endless maze of winding rivers, sometimes widening, interconnecting canals and underground rivers, and seemingly impenetrable swamp areas and flowages. There are exceptions, of course, such as Lake Jackson, Lake Talquin, and others. But in most cases an angler may have to check a map or chart in order to determine accurately whether he is fishing a swamp, lake, river, backwater pond, or other type of water, since all seem to perpetually wander and in one way or another connect with some other body of water.

It should be noted that few manmade reservoirs exist in Florida. One of the few such impoundments, and perhaps the most productive, is the Rodman Pool, which was created in 1971 when the Oklawaha River was dammed as part of the Cross Florida Barge Canal project. Already, this reservoir is yielding large numbers of bass in the ten-to-twelve-pound range.

The thing which often makes for tough fishing in Florida is the preponderance of visible cover. Most waterways contain extensive grass-studded, hyacinth-infested areas. There are also expansive fields of reeds, lily pads, standing cypress and willow trees, button-bush, and other vegetation. Plenty of large bass are taken from this cover. But except during the major spring spawn, or at other times when occasional bedding fish may be located, the largest number of Florida bass are not attracted solely by the vegetation and other types of swamp cover. Most anglers fail to realize that usually it is the presence of some associated bottom contour that is holding the fish.

For example, look at two hypothetical weedbeds. One is situated on a rather barren flat. The other is situated on an underwater ridge that juts up from the bottom, extends for some distance, and then drops off again into slightly deeper water. You fish both areas and no bass are taken from the edges of the first, but several monsters are derricked aboard from the edges of the second. In the case of the second weedbed, what attracted bass to the area and held them there? Was it the weeds? No! If that were the case, there probably would also have been bass along the edges of the first weedbed. It was the bottom contour, in the second situation, which was holding the bass; the presence of weeds was only incidental.

Canals are one type of structural formation found among Florida waters that are not too common in other areas of the country. These are channels constructed either to facilitate the flow of water by straightening a section of winding river, or to connect two or more larger bodies of water. Generally, the water in the canal will be deeper than the water in the old river channel, and it will be moving faster, yet both waterways may afford good structure-fishing opportunities.

We know from our discussion of flowing waterways that the outside bends of smaller rivers will be washed out and undercut and are therefore deeper, while the inside bends will have shallow shoals formed by settling sand and gravel. And we know the largest bass will usually be where the water is deepest, which means in the vicinity of the outside bends or perhaps where there is an occasional deep hole. The canal is probably no more than a long, uniform trench, but structure may have been created at those locations where the canal cuts across or through the old river channel. The most noticeable structure will be in the form of land points and underwater shelves or drop-offs where the edge of the canal meets the edge of the old riverbed. What is important is that not only are these good bass structures in themselves, but they are directly adjacent to the deepest water in the area. The best way to fish the deep outer bends in the river channel, and also the points, is with bottom-jumping techniques. To work the shelves, I would recommend speed-trolling, fishing the structure just like any other breakline. But all of this is something you'll have to determine on location, depending upon the water depth and clarity and whatever cover may be in evidence. Chart 30 shows such a canal situation.

In the large lakes, and also in the swamp areas, where the water is predominantly shallow and choked with cover, the fish will again be in whatever deep water exists. It may be a sinkhole which gushes forth spring water. I once found a sinkhole twenty feet long by ten feet wide, but they are usually much smaller. While the surrounding water may average from four to seven feet deep, the sinkhole may drop off to a depth of fifteen or twenty feet. Guess where the largest bass in that immediate vicinity will be found? Next to a cypress tree somewhere in the shallows? In the weeds along the shoreline where the water is two feet deep? Under a bush on the flats where the water is four feet deep? Not on your life! The very largest fish will be in or very near the sinkhole. And you can find such holes by carefully checking bottom-contour maps or through

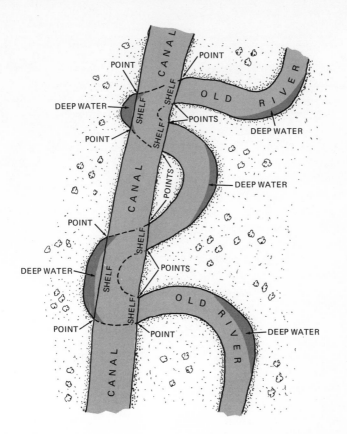

Chart 30. The creation of structure when a canal straightens an old river channel

random exploration by boat with your eyes glued to the dial of a depth sounder.

Other types of cuts, depressions, or drop-offs, while not necessarily associated with springs, may also produce fantastic catches offshore while your buddies are back in the swamp pitching plugs at the shallow weedbeds. And again, it is the change in bottom contour and the slightly deeper water which will attract the fish. Keep in mind, however, that these changes do not always have to be radical, such as the types one might find in a highland reservoir. In a Florida swamp lake where the bottom consists of endless flats in four feet of water, a one-foot drop-off to the five-foot level may be the home of most of the lake's lunkers if that drop is the only noticeable variation in bottom contour anywhere in the area.

In the great majority of cases, heavy cover along the shore-

These types of lures are the most popular with Florida bass-anglers, simply because they can be most effectively worked in the places where the fish usually live.

line of any lake is an indication of very shallow water with little in the way of interesting bottom structure. But sometimes just the opposite may be true if the cover is found in some midlake area and is surrounded on all sides by open water. A small patch of reeds or water lilies may signal the presence of a hump. A long, narrow weedbed may indicate the location of a bar, or a row of trees may signal the presence of an underwater ridge. If there is no depth change, but brush, bushes, or stick-ups are present in some midlake area, the cover may be indicating a place where a very soft bottom yields to a hard bottom. This location could hold a bonanza of big fish during the primary spring spawn. In all of these situations, the best techniques would probably be fan-casting crankbaits or bottom-jumping lures. The very shallow water and perhaps the presence of heavy cover would probably eliminate speed-trolling from consideration. But speed-trolling could be very effective in deeper-water situations, such as when working the edges of sinkholes, drop-offs, or cover-free structures such as bars.

There. is a type of live-bait fishing in Florida which also deserves mention. This method involves the use of shad or minnow species which may often be from six to twelve inches long and weigh upwards of three-quarters of a pound. The method is especially popular on waters such as Lake Jackson.

Jackson's depths average only seven or eight feet, and almost . the entire bottom is saturated with moss and weeds growing up to within a few feet of the surface. The floor of the lake is dishpanshaped, and the few holes or other variations in bottom contour are almost impossible to locate because the electronic signals from the depth sounder's transducer will not penetrate the thick weed layer to reveal what lies below.

An oversize baitfish is hooked once through the lips with a 4/0 or 5/0 hook, and just enough weight is added to the line to prevent the minnow from swimming to the surface. The rig is then suspended from two to four feet below a large float and drifted across open expanses of water just above the tops of the weeds.

When a fish takes, he is permitted to run a short distance before the angler sets the hook with as much gusto as his tackle will stand. Stout rods are the rule, and lines should test from twenty-five to thirty pounds. When the angler has completed his drift across the impoundment and reached the other side, all drifting baits are brought in, the craft is quickly motored to the other side of the lake, and another drift over new water is commenced. The bass lie deep in the weeds on or near some type of bottom variation, occasionally rising to pick off a baitfish cruising the tops of the weeds. When a good fish is brought aboard, it often means that some bottom contour or other structural configuration beneath the weeds is attractive to the fish, and many anglers quietly anchor to work the area. They may lob-cast their shad or minnow offerings, continuing to work the same area from which the first fish was taken. Or they may switch to topwater or shallow-running plugs. Sometimes plastic worms or weedless spoons can be used to work occasional potholes in the cover.

After the spring spawn, the critically important thing in Florida bassing is that the angler must try, difficult as it may be, to overlook the myriad types of bassy-looking cover he will almost

One unique type of Florida bass-angling involves drifting oversize shad or minnow baits over the tops of submerged weeds. Baits the size of this three-quarter-pounder account for some of the largest bass of the season.

certainly encounter. He should seek out structure and bottom-contour changes associated with the deepest water any given area has to offer. These bottom conditions, whether or not cover is present, will be the home of any particular body of water's largest fish.

Structure fishing isn't any different in Florida than in South Carolina, Tennessee, or Ohio. In Florida there are just more distractions to lure the angler away from his appointed task of finding the fish.

CHAPTER 14

Go Fishing When the Fishing Is Best

Owing to job responsibilities, family activities, and mundane household chores, few anglers have unlimited time for fishing. We usually do have some latitude, however, as to when to work our fishing outings into otherwise cramped schedules. The specific days one should go fishing, and the specific times each day when one should ply one's most diligent efforts, require careful thought because many time periods are vastly more productive than others.

We already know how weather influences bass behavior, and how the season will determine the various locations where the majority of large fish will be found in any body of water. And in several previous chapters we saw how bass can either be tempted into biting or provoked into striking. But the success of either approach is largely dependent upon the current activity level of the fish.

Except in the cases of river and stream bass, the fish spend the majority of their time in a rather inactive state, either resting in schools in deep-water sanctuaries or hiding in very heavy cover. And the angler who fishes for bass during these times is not likely to enjoy as much action as he who is on the water when the fish are in a hyperactive state (migrating on structure or prowling the perimeters of cover).

All living creatures possess mysterious, internal biological clocks which govern various types of behavior. These timing mechanisms operate involuntarily due to a combination of planetary forces to be discussed later. These forces affect every living creature from the lowest insect form to mankind himself.

You may have already observed this phenomenon, for example, while hiking through some woodland. There are times in which all is quiet and still, whereupon suddenly the forest comes alive with birds flitting about, squirrels rustling in the leaves, and deer on the move. Then, some indeterminate (or so it seems) time later, all is quiet again. There are quiet times on trout streams. And then suddenly, without warning, rainbows and browns are rising everywhere. Psychologists know there are various times of day when mankind is more enthusiastic and responsive, and certain other times when he is prone to daydream or retreat from engaging in highly active behavior. Factory supervisors notice there are certain shifts or seemingly random times when a lot more work comes down the assembly line without error.

What is important in all of this is that scientists have discovered that creature activity levels (including those of bass and other fish) can be charted in calendar form with a predictable degree of accuracy. The most notable such accomplishments resulted in the formulation of what are called Solunar Tables, by John Alden Knight, many years ago, and the Actiongraph Sportsman's Timetable, by the DataSport Computer people during late 1973.

Using either or both of these calendars, any angler can schedule his bassing trips so they will coincide with peak bass activity levels. For example, let's say each of Joe Angler's typical bass outings see him rise early in order to be on the water before dawn. And he usually calls it a day and heads for home around 4 o'clock in the afternoon. On one particular day, however, he consults either Solunar Tables or Actiongraph, and there is a prediction of major fish activity beginning around 5 o'clock in the evening and lasting until about 7:30. If Joe adheres to his rather standardized routine today, he may miss out on the best action the day has to offer. On this occasion it would be wise for him to sleep late in the morning and plan on staying on the water later than usual.

Or let's say Joe has planned a week-long fishing vacation for sometime next month. He plans to leave on a Friday when he gets off work later in the day. His boss says, "If you want to work late on the previous Thursday, I'll let you leave early on Friday, at noon."

Joe checks ahead in his tables and discovers, sure enough, a major fish activity period is scheduled to begin at three o'clock in the afternoon on that particular Friday. He takes his boss up on the offer, and works late the evening before his scheduled departure so he can hit the road early Friday to cash in on the fish activity period.

CONSIDER SOLUNAR TABLES

In February, 1926, a New York stockbroker by the name of John Alden Knight was feeling restless, as do so many who reside in northern latitudes where most fishing ceases during the winter months. And eventually he decided to set his work aside and drive south to Florida for a bass-fishing vacation on Lake Helenblazes, which is the source-water of the St. John's River. His guide was a young fellow by the name of Bob Wall who was reputed to be one of the most knowledgeable bassmen in the area, but by 11 A.M. on the first day both anglers had lashed the water to a froth and succeeded only in boating several yearling bass. Finally, Wall suggested they break for lunch on a nearby island. With the thought of perhaps napping in the shade of some tree, Knight readily accepted the offer.

As they sipped tea and munched sandwiches, few words were spoken. Knight, especially, was hot, tired, and discouraged. And though curious, he didn't bother to inquire why Wall continued to check his watch every few minutes. Then, however, Wall said something which was very puzzling.

"In one hour the moon will be down. And that is when we'll start catching some big bass."

They sipped the last of their tea while Wall explained that when the practice was still legal, his grandfather had been a market hunter in southern Georgia. "Market hunting" was the harvesting of fish and game for sale, and during those times, men who made their living by rod or gun were not given to wasting valuable time; they'd learned to take full advantage of those times each day when the pursuit of fish or game was likely to prove most productive. One of the many facets of this art, as passed on to Wall by his grandfather, was to be afield or on the water only when the moon was either up or down. Translating this rather bucolic philosophy into more scientific terminology, "up" means that the moon was crossing the meridian of longitude of Lake Helenblazes overhead. The moon would be "down" when it crossed the meridian on its return trip underneath. And during these times, in contrast to all others, substantially greater numbers of fish and game were sure to be encountered.

At first John Knight dismissed the matter with a chuckle and a wave of the hand. But Wall continued to describe his theory anyway, further relating that he had devised a series of charts which allowed him to determine the exact position of the moon during any time of any given day. When he added the comment that his "tables" had enabled him consistently to put clients into big bass over the years, and that the charts were solely responsible for his being the most sought-after guide in the entire state, Knight's ears perked up.

As predicted, the fish began hitting shortly after high noon, and within two hours the anglers succeeded in boating nine bass which tipped the scales at an almost unbelievable seventy-eight pounds! Then, and this was predicted too, the action quieted again. The bass would not go on another major feeding spree for about another twelve hours, though there would be a minor period of activity about 6 P.M., so they might as well reel in their lures and head for the dock.

That Florida bass trip, in which Bob Wall's unique tables accurately predicted when the two would catch their bass during the week, had a revolutionary effect upon John Knight's lifestyle. He drove home to New York and promptly resigned from his job and launched upon a full-scale investigation of moon phases and their effect upon all living creatures.

John Knight's research findings over the years startled the outdoor community, including trained fish and game biologists. Today, hundreds of thousands of sportsmen so thoroughly believe in Solunar Tables that they are regularly published as a syndicated feature in 175 major newspapers across the country.

In attempting to account for the apparently well-ordered way in which all creatures exhibit periods of activity, Knight suspected the controlling influence of some common, external stimulus. He then sought to identify the nature of the stimulus and predict probable times when it could be seen to exert its greatest influence. Solunar Tables, then, offer no iron-clad guarantees that an angler will be able to find or catch fish. What they guarantee is the accurate prediction of time periods during any given day in which an angler is likely to see action, if any action that day is to be had at all.

Bob Wall believed the moon was the sole governing factor or stimulus. But Knight's research revealed it was not the moon's influence alone that regulated activity periods, but the combined influence of both the sun and the moon. The term "Solunar Tables" was subsequently coined from "solar" (pertaining to the sun) and "lunar" (pertaining to the moon). The tables themselves are charts which indicate time periods during which the gravitational effect of the sun and the moon exert their greatest influence. As we all know, these forces are indeed strong, as they daily regulate the ocean levels of the world.

Following his initial investigations, Knight began fishing almost daily and keeping meticulous notes. In compiling his figures and notations some two years later, he discovered that when weather phenomena such as radical barometric fluctuations, rapidly changing air temperatures and frontal conditions were in evidence, fish activity was minimal or at best unpredictable. But on the great majority of other days in which conditions remained stable, there was conclusive evidence that the fish activity periods and the oceanic tide times approximately coincided. Knight further discovered that any angler could use a knowledge of tide times (Solunar Periods) to insure that he was on the water during those predicted times when fish should be exhibiting their greatest activity during any given day.

John Knight was baffled as to why Solunar Periods should so strongly influence fish behavior, and during his lifetime he never fully resolved this mystery. There was no doubt, of course, that Solunar influences were indeed powerful. But finally, he accepted the fact that the "why" would be almost impossible to explain (much like other natural phenomena that have eternally puzzled mankind). The remainder of his work saw him focus upon the "when" factor in the accurate prediction of various times in which the phenomenon could be expected to exert its influence.

Looking at the Solunar Tables on a daily basis, various fish-activity periods can be seen to arrive each day approximately one hour later than the day before. This is because a "moon" day is nearly one hour longer than our twenty-four hour long "earth" day. Each day usually sees the occurrence of four Solunar Periods (two minor periods and two major periods, with respective degrees of fish activity). Generally a major Solunar Period lasts from two to three hours and is followed by a six-hour lapse in fish activity, whereupon a minor Solunar Period of about forty-five minutes takes place. After still another six-hour lapse, another major period can be expected to occur, and then still another minor period. Because of the "earth" day being an hour shorter than a "moon" day, however, there will be an occasional day which sees only three Solunar Periods.

As an example of the appearance of activity periods, here are one day's predicted fish activity periods. Though it is not really relevant, the date is Monday, October 7, 1974. On this particular date a major period of activity (lasting about three hours) was scheduled to begin at 3:20 A.M. This was followed by a minor period of activity (lasting about forty-five minutes) beginning at 9 A.M. Another major period was then scheduled to begin at 3:50 P.M., again lasting for about three hours. And this was followed by still another minor period predicted to begin at 9:25 P.M. I fished on this particular day, electing to be on the water about three o'clock in the afternoon, and staying until about ten o'clock at night. And I boated a total of seven bass that day: six during the major period, and one during the subsequent minor period! But one thing I've discovered is that bass-anglers all too often fall into the trap of relying too heavily upon the tables while discounting the importance of knowing how bass live and move. The tables will *not* make you a better fisherman! Almost never, for example, will an angler find a school of big bass in two feet of water, over a muddy bottom, under a bright midsummer sun, even if the tables indicate a major Solunar Period is in force.

In order for Solunar Tables to aid consistently in bettering your fishing results, then, they must not be looked upon as a cure-all but only as another tool to be used in conjunction with your storehouse of bass skills. They are only a forecast of the probable periods of activity, based upon gravitational influences of the sun and the moon, which may be expected to occur on any given day when weather and water conditions are stable.

It should also be noted that the history, experiments and verifications surrounding the development of Solunar Tables have been presented here only briefly. For a more detailed account of how and why Solunar Tables work, it might be worthwhile to examine John Knight's book on the subject, which is listed in this book's Selected Bibliography section.

When John Alden Knight died, his son Richard further refined the Solunar Tables until he, too, passed away. Now Mrs. Richard Alden Knight, who was diligently schooled in the formulation of the tables, continues their publication. If Solunar Tables are not published in your local newspaper, they can often be had at tackle shops. Or you can obtain them for the modest price of $1.65 postpaid by writing to Mrs. Richard Alden Knight, Box 207, Montoursville, Pennsylvania 17754.

In these days of inflation it's difficult to go too far wrong with a dollar investment. So why not keep a copy of the tables in your tackle box, and after each day on the water compare the times you saw your best bass action with the predicted activity levels of the tables? My guess is that not too many outings will pass before your bassing adventures take place in accordance with the tables' predictions.

A LOOK AT THE COMPUTERIZED "ACTIONGRAPH"

Denny Gebhard, Jim Halverson, and Don Lomax all have several things in common. They all live in Minneapolis, Minnesota. All are computer experts by trade. And all go fishing whenever they have spare time. This probably explains why one day in late 1971 saw them fooling around with an IBM Data-Sorter, feeding the massive complex of wires, circuitry, and buttons some very specific fishing-related information. They were mostly curious as to whether the computer, having digested complex tide-prediction formulas obtained through the U.S. Department of Commerce, would burp data agreeing with the Solunar Tables or perhaps come up with a different pattern of predictions.

The computer predicted the best times to go fishing were during the hours of dawn and dusk, which is not in complete harmony with the Solunar Tables but is indeed in agreement with experiences anglers have had for generations. What is important is that the computer suggested that analysis of massive amounts of data pertaining to factors which determine fish and game activity levels might yield more consistently accurate predictions than the Solunar Tables.

The amount of data fed into the computer during the following two years was almost staggering. And the machine's scanner (a type of inking-stylus which passes over a continually turning roll of graph paper) responded by drawing a computerized curve plotted against a horizontal time axis showing predicted highs and lows of fish and game activity on a daily basis. Gebhard, Halverson, and Lomax promptly dubbed their brainstorm the "Actiongraph."

Every easy-to-read daily Actiongraph is cross-marked to identify each hour of each day, while also being fully adjustable for time-zone differences (including standard or daylight-saving time). On each daily graph, the farther the curve moves above or below the line, the greater the degree of fish and game activity predicted for that time period.

The reason tide-predicting formulas play an important role in the Actiongraph's daily curves is that, like John Alden Knight, the three computer experts have always believed in the theory of tidal activity coinciding with peak activity in all forms of animals. The Actiongraph is not simply a listing of tide-tables, however, but rather a measure of the strength of gravitational forces exerted upon the earth by the sun and moon on an hourly basis. Denny Gebhard believes this makes Actiongraph more precisely accurate than the Solunar Tables.

"The method used by fish and game to sense gravitational attraction," Denny explained to me in a recent letter, "is still unknown. But the fact that they do react to it in their normal daily patterns is fairly well accepted. It's been thought that simply by observing the tides it is possible to figure out when the gravitational effect peaks or bottoms. This is partially true, but there's a lot more to it than that.

"First, the gravitational attraction is stronger some days than others. When the moon and sun are in conjunction or opposition (lined up with the earth) the force is strongest and the tides are the highest. But the gravitational attraction varies widely throughout the day. Usually the tides do not reflect this variance accurately enough to explain why fish and game seem to react at some times and not at others.

"Second, there is usually a lag between the pull of gravity and the movement of the tides. Depending upon the size and shape of the body of water, and the distance from the equator, the tides can lag several hours.

"By using the computer, we can avoid studying the observable effects of the gravitational force (tides) and go directly to an evaluation of the force itself."

In addition to the tide-prediction formulas, other data were also fed into the computer in the hope of evaluating or at least taking into consideration as many possible factors which, in various proportions, may influence fish and game movements. It has long been known that light has an influence upon fish behavior, so sunrise and sunset schedules were added to the computer's memory bank. Next, the results of twenty research reports dealing with living organisms and their biological clocks were programmed into the computer. Fish-movement studies conducted by state universities, the Canadian government, and even scientists in Japan were added to the continually growing amount of data, making the graphs more accurate (since based upon more information) than the ones before.

"We found," says Lomax, "that unlike the Solunar Tables, the computer did not always select two major and two minor periods a day. Sometimes there would be only one period you could describe as major."

As of this writing, the Actiongraph Timetable has not been in existence long enough for extended accuracy determinations; they were first officially printed and distributed in 1974. Yet even during the short amount of time in which the tables have been available, the DataSport offices have been flooded with reports from sportsmen around the country, attesting to the Actiongraph's uncanny predictions of fish and game activity.

One question presented to Gebhard was, "What if the computer has finally solved the mystery as to the best time to go fishing?"

"We're not really worried about anglers suddenly devastating fish populations," Gebhard answered. "A fisherman must still know how and where to fish. And he must be proficient enough in angling knowledge and skills to take into consideration localized conditions such as weather. If a guy has only part of the day to fish, we think the Actiongraph can help him make the right choice."

The Actiongraph Timetable is sold in a package which includes weekly (seven-day) graph plots and adequate log space so the fisherman can keep track of his personal results versus the Actiongraph's predictions. Each package, with graphs for the entire year, costs about $5.00. Write to DataSport, 5636 Abbott Ave. South, Edina, Minnesota 55410. I have used the Actiongraph, and it works!

CHAPTER 15

By All Means, Join a Fishing Club

Any angler who desires to increase his bass-fishing proficiency and enjoyment can find no better opportunity than through joining a local fishing club—especially if that club has earned a reputation as an organization dedicated to encouraging the development of bassing skills.

One of the best guidelines in seeking out a quality club comprised of enthusiastic anglers is to inquire among fishermen whom you consider to be very accomplished. Usually they'll be able to steer you in the direction of the best clubs in your region. The next step should probably be to sit in on several meetings as a prospective member.

There can of course be no doubt that fishing clubs are organized primarily for fun—for people of all ages and backgrounds to get together to share common interests. But perhaps the foundation or philosophy underpinning the most active organizations is in the area of education. And this may be why membership cards in certain clubs are so highly valued; they allow dedicated anglers—whether beginners, intermediates, or experts—to increase their fishing experience and knowledge, and to do so in a way which would probably not have been possible had they not been members of the club.

Films are often shown at various club meetings, for example. These are usually received on a loan basis from major tackle companies and manufacturers of boats and motors, featuring some nationally recognized expert who passes on instruction on using certain types of fishing equipment or putting into play various angling techniques.

There are also sure to be various seminars, lectures, and chalk-talks from time to time. These are usually presented by an invited guest who is especially accomplished in the field he'll be discussing. First the speaker will pass on valuable "how-to" information, using a variety of visual aids such as charts, slides, and actual fishing equipment. Later there will probably be a question/answer period during which club members can ask for clarification of certain points they may not have understood during the discussion.

Crafts projects often take place during the course of fishing-club meetings throughout the year, too, with individual club members usually being asked to "teach" some of their particular skills to the others. These craft sessions may be almost endless in subject matter but frequently include talks and demonstrations on subjects such as how to tune an outboard motor, how to read a bottom-contour chart, how to rig and fish plastic worms and other bottom-jumping lures, how to interpret the signals sent out by an electronic depth sounder, how to clean and cook fish, how to evaluate oxygen-saturation levels in any given body of water, how to catch small-mouths in streams, and many, many more. All of these activities serve to round out each club member's fishing knowledge, and as we've said many times before, fishing knowledge is the key to fishing success.

One very important activity of fishing clubs is actual on-the-water fishing, often in the form of tournaments, with club members paired for the day's fishing. To provide an incentive for less-accomplished anglers to participate, the club secretary may compute past catches of individual anglers and award handicaps, so that all tournament entrants have an equal chance of winning whatever prizes may be given. In so doing, an angler who has never caught a three-pound bass before in his life might bring his very first to the dock and be awarded first place, even though another angler may have strung a five-pounder that day.

But in any case, it is common for highly skilled members to be paired with less-skilled anglers, so learning can take place. I've fished in many such tournaments and never have I spent a day on the water with someone either less skilled or more proficient than I in which we didn't both come away learning something. Book-learning plays an important role in acquiring fishing knowledge, to be sure. But there is absolutely no substitute for spending plenty of time actually on the water. And if that time is with someone who differs in his approach to finding and catching bass, and is willing to exchange knowledge, experience, and tips, your level of expertise will increase at a rate far exceeding what could normally be achieved by learning on your own. Fishing clubs provide this very learning atmosphere.

We should probably also say a few words about joining national fishing clubs. Presently, there are three which I can highly recommend, at least as far as bass-anglers are concerned. They are the Bass Anglers Sportsman Society (P.O. Box 3044, Montgomery, Alabama 36109), The Bass Caster's Association (Box 487, Ballwin, Missouri 63011), and The American Bass Fisherman Organization (P.O. Box 908, Cocoa Beach, Florida 32931).

These organizations are membership societies which publish bi-monthly magazines dedicated to bass know-how and conduct national tournaments each year. The magazines are especially worthwhile because they will keep you up to date on the latest tackle on the market, the latest fishing techniques that the guides, tournament pros, and other experts are using, and the latest research findings pertaining to bass behavior.

Still another organization is the Bass Research Foundation (P.O. Box 3385, Montgomery, Alabama 36109), a nonprofit society which seeks donations from anglers. This money is channeled solely into research projects designed to aid in fishery-management practices in the hopes that tomorrow's bassing will be still better than today's.

There may be some doubt in many anglers' minds as to the worth of joining a national bass organization, at least in regards to specific benefits individual members may derive. I believe the importance of belonging to a national organization should not be mea-

National fishing clubs look out for anglers' interests on a nationwide
scale. Here, anglers take off in search of bass on Lake Mead, Nevada,
during a tournament staged by the Bass Anglers Sportsman Society.
(*Courtesy of B.A.S.S.*)

sured in terms of personal gain but as an acknowledgment of your
support of organizations which look out for fishing interests on a
nationwide scale.

This is important because when confronting politicians or cor-
porate industries, individual voices usually go unheard. Anglers
nationwide need a unified voice to insure their fishing remains of
top-notch caliber. And the larger national organizations serve as

powerful political lobbies which influence national fish-management policies, gamefish laws, commercial netting restrictions, and the activities of those in charge of constructing new waterways or altering existing ones. Annually, they file hundreds of lawsuits against industries which pollute or otherwise destroy waters you and I would like to fish.

Supporting such organizations, then, may well help to determine the trend of fishing in this country in future years. With national membership fees averaging only about $12 per year, they are worthwhile contributions if to no one else than our children and the fishing heritage we pass on to them. In fact, belonging to one of the national membership societies is now even a frequent prerequisite for membership in many top-notch local bass clubs.

CHAPTER 16

The Modern Bassman as Sportsman, Conservationist, and Community Member

The modern bass-angler with his storehouse of bass knowledge and his sophisticated array of fishing equipment is a far different breed of piscator than his predecessors of generations past. For one, he's now fully capable of precisely evaluating weather and water conditions through the use of a variety of electronic aids. The interpretation of bottom-contour maps, followed by the use of a depth sounder, offers tremendous help in further narrowing the search. Sleek, comfortable craft with high-horsepower outboards allow quick access to the most distant sectors of any given body of water.

Compared to his forebears who angled primarily with a hit-or-miss approach, which commonly saw them go fishless during all but the brief spring weeks, the modern bassman can frequently make an accurate prediction as to where the fish should be, and how to

241

catch them, before the day's first lure is cast. There is also the distinct possibility that any day of the year he may return to the dock in the evening in possession of numerous bass with broad green shoulders and underslung bellies.

All of this has been the by-product of science, technology, and the perseverance of ever-inquisitive anglers in prompting Mother Nature in recent years to unlock many of bassdom's previously guarded secrets. Having achieved this stage of development and awareness, however, the modern bassman must now launch upon a continued effort to insure that her trust is not violated, because the underwater world of bass is a very fragile environment. And the bass species themselves are a precious natural resource which depend upon mankind's thoughtful and well-planned management practices.

Indeed, to be a sentinel of bass conservation is to be a concerned watchguard over mankind himself. The life-chain on this planet, it must be remembered, is wholly interrelated. And allowing the unwarranted disturbance of the delicate ecosystem in which bass live, whether intentional or inadvertent, signals a marked lack of regard for something which is living. Too much of this may even be an imminent forecast of man's eventual doom as well. The needless channelizing or trenching of winding and scenic rivers by the U.S. Soil Conservation Service, the outrageous building of dams where they are not needed by the U.S. Corps of Army Engineers, the dumping of acids and other poisons into our waterways by politically favored industries—in short, the selling of the environment for a handful of dollars to line the pockets of a few—are just a few of the many examples of ways in which our environment is being degraded.

Bass-anglers can help to reverse this trend by keeping abreast of political platforms and personal viewpoints held by candidates running for various positions, all the way from the village or township level to the highest office in the land. Then, vote the straight conservation ticket, because it is as crucial to our eventual survival as it is to our fishing right now. The elected official who is a known ally of big business, with favors to repay, is hardly likely to place bass and clean water before other interests. Writing letters to elected officials, or gathering names on petitions pertaining to local or national issues, is another way to express your desires for intelligent water- and fish-management practices.

To promote community interest and respect for our outdoor

heritage, many local fishing clubs are now engaging in conservation
and other projects, and this is something every angler and club
member should enthusiastically participate in. Such activities often
include clean-up campaigns around the shorelines of local waters,
fishing clinics for area youngsters, and fund-raising drives for
worthwhile conservation and beautification projects.

The personal conduct of individual bass anglers, especially
while actually fishing, is also immeasurably important. Any angler
who is seen littering, operating his craft recklessly, exceeding his
state's bass limit, or engaging in other illegal or unsportsmanlike
conduct may totally defeat the efforts being put forth by others who
are trying to present the modern bass-angler, in the community's
eyes, as a sportsman, conservationist, and respected citizen.

Finally, in previous chapters we've made frequent mention of
catching large numbers of big bass, and we've shown several pic-
tures of large bass catches. Now we need to say a few words about
the bass you catch, and the ethics of keeping them.

We have continually encouraged the viewpoint that it is virtually impossible for anglers, using conventional fishing tackle, to
make serious inroads upon bass populations in the larger bodies of
water. This attitude has been perpetuated for the purpose of helping the reader to understand that his lack of fishing success is almost never a result of his chosen water being "fished out," and that
through the acquisition of knowledge of bass behavior he may begin
consistently catching big bass during every month of the year.

The reason why almost none of our waters are presently in
danger of being fished out is that the great majority of this country's millions of anglers simply do not possess knowledge or experience of advanced fishing techniques. But as more and more
anglers each year continue to educate themselves, it is indeed con-
ceivable that in the near future many of our bass waters could be
in trouble.

Therefore, it is now time to shift gears. Having acquired an
intimate awareness of how bass live and move and feed, and the
consequent ability to catch many more large fish than he ever
dreamed possible, the angler reader must now accept certain responsibilities which are inextricably tied to those privileges of
which he has been or will be the beneficiary.

This is certainly not to imply that there is anything wrong with
any angler keeping, upon occasion, some or most of the bass he
catches, especially if they are fish which for one reason or another

probably will not survive release. Nor should an angler who boats a real trophy be admonished if he decides to have his prize mounted for the wall. The point to be made here is that we are presently witnessing an angling renaissance—and I am fully in favor of it— in which emphasis is now being placed upon quality fishing experiences rather than quantity catches of bass being killed. Many of the fish seen in this book are still alive, having been released after briefly posing for the camera. And some of the others pictured, which were kept for either the table or the wall, in many cases represent only a small portion of what was actually caught on the day in question.

What we should strive to promote in coming years, then, is the new attitude held by the modern bass-angler. The advanced bassman does not need the false and only temporary ego boost derived from having curious spectators, standing dockside, uttering oohs and aahhs over a string of more dead fish than he can possibly make good use of.

His "high" comes from the learning process and subsequently putting into use skills acquired to find and catch bass. The chase is what takes on greater and greater importance. And when the chase has been concluded, the modern bassman knows he does not always have to kill his quarry, because the sweet taste of success is already his.

A Glossary of Bass-Angling Terms

Biting: The voluntary act of feeding or seeking forage; a predatory response.

Break: Some change or noticeable interruption in the smooth contour of a breakline, such as a pile of rocks sitting along the edge of a long, continuous drop-off.

Breakline: A major change in depth, such as a drop-off; a major change in structural composition, such as the edge of a weedline; or a change in bottom make-up, such as where mud changes to gravel.

Contact Point: That location or piece of structure bass first associate with when commencing a migration from the depths to the shallows. A contact point is usually a break on a breakline.

Deep water: For practical purposes, water deeper than eight feet.

Epilimnion: During summer stratification, the upper layer of water.

Holding Area: Any location where bass instinctively wait or pause during the course of any exhibition of behavior before consummating that activity.

Hypolimnion: During summer stratification, the lower layer of water.

Ichthyologist: One who engages in the biological study of fishes.

Limnology: The study of physical, chemical, and biological characteristics of fresh water.

Migration: The act of moving from one location to another. With bass, this may be a seasonal migration during which the fish often travel substantial distances, or a daily migration in which the fish move from a particular seasonal home to an adjacent, nearby area.

Migration Route: That series of objects, changes in bottom contour, or other readily identifiable "signposts" which bass follow or travel along during the course of a migration.

Off-Structure: Some type of object or bottom configuration which is not in some way related or connected to the shoreline.

On-Structure: Any type of object or noticeable bottom configuration which is related or connected to the shoreline.

Oxycline: A grouping or combination of the upper two layers of oxygen-rich water (the epilimnion and thermocline layers); used in discussing summer stratification.

Piscatorial: Having to do with fish or the sport of fishing.

Sanctuary: That place, nearly always small in size and located in deep water, where a school of bass spends most of its time in an inactive state.

Scatterpoint: That place, usually in relatively shallow water, where a school of migrating bass is seen to disperse.

School: A grouping of bass, usually with fish comprising each school being of approximately the same size.

Shallow Water: For practical purposes, water less than eight feet deep.

Straggler: Any bass which, for one reason or another, has become separated from any school of which he was previously a member.

Stratification: The physical separation of the water into temperature zones; a natural process which occurs during the summer months in bodies of water possessing depths to at least twenty-feet feet.

Striking: A nonfeeding, involuntary act of hitting or taking a lure or live bait; an aggressive response.

Structure: Any place or object on the bottom which is noticeably different from surrounding bottom areas.

Substructure: A change or noticeable difference in structure. If the edge of a long weedline is structure, a gap in the weedline is substructure. Also known as a break on a breakline.

Thermocline: During summer stratification, that middle layer of water which separates the upper, warmer layer from the lower, colder layer.

Selected Bibliography

DALRYMPLE, BYRON. *Modern Book of the Black Bass.* New York: Winchester Press, 1972.

DANCE, BILL. *There He Is! Bill Dance's Book on the Art of Plastic Worm Fishing.* Montgomery, Alabama: Bass Anglers Sportsman Society, 1973.

FAGERSTROM, STAN. *Catch More Bass.* Caldwell, Idaho: The Caxton Printers, Ltd., 1973.

GRESHAM, GRITS. *Complete Book of Bass Fishing.* New York: Harper & Row, 1966.

HEIDINGER, DR. ROY C. *Largemouth Bass Bibliography.* Montgomery, Alabama: Bass Research Foundation, 1974.

KNIGHT, JOHN ALDEN. *Moon Up—Moon Down.* Montoursville, Pennsylvania: Solunar Sales Company, 1972.

KREH, LEFTY, and SOSIN, MARK. *Practical Fishing Knots*. New York: Crown Publishers, 1972.

LIVINGSTON, A. D. *Fishing for Bass*. New York: J. B. Lippincott Company, 1974.

PERRY, BUCK. *Spoonplugging*. Hickory, North Carolina: Clay Printing Company, 1965.

PFEIFFER, C. BOYD. *Tacklecraft*. New York: Crown Publishers, 1974.

SOSIN, MARK, and CLARK, JOHN. *Through the Fish's Eye*. New York: Harper & Row, 1973.

———, and DANCE, BILL. *Practical Black Bass Fishing*. New York: Crown Publishers, 1974.

Index

About the Author

John Weiss was born in Akron, Ohio, and educated at Ohio University at Athens, from which institution he holds a master's degree in education. A nationally known fishing writer, he has published over two hundred feature articles in major sportsmen's magazines such as *Field and Stream, Sports Afield, Fishing Facts, Fishing World,* and many others. He has been a pioneer in many aspects of fishing and was the first to publish material on "oxygen-structure fishing" and light penetration of water in relation to bass angling. His research work and love of fishing take him each year to all parts of the country and often beyond the borders. Aside from fishing, his great hobby is wildlife photography, and his work in that field has appeared in many magazines. In 1974, John Weiss received a first-place citation from the Outdoor Writers Association of America for the best conservation article to appear in a national outdoor magazine. The story appeared in *BASSmaster Magazine.* John Weiss lives in Athens, Ohio, with his wife, Marianne, daughter, Lisa, and son, Michael.